Language
and
Human Nature

Toward a Grammar of Interaction
and Discourse

Language
and
Human Nature

Harvey B. Sarles

UNIVERSITY OF MINNESOTA PRESS

Minneapolis

Published by the University of Minnesota Press, 2037 University Avenue Southeast, Minneapolis MN 55414
Printed in the United States of America

Library of Congress Cataloging in Publication Data

Sarles, Harvey B.
    Language and Human Nature.

    Reprint. Originally published: After Metaphysics. Lisse: Peter de Ridder Press, 1977. (Studies in semiotics; v. 13) With new introd.
    Bibliography: p.
    Includes index.
    1. Language and languages—Addresses, essays, lectures. 2. Animal communication —Addresses, essays, lectures. 3. Human behavior—Addresses, essays, lectures. I. Title. II. Series: Studies in semiotics; v. 13.
P106.S224   1986   401'.9   85-1175
ISBN 0-8166-1353-2 (pbk.)

To Hattie R. Sarles
...my first teacher

CONTENTS

FOREWORD
WILLIAM C. STOKOE

The fourteen essays in *Language and Human Nature* were written by Sarles in the late 1960s and the early 1970s. They take on a remarkable timeliness eight years after their republication in 1977. Thus, Resnick (1983) in *Science* reported a shift from the teaching of science as the transmission of facts to student minds toward teaching as the interaction of a consistent and verified schema with each student's own naive but stubbornly held schema to explain to him or her how things work; and Scherer and Ekman (1983) began their handbook on the study of nonverbal behavior with a clear statement of the validity of studying social interaction as an alternative to quantitative studies of individual behavior. What Sarles says here may differ from these statements more than it reinforces them, but the book is nevertheless in the current trend of looking for more systematic, more embracing paradigms. The central theme is that our traditional ways of looking at language, at thought, and at communicative behavior need to change. But while many agree that change is needed from reductionist, static, dualistic formulations of linguistic and psychological problems, the precise direction of the change to be made and its philosophical implications are what makes this book especially interesting.

Sarles became impatient early with the efforts of linguistic study to explain human behavior either as the structure of abstractions or as something innate and unobservable. Part of his quarrel with business as usual of the anthropological linguistic kind or of the generative kind is occasioned by its exclusion from focus of all the phenomena that usually constitute social interaction but have been pejoratively labeled "nonverbal." His impatience for a human ethology, or a broader linguistics, is predictable enough in one who has studied with Birdwhistell. The idea that only the portion of human interaction capturable in conventional alphabetic or phonetic notation can be called language, and the corollary idea that language so defined is the only sure distinction between human and other animals, are ideas that Sarles attacks with vigor and effect, particularly by using biologically based criticism of Platonic and Cartesian dualism.

Sarles's quarrel with dualism goes deep. It is bodies after all, he insists, that distinguish one species from another; difference in bodily form is all that biological science has to work with. To Sarles the *assumption* that the human animal can be distinguished from "(other) animals"—a regular feature of his careful diction and punctuation—by its possession of mind and language is a retreat from objective science. He would like to see linguistic science reject its old theological and political arguments and demonstrate empirically the special nature of language, if it has one, the better to explain language as one kind of interaction of a social animal.

By forsaking a presumption of supernatural explanation for language and humanity, Sarles believes modern science could escape an old dilemma. In trying to ride both horns, he says, "the issues have been obscured. Knowledge is either in-built and learning is chimerical; or experience is the be-all of existence. The notion of life-as-interaction contains the seeds, I believe, of alternative conceptualizations and paths of study of human behavior" (p. 231).

Some of these conceptualizations and paths are described in the essays in *Language and Human Nature*. First is a new approach to "the study of communication across species" (title of the third chapter and subject of the first two). A second path of study begins with the human face. A third would make body movement not peripheral as it now is to studies of language but central in the study of human and (other) animals' communication. The major change in direction is to put interaction at the center of investigation and to investigate it by observing body changes (and changes that may become observable with advances in biochemistry).

Questions about the philosophical basis of scientific procedures are always in order, but the questions Sarles asks in the first two chapters were particularly pertinent in their original contexts. "Could a Non-H?" was contributed to a 1972 American Anthropological Association symposium on language origins (Wescott, Hewes, & Stokoe, 1974; Hockett, 1978); it asks whether a nonhuman E.T. linguist could possibly distinguish from observable human behavior enough of what we glibly call linguistic to discover that the human species was capable of and used language. His conclusion is too well argued to give away here. "On the Problem: The Origin of Language" was written several years later and addressed to the New York Academy of Sciences Symposium, before it convened (Harnad, Steklis, & Lancaster, 1976). Here also, Sarles finds both "animal callists" and linguists agreeing on the a priori assumption that there is no continuity between the calls of other animals and the language of the human animal. His prediction that not much new would come of this symposium because of its participants' commitment to traditional assumptions can be judged by readers of its 913-page proceedings.

In considering the importance of the human face to identity, memory, communication, and human life generally, Sarles suggests a quite unusual path for study: the inside as well as the outside of the face, for the tongue "knows," as he puts it, all that there is to be known about "the management of saliva''; that is, about the articulation of vocal sound. This kind of focus on faces and bodies penetrates to the major theme of the book, interaction, not individual actions, and Sarles sees it as a clue to some of the mystery of language. One test case for his theory is still on trial: If he is right, the mental retardation associated with Downs syndrome, like all development, is not solely genetic but results in this case from reduced and abnormal interaction. The affected child's face *looks* so unresponsive that parents and caregivers do not like to and so do not facially interact with it; their eyes and faces do not treat it as a face. Consequently the child's face grows still more unreflective of intelligence. With Sarles's interactive approach, of course, this vicious spiral is thought of as reversible, and while the effect of engaging Downs children heroically in facial interaction has not yet been fully determined, Sarles in personal communication is sanguine about the results he has seen.

He is equally innovative about the study of body movement. How and why do so many of our muscles, usually without our willing it, mimic the actions of the facial, postural, and upper limb muscles of others? As a musician, Sarles is aware to an unusual degree of "knowledge" in hands: A violinist's fingers, hands, and arms must do difficult and different tasks with exceptionally precise coordination. Such behavior, as well as the rhythmic synchrony of human interactions (and of course other interactions), can hardly even be talked about in ordinary or in scientific language, yet this mimicry communicates and surely has much to do with our awareness of self and others. It may even help us arrive at the basis of distinguishing self from others and so illuminate the state called consciousness. But study of these fascinating behaviors cannot continue to be isolated from study of "language," Sarles is saying in this book, and he insists that it would be a mistake to go on any longer treating language as a system unrelated to bodies and other natural systems, and treating language sound as the unimportant and uninteresting "carrier" of reified and deified language.

In this volume Sarles challenges a great deal of common wisdom. He wants a dynamic science of life-as-interaction, and I applaud his philosophic depth and hands-on knowledge of faces, hands, tongues, and bodies. Also to be admired is his prescience. His is a book to be read along with Bateson's *Mind and Nature* (though they do not always agree) and Neisser's *Cognitive Psychology,* to name but two. As early as the 1960s, Sarles began forecasting the changes in anthropology and linguistics required by a dynamic logic; that is, by a view of life as becoming through interacting, and by increasing knowledge about cybernetic systems. Collected here into a challenging book, his thinking helps one to see what is happening and should happen in the science of communication.

References

Bateson, G.
   1979   *Mind and Nature: A Necessary Unity* (New York: Dutton).

Harnad, S., H. Steklis, and J. Lancaster, eds.
   1976   *Origins and Evolution of Language and Speech* (New York: New York Academy of Sciences [= *Annals of the New York Academy of Sciences* 280]).

Hockett, C. F.
   1978   "In Search of Jove's Brow." *American Speech* 53, 243-313.

Neisser, U.
   1967   *Cognitive Psychology* (New York: Appleton).

Resnick, L.
   1983   "Mathematics and Science Learning: A New Conception." *Science* 220, 477-78.

Scherer, K., and P. Ekman, eds.
   1983   *A Handbook of Methods in Nonverbal Behavior Research* (Cambridge: University Press).

Wescott, R., G. Hewes, and W. Stokoe, eds.
   1974   *Language Origins* (Silver Spring, Md.: Linstok).

PREFACE (1985)

Since the earlier publication of this book, concentration on the formal aspects of language has yielded to a renewed quest for meaning. An overconfident promise to illuminate the workings of the human mind by the analysis of the structures of language is now being replaced by more cosmological and ontological concepts of language in relation to human nature. Questions concerning the very nature of language have arisen, replacing a commitment to language as the principal entry into what is particularly human. These conceptual changes are emerging both in academic circles and in the general population.

The increasing sense that we are tied to the entire earth in vague, yet intimate, ecological ways poses the question of who we are in conjunction with all of the earth's inhabitants. The Old Testament injunction of Genesis 1:26, of human "dominion" over all other species, refills itself with new awareness of "rights" and "responsibilities" we have toward other species. This is augmented by research that demonstrates that other species are at once more complex, that they are social (much as we), and that companion species (dogs, cats, parrots, etc.) are more important to human well-being than we had previously imagined. These researches, as well as "animal right's" movements, support an increased interest in the "animal-human bond."

The quest for meaning opens a set of new perspectives and problematics concerning language: how and what to pursue. The notion of language as some essential "superorganic," an independent object which stands above and outside our lives, can now be seen critically. Language is more dynamic, a relation between persons; in a cultural context—a common knowledge. Language is embedded in contextual issues, not merely a thing in-and-of itself nor a direct entry into each mind. This outlook places the relation of language and meaning into a general inquiry about the nature of being human.

Inquiry into human nature leads to a new view of the history of ideas, reflecting the puzzle of what is particularly human, and pointing to the development of assumptions and beliefs about what is nonhuman. It has become clear that the Western notion of language has been utilized, historically, to defend or to justify particular political, religious, and metaphysical theories, as well as to account for itself. This broad application of the function of language beyond its habitat also affects how we think about language's structures, placing the notion of grammar into new perspectives.

As these historical ideas are reviewed critically, the Western dualism of mind and body becomes problematic. Accepting the human body as more than a vehicle for the mind and the mind's language diminishes the dualism. It leads as well to the study of other persons as we realize and admit the concept of an active body, a body which is present, expressive, and reflected in the expression of others. This aspect of the inquiry into meaning places language within the examination of interaction and discourse, where the important function of language is toward understanding and experience of others and of the world.

This turning toward experience as a locus for the meaning quest, the experiencing of increased change and complexity in our lives, demonstrates that much of our lives remains poorly understood. It appears that the earlier essentialist, unchanging notion of a superorganic language has contributed to a poverty of theory and interpretation of experience.

As the essentialism of language theory is explored, the question of evaluation and judgment of self and others is also raised. The notion of an ideal, essentialist language led us to judge others (hence ourselves) with respect to how we regard (their) language. These ideas were used to justify a self-elevating moral stance, which raises us while diminishing others. Essentialist language has been used as an "ideal" in which we cloak ourselves, an "ideal" from which to judge those who differ from us as well as the handicapped and damaged among us. In the newer sense of language and bodily experience, we are more prone to yield to others the same fullness of self that we have granted to ourselves. Within the context of what meaning means, many of us are now willing to grant that others also seek meaning, much as ourselves.

In a global context, the quest for meaning leads to an examination of life or world visions: answers and solutions, frameworks of questions by other than Western traditions, to the meaning of life. There are now, and have been historically, a variety of approaches to life and living that have sustained life—some quite richly, some for very long periods. These include theories and philosophies of the world, life, and of oneself. The quest for meaning leads us to ask, in a comparative mode, what these other life approaches contain, how they developed, how they function; can they help us interpret these times of change, on a world scale? Language in the context of human nature now includes all humans, perhaps all others.

The dark side of the quest for meaning also affects thinking about language and human nature. A realization of differences among philosophies, religions, or life approaches often translates into believing that meaning has been lost, that an (apparent) plethora of truths translates into a sense of no truth at all. To understand this "relativism" and the "absolutism" that messianism and religious fundamentalism attempt to substitute for it, it is again essential to enter into history: to learn how Western concepts of language and human nature have developed, to probe our conceptual debts to this history, to discover the "howness" of earlier dark periods, to dig back in history before Plato, before the Christian era, to begin to understand why Western thought proceeded as it has, to probe how it might have gone in other ways.

Here it is possible to balance our knowledge of life experience with the ideas that have provided its informing and particularities, to note that it has not "lost" meaning. The sense of any loss of meaning resides in outlooks and presumptions that weaken resolve when we move into an era of impelling change of sufficient dimension. As an antidote to the felt loss of meaning, it is useful to examine our being in the world to note that language is an aspect of the body, that we are in the world with others, that meaning is located in this being and interacting with others. Especially, meaning is located in the relationship to each next generation. Meaning is not merely what words or ideas or languages mean, but how humans construct, sustain, and act within that notion of meaning. Nonetheless, the dark moods of our times are frightening and dangerous, since they cause us to question the very nature of existence, thence to cheapen life as the drive to find personal meaning overrides all else.

Other directions: the quest for meaning may lead away, outside life processes on this earth, into the universe of extraterrestrial intelligence and into the intelligence of robots, computers, and other machines.

The quest for meaning is cosmic literally when we turn away from terrestrial roots and seek some informing notion of a universal "consciousness." In the context of extraterrestrial intelligence, the notion that human intelligence is unique upon this earth, in tune with some celestial force of knowing, denies that we have much to learn from other earthly species or from our own human histories. It pushes the quest for meaning away from ourselves, away from experience, into other notions of time and of place.

The human relationship with technology deeply underlies a proud, but anxious aspect of the inquiry into meaning. We virtually dance with "techne": in cars, driving, listening to sounds we design, seeing through ground lenses; living longer. We may seek some sense of meaning in artificial intelligence, in the robots we tend to humanize, in the destructive forces we have unleashed. Technology, the result of earthly human intelligence, is at once awesome and simple, helpful and destructive. It reflects the human context and problematics ever more clearly. Where we have used technology as an evil, it now becomes our mirror image: often more real in reflection than we are, looking. For those who are anxious, for the anxious moments within us all, it seems possible to find ourselves reflected back from our own technology, often more possible than from within. Will we train thought to become servile to this technology, or will we enter more deeply into the human quest that we may find the meaning in our lives? Will we use our technology or be used by it?

The importance of the quest and yearning for meaning, carried to the scope of the world, underscores the thoughtfulness and confidence with which we must approach current problems. The temptation of meaning's obverse—meaninglessness—deflects us from approaching problems in mutual and in self-understanding. In this context, the quest for meaning derives from a mistrust of self which directs itself toward a mistrust and scapegoating of others.

What directions emerge within this quest? What meaning? Language? Human? Whence did these notions derive? How did they frame our conception of the present problematics? Who will control the definition of what it means to be human as we enter this phase of the entire earth, lacking understanding, attempting to interpret, to understand, and to control the forces upon the lives we find ourselves living?

H.B.S.

PREFACE (1977)

This volume is a set of my essays which discuss the nature of language in the context of a human ethology. They attempt to extend the view of anthropology beyond the comparison of other human cultures to that of other species: real or imaginary. How would 'they' describe human beingness and human behavior? Would their view jibe with ours, or would there be differences in perspective which would challenge or extend our thinking about human nature?

If language and thought are the pivotal issues in the construction of most of our theories of human nature, changes in perspectives concerning these issues may affect our conception of man in interesting, probably deep, ways.

In these essays I explore these issues, trying to 'account' for them, to place them in a variety of contexts and to offer antidotes to (older) ideas when an ethological perspective suggests it.

During the many phases of writing these essays, a number of people have contributed to the formulation and criticism of the ideas.

While the subject matters of language, behavior, and bodily form have been my special interests, the critical acumen of Janis Sarles has sharpened the ideas and kept the enterprise afloat and moving.

Mischa Penn has helped teach me to think historically and philosophically, taking the ideas and placing them within the traditions in which they may gain meaning.

As field worker and academic, I have been fortunate to have time to study with our children, Amy and Stefan. They have taught me a great deal.

Others who have been willing to discuss ideas with me at length include: Ray Birdwhistell, teacher, then for two years, mentor, at Western Psychiatric Institute; Martin Q. Peterson, who argued with me about Human Biology; Joan and Stephen Baratz and William Stewart with whom I discussed racism, reading, and public policy;

William Stokoe and Alan and Trixie Gardner who are willing to pursue ideas wherever they have to go; Thomas A. Sebeok, who trusts his own judgments; Robert Jamieson, cellist, who has tried to tell me how a musician thinks; and Burton Shapiro, oral biologist, for the toughness of his criticisms.

Persons who studied with me during the period in which these essays were written include Chet Creider, Gail Rhian Benjamin, Dean Oyen, and Spero Manson. It is difficult to say, now, where all of our ideas and criticisms intermingle and separate.

Betty Williams has been patient and careful in typing the edited form of this book. Terri Valois, Debb Luebke, Mary Lukaska, and Debbie Boyles have dealt kindly with varying forms of my scribblings. Eileen Flory drew the illustrative examples in (6) and (7).

Finally, thanks to Martin Krieger. His advice and thoughtfulness continue to enrich my thinking.

Several of these essays are reprinted here in slightly abridged form. The publishers have kindly granted their permission for reprinting in this volume. The original titles and place of publication are:

I (1) "On the Problem: The Origin of Language", *Sign Language Studies* 11 (Silver Spring, Md.: Linstok Press).

II (2) "Could a Non-H?" *Language Origins*, Hewes, Stokoe, Wescott, eds., 1974 (Silver Spring, Md.: Linstok Press).

II (3) "The Study of Language and Communication across Species", *Current Anthropology*, Vol. 10, No. 2-3, April-June 1969, 211-21 (Chicago, U. of Chicago Press).

II (4) "Language and Communication II: The View from '74", *Nonverbal Communication of Aggression*, Pliner, Kramer, Alloway, eds., 1975, 1-19 (New York: Plenum Press).

II (5) "Critical Naturalism and the New Linguistics: Back to Phonology", *Studies in Linguistics, in Honor of George L. Trager*, M. Estellie Smith, ed., 1974, 64-73 (The Hague: Mouton Press).

IV (7) "The Study of Intelligibility", *Linguistics* 34, 55-64 (The Hague: Mouton Press).

V (9) "An Examination of the Question-Response System in Language", *Semiotica* II, 1, 1970, 79-101 (The Hague: Mouton Press).

VI (12) "Facial Expression and Body Movement", *Current Trends in Linguistics*, T. Sebeok, ed., Vol. 12, 1974, 297-310 (The Hague: Mouton Press).

VI (14) "A Human Ethological Approach to Communication: Steps in Transit around the Cartesian Impasse", *Organization of Behavior in Face-to-Face Interaction*, A. Kendon, ed., 1975, 19-45 (The Hague: Mouton Press). (IX ICAES)

Two of the essays were originally written to be read and have not been published.

V (11) "Toward an Anthropology of Development" read at the symposium in honor of the retirement of Dr. Hyman Lippman, 1968. Wilder Foundation.

VI (13) "The Dynamics of Facial Expression" read at a craniofacial Biology Group Symposium, International Association for Dental Research meeting, Las Vegas, 1972.

INTRODUCTION

What is particularly **human** about human beings? **Language** is often
thought to be the major feature of our uniqueness. Its possession is
not merely what separates us from (other)[1] animals, but it has
occasionally been elevated to a position of centrality in probing our
innermost nature. Language is also a transcendent notion, a metaphor
carrying concepts which range from 'mind' and 'soul' to 'consciousness' and 'rationality.' Language is virtually coterminous with being
human.

With the recent development of a biology of behavior, questions
of cross-species communication have arisen. These questions have,
in turn, led to quandaries about the language and thought of species
other than man; how to do behavioral-linguistic comparisons which
might shed new light on human communicational processes? Thinking
about humans from the perspectives of observing (other) animals
has expanded our thinking about human language, and has opened
discussion about the nature of language — subsequently the nature
of being human.

It is apparent in this discussion that the definition of language is
borne upon the duality: what humans are, and (other) animals are
not. As language, mind, and reason are aspects of what is presumed
to be uniquely human, the body is left over, a conceptual residuum
which we are said to share with other species. Comparing language
across species is thought to be futile, because a basis for comparison
does not even exist. This view puzzles me and has led to the writing
of these essays, in which I explore the foundation of the concept
of language, and suggest alternative ways of thinking about language,
and what is human about human nature.

The accounting for human nature by language has relied heavily
on the idea that the human mind or the soul, in each individual,
uniquely possesses language. (Other) animals' (souls) do not have
language, nor the capability of learning words, sentences, and
grammar. Within this construction of human nature, man (alone)

was either given his propensity for language, or he attained it at some point in an historical, evolutionary development. When he gained language, he became capable of knowing. As he knew the external objective world, he could know others and gain a new view of self. Language enabled society as we could know and understand other minds.

The depiction of human-nature-as-language has come into serious question recently on two grounds: first, Gardner and Gardner (1969, 1971) have shown that two-way communication with another species (chimpanzees) is not very difficult if one is not overly specific or literal about what language is. Apparently, knowing is not solely dependent on possessing language. Secondly, as behavioral biologists/ ethologists have actually studied other species on their home grounds, it has become clear that man evolved as a social species (Crook, 1970). Language, whatever it might be, is not some force which first enabled us to become social.

If there are some senses in which humans are unique, language must be an aspect, not the cause. Whether (other) animals possess language in any clear-cut sense remains moot. What is clear is that the ideas of language and language behavior to which we cling are themselves being opened to question. It is not language which makes humans unique; it is language which we use as a cover term for what we already assume to be unique.

I join an argument that Nietzsche leveled at Plato:

Nietzsche: But the awakened and knowing say: body am I entirely, and nothing else; and soul is only a word for something about the body (TSZ, I, *On the Despisers of the Body*).

Plato: And he attains to the purest knowledge of them who goes to each with the mind alone ... he who has got rid, as far as he can, of eyes and ears, and so to speak, of the whole body (Phaedo).

Traditionally, language has delineated man's uniqueness as **mental** superiority. Instead, these essays entertain seriously the idea that humans (as all species) are unique because of their bodies, their forms. But the body is not merely a vehicle for cerebral resonance. Body is the observable surfaces we study, remember, and love; body is the form by which we identify and know species. Calling bodily form useful only for identification is to jump to mentalist solutions, and to bypass most of the facts of living behavior. It construes the human condition as static: virtually timeless and lifeless. Moving toward the final section in which the 'knowing body' is proclaimed, I argue against the mentalist position.

As the first paper (*On the Problem: The Origin of Language*) points out, our views of human nature lean heavily on an implicit comparison of humans with other animals — which is pseudo-comparison. It rests on beliefs that only humans are intelligent, have minds, souls, rationality, consciousness. We do not know how to compare human languaging with (other) animals' communicational behavior. To do more than speculate on a genesis of language requires knowledge and facts. Recent animal studies hint at the possibility of true comparison, but it is not yet possible. To state that (other) animals cannot think, do not possess language, is to defend a prior view of human nature which is heavily laden with politics and theology. The strength with which scholars defend the unknowable suggests, to me, that more is at stake than appears on the surface.

It seems clear that any attack on earlier definitions of language also entails an equally vigorous attack on earlier definitions of human nature. The essays in Part II venture into this arena, plunging deeply into the turbid waters which enshroud the problem of language.

Could a non-H? queries whether any intelligent being could possibly discover that we humans have language if that being utilized the techniques which **we** use to examine the languaging propensities of other species. We have abandoned the field of interspecies understanding, of further conceptual knowledge of human development, to the fiction of the 'intelligent Martian'. To say that we humans are superspecial and advanced, is to deny our kinship with other terrestrial creatures. We have assumed that they are stupid. I suggest that this may not be true. No Martian, I argue, could possibly discover our languaging abilities; nor can we, if we already assume noncomparability. The ultimate costs have been to depreciate the complexity of human existence by juxtaposing us with creatures we believe to be comparatively 'simple'.

Essays (3) and (4) express an intellectual kinship with *Darwin's Expressions of the Emotions* ..., outlining areas of agreement, arenas for research, and pointing out difficulties with an overly literal interpretation of his positions. Many modern biologists have considered (other) animals from the position of their inferiority, especially mental inferiority, with respect to man. Lorenz (p. 29)[2] and Simpson (p. 84) **use** language to exclude man from Nature. As a result, the behavior of (other) animals appears, in their constructions, to be simple, usually instinctual and genetically fixed.

Such arguments for uniqueness-by-exclusion essentially prior to study are, in fact, assumptive and debatable. Their entailments are potentially racist, and may be used to reconstruct a progressive Social Darwinism in which the 'fixed' components of human nature will come to appear more important than our learning and flexible features, merely because this form of thinking leads in these directions.

The final paper (5) in Section II suggests that a perspective of 'Critical Naturalism' is a possible antidote to the simplistic empiricism by which many ethologists/behavioral biologists study feral species. It is simply not clear what might constitute 'objectivity' in the study of behavior. The ethologists carry into their observations a great deal more intellectual baggage than they admit. In my experience most of them appear to be unaware of the theology and politics and intellectual history which underlie their thinking.

Part III, a single paper (6), is an attempt to explore the thinking of many behavioral biologists and of most behavioral scientists: dualists that they are. Within the fundamental dichotomy of body and mind, the 'mind side' since it is ultimately **unexaminable** (shades of Plato's *Cave of Shadows*) lends itself to a variety of sorts of **ideal** states, essences. Depending on where one's primary observational focus resides (e.g., in pathology and medicine, on [other] animals, on the 'retarded'), he will likely juxtapose what he observes with some construction of ideal-typical. It seems inevitable, as this essay tries to show, that there be winners and losers within this formulation of existence. A purely intellectual endeavor turns out to carry a politics in its working out and thinking through.

The essays in Part IV represent my conviction that language, sound, verbal behavior is much more complicated than we linguists have previously thought. The reasons for sound-as-language having appeared simple are several: (1) a presumptive dualism claimed a distinction between a more central, examinable, systematic message, *langue*, and a peripheral 'speech', paralinguistic, *parole* aspect which was considered epiphenomenal to 'language per se', or commentary upon it; (2) linguists assumed an implicit semantic while claiming that they (already) knew that words exist and are same/different in intuitively obvious ways. The bedrock task of linguistics was to account **minimally** for sound differences between otherwise similar words. Here sound merely keeps words apart; (3) sound comparison was done principally **within** sentence units, mainly with respect to contiguous words or phrases. Context is severely limited or not taken into account.

The essay on *Intelligibility* (7) argues for a view of sound-as-language which differs deeply from earlier ones. In a Nietzschean antidualist sense, sound (like 'body') is what there is and **must** be itself semantic. Previous assumptions must have limited observation and inference.

Essay (7) shows that the 'same' words sound different as they are **located** differently within any larger structure; that they sound different, at least in part, because location itself is functional in promoting continuity; e.g., initial words in a sentence not only **are** themselves, but tell us a good deal **about** the nature of what is to come (and what is **not** to come). Entire words can be excised from a stream of sound with little or no effective loss of sense. This essay suggests how this may happen.

This essay also shows that a naturalistic, ethogram-type of observation, no matter how carefully done, will be severely limited in truthfulness. Speakers carry in their talking selves extremely complicated contextual, historical, interactional pictures of what and how they speak.

The problem of comparison, of what is same and what different, is shown to be of extreme import in the study of language processes. The very 'same' word, repeated in a phrase, (e.g., dog, dog, dog, dog!) get considerably **quieter** over the phrase. An external Martian-observer, hearing these, would likely regard them as different 'words', whereas we regard them as the same. The minimal theories of sound-keeping-words-apart simply do not notice these sorts of pervasive features of sound in language.

Finally, this essay implies that cross-species comparison of verbal behavior is possible only if we have a deeper, more critical, and careful description of human language in its processual, as well as static, senses. What we have regarded as language may well be only a very small percentage of the amplitude of speech. To compare what we hear in other animals' speech with very limited features of human language is unsound and can confirm whatever the comparator desires.

A number of limiting aspects upon our observational predilections and powers are examined in the accompanying paper in Section IV. This essay (8) elaborates upon (7) and attempts to point out some of the senses in which we are contextually-bound observers in our own ongoingness. Antidotes include the purposeful 'breaking' of context, constant reexamination of one's assumptions, finding new observational positions, directly attempting to study contextual variables, and abandoning the view that the nature of language is already well understood.

Part V represents my explicit excursions into metaphysics. In opposing the notion of man as extranatural, *cum anima*, I question the view that grammar is some 'infinite' set of sentences, independent of causality (Chomsky, 1968: 11). While grammar may, indeed, be a way into the human 'mind', the claims of infinity and creativity which sentence grammars imply ought to be questioned. Not only do they direct the study of grammar to deep and hidden processes, but they are also directly theologically motivated. This portrayal of grammar is an accounting for how humans can know an infinite God; there are no observables in this construction of grammar-as-language; there is no possible comparison between man and (other) animals within this conceptualization of language.

Instead, essay (9) is a proposal for a different sort of grammar, a grammar of interaction and discourse: *The Question-Response System*. It is generative, infinite in several senses, but intrinsically finite and examinable. As (10) points out, it may well be **the** grammar of human mother-infant interaction. It can account for the development of **sensibility** in the human condition — which, in sentence grammar, must remain built in, essentially prior to experience. It is context-sensitive and can itself direct the scholar to differentiating its syntactic and semantic structures. It is nowhere 'indefinite', yet it remains 'open' — and, I believe, provides a much better accounting for human development than can sentence grammars, or, for that matter, any S-R theory to date. At the least, it suggests that there may be multiple grammars.

The final paper in this section (11) is a circumambulation around the problem of human development, particularly with respect to how one comes to 'have' meaning. Development is statement and process both from the perspective of parental-societal assumptions about growing up to be, and the child's **active** participation in his own changing sense of being. Development is not merely toward becoming 'rational' — as Piaget et al. would have it — but in becoming adult; much like the present adults. Parenting, like teaching, is both present and projected future; perspectives change as children grow and learn in interesting and complicated, always interactional, ways. The process is more fragile than it usually appears to scholars. A great deal of 'pathology' is interactional in origin, not due to congenital damage, as it tends to appear in dualist thinking. We are all active observers and strategists in the game of life.

The concluding section of three essays on the **Body** represent attempts to transcend the mind-body dualism by concentrating on the body as an interactional-communicating device. In what senses do we know about our own and other persons' bodies? What do infants see and study as other people? How does what they see affect how they are? How they become?

Essay (10) sets the problem by claiming that language is an aspect of the body, that the body is expressive in ways that interactors 'read' constantly. Language does not exist in any sense, disembodied. We watch others as they speak — early childhood poetry, particularly, is explosively **visual**. We speak to 'faces', not merely to ears.

We are students of others' **faces**, as they are of ours. But what is a face? Why do we look like we do? In what senses can one face mimic another?

Is facial expression an external playing out of some basic, inbuilt emotions? Or is facial expression how we are, how we imagine ourselves and others, how we remember others?

I argue for the latter view: that people come to look like they do principally in terms of their interactional ongoingness; that why we look like we do is not principally 'genetic', but is made explicable by new developments in dynamic, functional anatomy.

The *Dynamics of Facial Expression* (11) considers more extensively the nature of the face-as-expression in interactional processes. How does it get shaped? What is a tongue; what does it 'know'; what does saliva have to do with speaking and thinking?

This paper also begins my ongoing exploration into the nature of 'odd-looking' people, the nature of 'normal' vs. 'retarded' persons. What is 'wrong' with Mongoloid (Down's Syndrome) persons? I am convinced that these persons have been misunderstood in ways that are directly implied by a mentalist-dualist view.

Granted that most Mongoloid persons appear to be intellectually retarded, is this due primarily to some congenital central nervous system 'damage', or to having a 'peculiar' body/face, which is interacted with **as if** retarded? I explore the latter view: that these persons have a body whose 'peculiarities' tend to place them in conceptually different worlds, than those of us we consider to be essentially normal, and suggest how this may occur. In this arena the political consequences of modes of conceptualizing minds and bodies are crystal clear. The civil rights of those we regard as 'retarded' are indeed tenuous.

The concluding essay (12) summarizes my views on the study of language and expression. It is written from the post-dualistic futurity in which Part I is a critical exposition of how and why a critical naturalist-human ethological mode of investigation may make sense.

In order to observe, yet transcend our historically determined senses of what we regard to be **common** sense, it is necessary to broaden and deepen our perspectives; to try to view humans as the porpoise, the Martian, the infant, the 'retardate', the enslaved, the classicist and futurist. ... Each ongoing species has a truth, a logic, a science, knowledge about the world in which it lives. To take man outside of nature, to aggrandize the human mind, is to simplify other species, and, I am convinced, to oversimplify ourselves, to constrict our thinking and observation about ourselves into narrow, ancient visions of human nature, constructed for other problems in other times.

Having (re)admitted the body – but, **the body-as-expression in interaction** – into the depth of human and (other) animal conceptual being, I try to catalogue a program of what we are and what we know: about ourselves and others.

It appears clear that we, as other species, are already communicating beings. If anything our sense of self, individuality, is emergent, not given. As we interact with others who treat us as consistent and constant, we become persons, existents. But this all has to be thought about, lived, tried – not assumed. Evolution is ongoing, even for humans.

In a deep sense, the admission of the body-as-human-being gives impetus to Whitehead's notions of process and reality. We **are** in process – the elusive problem has to do with the nature of continuity; the world as phenomenal, not merely as phenomena. What do we 'know' as bodies; what do we know of others; how do we study, strategize, grow and become? The phenomenology is embodied and occurs in the effective presence of others – also embodied, also embodying us.

This final essay, Part II, is a set of 20 aphorisms, each of which is an exploration into Nietzsche's claim that 'body' is what there is, and 'mind' some statement about it: the nature of mimesis, rhythm, body image, excitement, fright, facial memory, as aspects of a theory in body-in-interaction. What shifts in focus, in data, in definition might be needed, in order to derive a complicated sense of mind from the moving human form?

In sum, these essays are excursions into the intellectual, theological, and political entailments of language. What started out to be some 'correctives' to theories of language which I felt to be somewhat inadequate, mushroomed as they gradually revealed their implications and assumptions.

As I am a 'body-person', these essays reflect my personal inabilities to sit still for any length of time, as well as my convictions that the body-in-interaction is of primary importance in considering the human condition. I am no less impressed by the beauty of (other) animals and feel that much of human understanding will become clearer only upon more deeply granting fellow terrestrial species a full measure of beingness.

PART I

(1) ON THE PROBLEM: THE ORIGIN OF LANGUAGE

The Occasion

The New York Academy of Sciences has decided to sponsor (in September of 1975) an extensive discussion on the origin of language. One wonders whether this issue, which arises seriously about once every century, will provide any 'news' this time through. Will it be an exercise, a convention of the high priests demarcating the arena of the 'problem'? Will it be a disputation; or is there a singular point of view which has been subdivided into corporations, all with different titles, all selling the same product, and colluding to limit competition?

This is a serious wonderment, not because the language origin problem is *de facto* so interesting, but because of what it seems to represent and to entail. While it appears in many senses a straight-forward issue, it is, in my experience, an epigram for a view of human nature: language is that which makes man unique. The view, which is implied by raising the issue of **language origin**, has increasingly been in flux on a number of grounds, for a variety of reasons. One suspects that such a conference, at this time, is an attempt to stave off change, and to restate in a very public way, that the human nature 'business' is in the same location, and peddling the same wares, stylized to fit the tastes of the 1970's.

I have tried, in the following paper, to state what is wrong with the 'problem' of the origin of language, to offer some alternative ways of conceptualizing the underlying issues, and to show why they might be interesting.

In my view, the 'origin of language' problem is a pseudo-problem. As it is conceptualized and treated it will not, nor can it, yield any new knowledge about language or about human nature. In the history of ideas, its elaboration already presumes a particular definition of human nature.

Discussion of the 'origin' of language only defends this definition — and embroiders it with a network of entailments which follow directly from its assumptions. It is virtually a **system of thought** about human nature, and consequently does not leave itself open to attack, or even discussion. It presumes that language and reason are essentially the same – a unity – in correctly describing the human condition; any attempt to reorient the 'problem' is considered to be against 'reason'; therefore, irrational.[3]

Any set of ideas whose ultimate defense rests upon such grounds seems, to me, to be very suspect. Nor can I find any grounds on which such a problem is open to the possibility of proof or disproof. It is no more than a particular descriptive system; one which is probably as consistent and accurate as, say, any particular geometry. This is not to say that the prevailing view about language is uninteresting or nonuseful. It is to claim that it is not necessarily an exhaustive or accurate system. There are different ways to think about language than the issue called 'the origin of language' would suggest.

What does the notion of language origin presume? Why is it interesting to question the very raising of this issue, particularly at this time?

Logically, the issue presumes a type of human uniqueness which is progressive; we are similar to other animals only in some respects. In the realm of language, humans are so different and **advanced** beyond other animals as to be noncomparable with them. The issue thus presumes an essential **discontinuity** between (other) animals and humans.[4]

In such a situation the presumption is that there was a (historical) jump between human predecessors and human beings. The origin of language problem is simply to **account** for the **differences** between humans and nonhumans.

The **logical problem** is that there is no way within this conceptual system to find out what nonhumans are like. Nonhumans are conceptualized as particular forms of deficient humans, not in their 'own terms'. We have **decided** that they do not possess language; the problem is to convince ourselves how a few of the have-nots could have come upon what we consider to be language.

Reading the history of this issue, it seems that different theories have **appeared** reasonable and convincing in different eras (Salus, 1969). Since, logically, there is no possibility of a knowledge base for such theories – on prior grounds of noncomparability – what appears reasonable or convincing must have to do with issues extrinsic to the so-called problem. Either there is no issue, or there is no possible solution. It thus behooves us to investigate the presumptions which lie behind this pseudoproblem and ask why it appears to be reasonable, even to otherwise reasonable people.

The first part will be devoted to unraveling the underlying presumptions. I offer an alternative view about the nature of animals and men. In light of the continuing observations that our ancestors were already social creatures, language did not **make** us social.[5] I attempt to develop the implications of this different conceptualization of animal sociality, how it might affect our view of human nature and of language. Along the way, I will also point out that some animal behaviorists have taken the prevailing (pseudo) beliefs about human language and have tried to promote **their** views about human nature, whilst appearing to derive these views solely from observations of nonhumans. Overall, I will attempt to show that we principally use the **form** of animals and man to tell one species from another. This fact of the existence of bodies has been bypassed and neglected within the prevailing conceptual construction of the problem: the **origin of language**.[6]

Individuals and Minds

The primary urge, which has pushed the development of our views of human nature, has been theological, metaphysical, and political.[7] What is the nature of human life; especially, of death? This construction of the problem of human life postulates that the 'soul' or 'mind' of man is the uniquely **essential** aspect of human nature. It not only differentiates us from (other) animals, but endures beyond the 'life' of the body.

With just one more assumptive piece, this accounting of the problem of human nature seems to have predetermined almost all of our thinking about humans, about language, about other animals, etc. The remaining assumption is that the primary **locus** of being, of the soul and mind, is the **individual** human being. This is sufficient to account for the language origin problem. An alteration in any one of these pieces will change the way in which we conceptualize human or (other) animal nature.[8]

It follows quite easily and directly from the notion that humans are unique **because** of our souls and minds, that we alone possess other unique facets of our being. For any number of reasons, but mostly on theological grounds, the perfectly obvious idea that our bodies are also distinctly human has been rejected as a focal area for accounting for human nature.[9]

How are souls and minds of humans unique? In several ways — and it is important to note that the ancient solutions to these questions still seem appealing and common-sensical. Once this **question** appears reasonable, its potential solutions follow.

If man has a soul which endures 'forever', then the conceptualization of human nature already takes on a particular viewpoint of the nature of **time**. Time must be made an **attribute of being**, rather than, say, a relationship among persons and the external world. If the soul is forever, it is most tempting to think that any particular moment is a mere step on the stairway to heaven.[10] If we view that moment from the perspective-of-forever-after, it is likely to appear infinitesimally small. It is one more small step to think of it as illusory, because an entire life is but a moment in the greater firmament. Who is to know but that all we observe is a shadow of some deeper reality? God only knows.

It also follows from this concept of soul and time that animals — not having souls — also do not 'have' time. How else can we account for claims that (other) animals exist only in the 'here and now'?[11] The other element in this thinking is that it is **minds** which give us a time sense; thus it must be that bodies do not possess such abilities. Bodies only exist in the here and now; sensation is in the body; we have bodies essentially like other animals. Bodies are 'natural', biological — the mind is what is unique to man. The mind is, in some sense, extra- or supernatural. If we want to find out what is **really** natural about humans, we must observe other animals.[12]

These ideas follow easily from the notion of time, which the postulation of human uniqueness and 'soul' seems to force upon us. In a complicated way, most of the elaborations of human nature have also derived from this picture. If we believe that animals live only in the moment, we believe that we do not. This, then, sets up a difference — an **opposition** — between mind and body; 'concrete' and 'abstract', 'subject' and 'object', and leads to a theory of knowledge in which the most important aspects of human nature are precisely those features by which we **presume** ourselves to **differ** from (other) animals. (Note that it is not at all necessary to know anything about other animals — we have been able to invent their capabilities fully without the necessity of consulting 'them'. Almost all our methodologies for studying other animals' 'language' already presume what they set out to 'discover'. Later I attempt to show how our methods of investigating their communication systems is set up in such a way that our theories about them cannot possibly be refuted.)

The roadway connecting language with mind is also quite direct, following from the primary locus of being-as-the-individual and from uniqueness: What is the mind? What is in the mind? Obviously, bits of being which make us unique — ideas, thoughts, memory; i.e., time and all it implies. Nonbody. We are the only animals who have language.

That seems clear enough, although I suspect it was derived from assumptions, not from observation. It simply is not difficult to note that many animals make complicated noises. Why do we assume and believe they don't have language? — not from any evidence, but because we believe that we alone have language, ideas, thoughts. And this is what makes us unique. Each step of the journey appears logical, but it is nonetheless circular.

The **individual** contains the ideas or thought which language represents. The mind or soul is that which is the essence of men; but, especially, of each individual man. One suspects, as Nietzsche points out (1967), that Plato was attempting to make time 'stop' in order to ward off the fear of impending personal-bodily death and to ensure (a theory of) immortality.[13] Thus, the notion of human nature as located in each individual was motivated not by a consideration or understanding of life/living processes, but by the attempt to manage and conquer the fear of death. This view has led to a virtual impasse in the development of theories of mind, thence of human nature.[14]

In the history of ideas the notion of (other) animals' understanding the world and one another seems not to have arisen seriously until relatively recently. Bestiality implied a sense of nonrationality, intemperence, lack of self-control and forethought, impulsiveness, etc. No wonder that the presumed road from nonhuman to human is strewn with so-called 'primitives', who are assigned an increasing dose of rationality, yet retain certain 'deficits'.

In 'origin of language' theory it is simply not possible for animals to communicate deeply; it implies a notion of the (other) animal world which makes only humans capable of understanding the universe and one another. Language and the 'gaining' of language enabled us to understand the objective or external world and one another. The ontogeny of the individual recapitulates the development of the human species. From nonlanguage to language, understanding, rationality, communication. Language **enables** communication, society, culture. Humans develop consciousness through understanding others, how others understand them; consciousness of the 'I' enables the 'thou'.[15]

In broad outline this is how the origin of language problem has been and continues to be conceptualized. Its 'solution' should show how nonthinking beasts could have begun to be rational, logical, and conscious of self.

It seems that certain stories which gradually extend what we believe to be 'animal' or bodily abilities, have been, and continue to be the most plausible. Physical or emotional gestures seem like reasonable **intermediary** steps from animal to human. **Before** we engage in offering such 'solutions', however, we must require that we know, in some deep sense accurately, about the behavior of other animals. We do not possess such knowledge. I do not believe that we can obtain this knowledge because this conceptualization of the language origin problem strongly suggests a particular view of other animals which is based on their not-being-human — which has meant not-having-language.

It remains unclear what goes on in (other) animals' 'minds'. What is clear, to me, is that our conceptualization of human nature and language forces us to believe a particular story about animals which is derived not from animals themselves but from our uniqueness theories about humans.

Objections: To the Problem [16]

My objections to the problem are of several sorts:

(1) Our predecessors were already social. What we call 'language' is a new (possibly) form of communication, but it is not necessarily what 'makes' us unique.

(2) Current formulation of the problem blocks the possibility of learning much 'new' about human beingness. It presents a view of language which focuses on 'differences' and obscures possibly valid comparisons. It is my experience that comparative work must proceed from similarities, not from differences or it will tend only to confirm, describe, and account for the observed or presumed differences. (It can only confirm or enlarge human-nonhuman differences; it cannot possibly cast new light on the human condition.) One wonders why people engage in this supposedly comparative problem, when they already presume strong human uniqueness. [17]

(3) It calls attention away from a series of potentially interesting ways of thinking about human nature; the notion that humans instantiate others as **faces**.

(4) It makes man appear to have stopped evolving when he 'got' language and urges a **static** view of the human experience.

(5) It enables the ideas of the view of man which seem plausible at any historical moment to appear to be exhaustively true.

(6) By setting man as unique **because** of his mind, it (language) idealizes the normal use of language and sets up a group of defective (or animal-like) humans, e.g., retarded persons, deaf persons, people who speak differently from the majority. The problem is implicitly, perhaps necessarily, **racist**.

(7) By setting up humans as more complex than animals, it has oversimplified most animals. It has also tended to permit us to oversimplify humans, since we were unique **only** because we had language. It has been tempting to seek simple and static solutions or schemata to account for, what in my life, at least, is a very complicated and ever-changing being-and-experiencing.

(8) The mere announcement of the problem suggests that we already know, in some deep sense, what language is. Thus it obfuscates the fact that our theories about human language remain relatively simple and minimal. Language, the 'target' of the process by which animal becomes man, tends also to be static; an entity, rather than the behavioral, muscular processes which language undoubtedly includes. The exciting thing about comparing animals and man is that we may gain new ways of thinking about man, rather than being forever locked into our ancient humanly derived ideas about ourselves.

(9) It 'blames the victims'. Animals are not merely different, they are 'defective humans'.

(10) By making humans appear to be especially unique, it forces us to lump all (other) species into a single nonlanguage-possessing universe. It is more likely that there are greater differences in the animal universe than the speaking propensities of humans would suggest.

(11) It implies or includes a theological and political view of man which is claimed to be wholly intellectual. Particular theologies and particular politics are borne on the wings of its proclaimed scientisms. (Any position about human nature which claims a purely scientific base is either very naive, or its proponents are attempting to wrap their prior views in new cloth — perhaps both.)

(12) It calls attention toward the individual in ways which obscure the social aspects of human existence or make them seem to detract from the possibilities of individual freedom.

On the contrary ...

Language as a Social Process

The major notion derived from ethology which has impressed me —
with respect to the language issues and why I believe the issue
arises at this time — is that it now appears clear that prehumans were
already social creatures. We did not **become** social upon becoming
humans, and through the use of language; humans were always social,
are always social.

What this implies for language origin is very deep and far-reaching,
because our origin theories rest in large measure on a story which has
language as the primary enabler in human society and culture
(Cassirer, 1955).

Many ethologists still entertain this vision: In K. Lorenz' hands,
language is a quality which virtually **removes** man from nature —
"the greatest gifts of man, the unique faculties of conceptual thought
and verbal speech which have raised him to a level high above all other
creatures" (1966: 230). For Lorenz the unique features of man are
so great that he is not directly comparable to other creatures. To
even find out about man's 'natural, biological, instinctual' state, one
must and can only infer from other creatures to man, **because**
language obfuscates man's inner, deep, true nature. Those particular
features of man (e.g., aggression, morality, territoriality), for which
part'cular scholars **claim primacy**, guide the research and interpretation of their work and their scholarly traditions. One must be wary
of the so-called biologist who has man as **more** unique than other
species because of a certain attribute such as language; because he
can use this story to characterize human nature pretty much as he
wants to, while it remains inobvious that many aspects of his animal
nature remain unnoticed, unnoted. We must be wary because the
nonobservers among us tend to trust the observations of a brilliant
biologist like Lorenz. We are less aware that his story which claims
to be **biological** is so similar to the theopolitical metaphors which
have guided our thinking that his behavioral biology may simply be
a new form of the same old story (Waddington, 1975).

Thus many ethologist-behavioral biologists continue to believe
man to be an especially peculiar form of demi-animal — due to his
'possession' of language and all that language has entailed in the
history of Western-thought-about-language. But it seems clear to
me that man, as all species (**by definition** if the biology of 'species'
has any real meaning), is unique. In attempting to understand the
problem of its 'origin', we must wonder what it might mean to be
already social, to have evolved as social creatures. For, the question

of language **origin** assumes that language 'came first', and thence **enabled** communication, understanding ... thence society.

Being social seems to imply that creatures engaging in social processes already possess some sense of knowledge of one another — 'who' is, and who is not a 'member' (who can or might be a member, etc.). Sociality involves communication, understanding, politics, law, morality. It implies a sense of being, a way of being, with respect to others of one's 'significant' grouping.[18]

As one begins to think through some of the implications of sociality, a number of questions arise about what human language might 'mean'. If all social creatures have some sort of knowing (an epistemology), then human language may simply represent another form of knowing — one among many. All species 'know' their universe — survival means, to me, a sense of knowing.

How can nonlanguaging creatures communicate? What might they communicate about? What does the notion of communication ultimately mean? Is language **used** to communicate? If we are (also) social creatures, then we could communicate before we had/could language. What **is** language, anyway?

Such thinking might lead one in a number of directions:

(1) If communication in humans exists 'prelanguage', e.g., between mothers and infants, what are the forms and nature of such communication?[19]

(2) How does language develop and change and/or enrich the nature of communication?

(3) How do deaf people understand one another (and the world)?

(4) What is animal 'noise' about — is it 'speech' as opposed to 'human language' (in a sign-symbol dialectic sense)?[20] Are its form and nature that different from language, or have our ideas about animal noise ('calls') been guided by our assumptions about human uniqueness, leading us to believe that animals are so unrich, stupid, nonabstract, unthinking creatures? If the latter, most of the current work in animal communication having to do with 'calls' must be anthropomorphic[21] (Marler in Stokoe, 1975).

(5) What do other animals hear and 'think'? Does this have anything to do with their 'limited' mental capacities? (Is it any less anthropomorphic to say other animals 'think' than to say that they don't think?)

(6) If animal being and communication have something to do with animal form, do human being and communication have much to do with human bodily form?[22]

(7) What is the human body as a communicative instrument; e.g., how do infants 'understand' their mothers' (bodies)?

(8) How do adult bodies influence their communication, being, understanding?

(9) How do people get to look like they do?

(10) What is the nature of 'gesture'?

(11) The 'innateness' of communication ...?

In thinking about the nature of sociality with reference to human and other animals, several features become apparent. We are not merely 'minds and bodies' in an individual sense; we are 'socially expressive' creatures whose presence and movements are available to, and actually noted (and monitored) by, others. 'Even' in the human condition, most of our behavior is nonverbal and is constantly 'read' by other people. Social 'adults' have 'in mind' the 'product' they desire in their children; a model of future being delimited by the way they see their young. If the concept of 'misbehaving' is available to social animals, and sociality implies such behavioral limits, then each animal who 'punishes' must enjoy a sense of being which is well defined. Social adults do not merely see and interact with larger or smaller bodies; they have some notion of other beings as proper or improper.

This notion of humans, as already social and communicating beings, points toward redefinitions and reconceptualizations of language. Our ancient, yet current, ideas about language and linguistics are clearly asocial, probably antisocial in their entailments. Definitions of language (all of which must be reconsidered in light of humans-as-social-creatures) include the very idea of grammar as the set of all (possible) sentences and of the words which compose them. But grammar has never led to the study of the body or communication.[23]

In the real-social world the sounds which emerge from our mouths and faces are merely a form of communication; they do not enable it to occur. Language, now italicized because its very existence is open to question, enables the forms of communication to expand, change. It helps us to manipulate space and time, gives a 'sense of permanence' to one's being and to the world of others, of objects, to 'make sensible' one's existence in others' terms.[24] I question whether it 'enables' us to be conscious, 'human', rational, intentional, logical, creative, or any other 'mind' terms which the exclusive definitions of language-as-distinctly-human have forced us to believe. In Western thought, Language and Reason are coterminous and tautological — they can tell us nothing 'new' about human beingness![25]

In the real-social world, individuals **emerge**; they do not preexist, bounded as their souls or by their skins. Current grammars imply that each individual is the (sole) repository of the rules for **generating** all possible sentences. Though in many senses **a truth**, it is a limited and misleading one. It makes, for example, the existence of **human bodies** become essentially inconsequential to human being. Current language theories are seductive. By making human uniqueness appear to be most clearly due to the uniqueness of the **human mind**, we are led away from the fact that the human form is quite special. It has led us, for example, to study facial expression as if it represents merely the external workings-out of one's inner being, rather than having a complex being which may be in some senses **causal** rather than caused.

Perhaps the first move in understanding the nature of language as part(s) of a social interactional process is to postulate a different form of grammar; a grammar, not merely of sentences, but of Questions and Responses. In sentence ('mind') grammar, questions are merely another form of **sentence**. In the social world of interaction, **questions get answered**!

I suggest that **the** Human Grammar — at least of early child development — is composed of parents playing a game of question and response with children **about** their relationships and the external world. They **use** the existing communicative-body relationship and extend it to the external universe (Wittgenstein, 1958).

It is interesting to notice that certain aspects of the languaging process have been almost totally overlooked, just simply missed or dismissed, because of our preconceptions of language as words and sentences, surface representations of the deeper mind. These 'surface' representations have a lot to do with what an infant is about.

Consider: the infant **watches** so carefully the mouth and other facial movements of its parents.

We have missed the fact that languaging **is** itself a set of facial expressions. "Baa, baa, black sheep" is explosively, contrastively facial — especially as we say it to an infant. It is engagement, practice in mouth moving and shaping — not merely words. How has it been missed in our descriptions of language?

In the quest for the origin of **human** language, it may well be that what is most important is not the mere size or 'complexity' of the brain or suitable types of vocal chords, but in the fact of having human faces, facial muscles. Why has this obvious fact of existence been omitted from our theories about being: i.e., the human propensity to 'personalize' and to remember people essentially **as their** faces. (One can only speculate about which bodily aspects dogs would choose to preserve in a 'Doggie Hall of Fame'!)[26]

As in any enterprise, one must be clear about what he thinks is important or primary about the nature of his subject matter. I am confident that the 'origin of language' problem would look quite different than it seems today,[27] if the (apparent) fact — that humans do most of their thinking about other humans in very complicated, dynamic terms of their facial expression — were elevated to a central notion of human behavioral theories (and why not?).

The fact is that linguistic descriptions of phonetic articulation discuss the 'how' and 'where' of sound formation but neglect to point out clearly that languaging is like other muscular movements. Talk is muscular process, not to be relegated to 'prelinguistics', but as how humans are. The body 'feels good' to move and exercise, and talk is a form of exercise (particularly satisfying to the lecturer, one would guess: the lecturer-as-marathon-runner).

Our mind theories of language have been so attractive that the fact that human bodies like their speech 'straight on' — full face — has never entered into acoustical theory. Somehow we have been deceived into believing that sound strikes only ears, thus auditory nerves, and that the shape of the human face is inconsequential to the shape of the 'message' it hears — **and feels**. Humans also tend to get their speech 'full body front' whereas many other animals' hearing apparatus are located essentially 'in front' of their bodies. The very form of our faces, as we come to 'look like we do', may have a lot to do with the sound we hear, or like to hear. Bodies are absorptive, and reflective, shaping surfaces as well as male or pretty or nonanimaloid.

The single largest change in the human body the first few days after birth — i.e., tissue change — is in the saliva glands. How is it that our descriptions of human language seem to overlook this fact: (muscular) control of saliva is crucial, if not defining of human talk, and possibly human mentation? Our talk — and our listening — only occur via a layer of saliva. Dryness and languaging are not compatible.[28]

The (mere) fact that these processes work so well, for most of us, that they go unnoticed, unresearched, and unthought about, does not mean that they are unimportant. That muscular device called the human tongue is quite meticulous in touching to talk, but also in spreading saliva (Language as a subtopic in the study of saliva? — Better the origin of language problem focused here!). The tongue 'knows' its domain so well that only changes in it will remind us that the tongue is constantly in charge – a dental carie, a bit of stuck food. The tongue is the major **shaper** of the mouth and face; it is constantly tensioned. It is visually available to infants, to see, and to feel their own tongue, to explore. The 'oral' stage of development may not only be 'mental', but also the major mode of exploration of the world for the first years of life – i.e., most of one's external contacts take place through the mouth.[29]

What are other animals' tongues doing while they wander in the forest primeval? Their saliva? No one seems to know much about tongues or saliva beyond a first, superficial attempt to characterize the proteins which may be found in the average bit of spit. The 'origin' of language may have principally to do with human tongues (and saliva).

The major point of this section is that all of this occurs not merely in one's mouth or mind and body, but also in the presence of other creatures in whom we show interest. Human babies spend a great deal of time and energy watching others' **faces**; not simply in psyching their minds, but in studying **faces**. How is it that they sense that their 'face' is 'like' their mothers'? If we want to understand the origin and development of language, is it not sensible to study the students – our infants?

Knowing as a Social Process

Granted that human children are involved with others' faces and bodies, how is it that they get to know about the 'external world'? How do they come to **know** objects, to name concepts, to become the sorts of conscious, abstract, creative, reasoning creatures we like to think of as uniquely humanoid? Are they?

In order to probe this issue more deeply, we have to consider what we imagine language to be and, again, to point out that its characterizations have been partial and particular. They follow **from** and justify the beliefs about human uniqueness for which they were constructed.

Language, for example, appears to be infinite in sentence grammar, 'because' we are creative and can expand our ideas way beyond our experience. For Thomas Aquinas, we are creative because God is infinite (Pegis, 1948). And other animals do not have souls, are not creative. It seems to me that one aspect of language has been raised to primacy, because it assisted in the human uniqueness-having-a-soul argument, rather than it being clearly correct. How can we possibly know whether other animals are creative, abstract ... whatever? Almost all of our methods for studying them have precluded this very possibility — with the exception of the Gardners' and some other current work with chimpanzees (Gardner and Gardner, 1971).

The arguments about human language have implicitly — occasionally explicitly — carried with them a description of how other animals think; rather don't think. I suggest that such arguments derive not from animals, but directly from human characterizations of animals-as-subhuman. The idea that animals have 'calls' which are more-or-less instinctual is not necessarily to characterize animals **in their own terms**, but to set off humans as especially special. 'Callists' are guilty of this sort of anthropomorphic reasoning that they often accuse others of employing. That they can turn around and use descriptions based on animals-as-defective-humans, to attempt to **characterize** humans, is only understandable if we believe that they already came to the study of animals with axes-to-grind about human behavior.

About the appearance of language being infinite,[30] I suggest that infants already relating — communicating with parents — begin somehow to be in a question-response relation with them. Given several dozen 'question words' — each yielding a distinct 'response set' — language would appear to be infinite. The set of all answers to even a single question as 'Where ...?' is itself infinite. It generates as many answers (sentences) as there are 'places' in the imaginable universe. If anything, there are quite a few infinitudes in language, but that fact does not make language any more mysterious or mystical or special than the facts of the existence of anything else (nor any less).

The primacy of the assumption of language-as-infinite has given a particular twist to the 'great' problems in Western thought. However, it has not yielded, and cannot possibly yield, any 'solutions', and very little if any insight into the human condition beyond what it already presumes. It is in this sense that language is merely a powerful metaphor which encapsulates a particular view of human nature. Its 'analysis' will not tell us more than the metaphor already contains.

A problem sentence grammar (S-grammar) cannot handle: why anything is **sensible**, beyond imputing it to each (normal) human individual, as innate, or its propensity as somehow innate. In a social-interactional view, sensibility is a statement about what society (e.g., a mother treating her infant as a representative of how a 'normal' person constructs the universe) means sensibility to be. Sensibility subsumes 'logic' or 'rationality', because it shifts these notions to the way in which one's society thinks and is a notion which permits change. Rationality is not then uniquely human, but it is a statement about how one's significant others think about the world.

The adult members of each community tend (within some limits) to literally see the world in approximately the same ways. The idea of language as a set of words referring to objects already implies that speakers of any language see objects in essentially the same way. Their minds might in some senses be very different, but the ability to consistently call a 'table' by that term implies sameness of properties and agreement on what it looks like. In this sense of language, there is essentially no arbitrariness or disagreement about what is seen in a visually 'busy' universe. In effect, each infant who will come to be called 'normal' must come to see and say in the same way as the adults whom he will 'join'. Sensibility is not some organismic propensity, but a statement about sociality: each child will come to see the world and understand it in about the same way as others; failure to do so will result in his exclusion from society, being labeled as defective, retarded, autistic, etc.[31]

Whether any nonnormal person is not willing to become sensible, or he is not able to become sensible, is one of the points on which S-grammar and an interactional Question-Response (Q-R) grammar will disagree. If one's view of language imputes sensibility and knowing to the individual, then it is the problem of the abnormal person. He was 'born defective' — poor genes, 'tired eggs', his mother got frightened by a goblin — the victim is blamed for his incapacity. On the other hand, even a physically unusual individual (and each of us is anomalous in some sense or other, I learned in Anatomy) can become a pretty normal sort of person.

It has seemed to me that becoming normal, staying normal, is a process which is part of the social scene. It would be difficult to know in a definite way whether abortion, autism, retardation are organismic or interactional and whether their therapies ought to be directed to the individual-qua-individual or to the individual in terms of some social reality (or both). But our theories direct us to one or the other direction, exclusively.

If sensibility, rationality, and normalcy are essential properties of the individual, then a lack of them or peculiar sorts of them are the 'fault' of the individual. In this view it becomes clear that the outside world and other persons in one's world are nothing more than stimuli which nurture one's being. But there are no other 'minds'. Time tends to be fixed; once is forever. An abnormal life is the payoff for a 'genetic accident'.

Instead, I propose that life-as-interaction is a very fragile, processual mode of being. We ought to be 'surprised' at how well it usually works. If an infant 'looks funny' (as, say, in Down's Syndrome), parents are highly likely (in my observation) to spend less time and energy interacting with that child. As I suggest later, it is impossible to know whether a child has a defective or retarded mind, or whether his treatment and subsequent 'internal' view are very different from what most of us call normal. (As someone who grew up as a partially handicapped person, I can give ample testimony that being physically 'unusual' is a small feature of being which tends at all moments to grow and pervade one's total existence.)

S- or mind-grammar leads us to postulate normalcy as an inherent/innate attribute of individuals; Q-R suggests that so-called normalcy, including what we have believed to be uniquely human (intelligence, rationality, etc.), are statements about a very complicated and fragile interactional process in which the theory makes a great deal of difference to how the behavioral scientist will regard the world to be observed. And it has very clear and definite implications for how we will regard all people who 'look different' or think differently from the majority. S-grammar, in my view, inevitably lends itself to a form of racism because it imputes those distinctly humanoid qualities of intelligence and reason to each organism, rather than to the form and quality of social processes.[32] In my view, S-grammar is a theological notion which may now be retired in the context of humans as intrinsically social beings — evolving, as we have, from other social beings.

In my view, individuality, self-personhood are **emergent** processes growing over time.

Toward an Existential Biology

Where, then, are we in considering the 'origin of language'?

The issue of the 'origin' of a putative entity called 'language' seems to have two senses: (1) a temporal, simple causal sense; and (2) a much broader, conceptual sense. Was there a singular event, such as the enlargement of the human brain, which enabled us to have language? Or was there a complicated nexus of processes which gradually changed the nature of human nature, language being but one of the resultant features of being?

The 'origin' problem tends to suggest the former, a singular clear course, akin to the origin of, say, a glacier. Attention to the dynamics of languaging, however, its development, and the dimensions of the interacting bodies suggests that language is one small part of a set of gradually accretive processes toward being human. There may have been many points of 'origin'.

It is in this latter sense that the isolation of some entity we call language is misleading. In our zeal for an 'accounting' of human nature, it has been tempting to capture an essence, and believe that it represents exhaustively, the essence of man. On the contrary, the view of man as unique because of language seems to have exhausted its power of accounting and explanation. These theories of language have no place to go that they have not already been.

The dilemmas of life, in terms of our social being, have to do with the nature of our sociality. If we are always — and already — communicating creatures, the development of body, languaging, thought, self are variations on the nature of such processes. It is not that our minds 'take over' from our body; it is that we grow and develop as unitary sorts of beings. There is no question that the processes of communication change and develop through life. It is the nature of these processes, the form and changes in them, which ought to be the subject matter worth probing — not a limited aspect of our development called 'language'.

The dilemma of life, as encapsulated by the 'origin' problem, is that it seems to tell us that only the 'mind' parts of our being represent the true person. Our bodies are either inconsequential to our being or less important in our lives. The problem, as I see it, is how to reconcile a theory of being human with our life experience. In effect, what we need to do is to admit our conceptual-beings 'back into our bodies'. We exist as biological beings and will continue to. But our theories of being seem to have denied this. The antidote has been to deny the 'mind' and talk only about 'behavior', but this has not jibed with our existence either. We are not one — or another — of mind or body, but 'all of these'. We are, in my view, much more complicated creatures than our theories have been leading us to admit or to realize.

In order to gain the sorts of insights and knowledge about being human, which the 'origin of language' problem has not permitted, observations about us and (other) animals must remain 'open'. It is not possible to compare creatures whom we have already decided are different in essential features of their being. Yet, to further our own objectivity about ourselves, it is necessary to observe other species and attempt to understand their 'terms', their space, their bodies. If the 'sound' one hears differs according to one's sort of body, then a comparison of sound instrumentally is pseudo-comparison. We need first to understand the relation of sound and body form. Current ideas seem to presume that a particular analysis of human sounds grants insight into other species' significant sounds. This sort of thinking is not true comparison but points toward and highlights differences, rather than similarities. All of us believe that we are different from (other) animals — the question that remains is: how are we different?

As Allen Gardner and I concluded together in a debate over this issue a few years ago with Marler and Geschwind, the discontinuity between (other) animals and humans has not been in language or thought, but in the conceptualizations we have brought to this issue.

The origin of language problem remains a pseudo-problem. I have tried to clarify why this is so and to suggest other ways of considering the issues involved. In my view, we are on the threshold of a fascinating era of discoveries about the nature of human nature, which an open comparative science may yield. What has, in effect, stopped us has been a firm belief in the uniqueness of man as the only creature with language.

How could we know that?

(2) COULD A NON-H?

On reading studies of verbal behavior of man and of other animals, one is struck by a number of similarities in methodology and of differences in approach, ideas, and theories. Perhaps this is natural and reflects the ambivalence that most of us feel in trying to compare processes which seem to be only more-or-less analogous. Most striking to me is the fact that human linguists tend to consider semantics as their most problematic area, while nonhuman callists proceed directly from meaning. Perhaps neither has a choice, given the nature of his subject matter.

Despite these outstanding differences, however, one is also struck with how knowledgeably many of these scholars regard their methods, definitions, and subject matters. In my experience — fairly extensive among both linguists and callists — each side tends to presume much more about the subject and results of the other than appears to be warranted. Especially striking is the willingness of callists to believe that human language behavior is well understood and explicable, thus the fairly uncritical adoption of some linguistic methods.

I believe that new insights, new theories, and ideas about all verbal behavior are long overdue. We are, at present, left with non-analogous data — not because the subject matters are intrinsically nonanalogous (this remains an open question) — but because the approaches are so different.

In order to underline this position I offer the following parable on the question of whether **any** nonhuman could possibly discover that humans have language.

Could a nonhuman possibly discover that humans have language?

Probably not. But this question has to be put in a number of contexts in order for it to take on any significance.

First of all, the 'outsider', the nonhuman of our imaginings, cannot simply be ordinarily terrestrial; like a dog, for instance. Dogs have already had untold centuries of opportunity and have not done any impressive work in this direction, so far as we know.

So we must mean a **special** type of nonhuman who might find out about language. What attributes would he (she, they) have, and what kinds of things might he observe that he would be able to adduce to his discovery that we have language (or that we don't — **we** cannot *a priori* rule out that possibility for **them**)?

The simple answer, perhaps the most direct one, is that he would observe our **verbal behavior**. Maybe he could relate it to our other behavior or to our things and our works. Anybody could look at our cities and figure out that we must do some pretty fancy languaging.

Yet if Mr. Outsider had dropped in on us, say, 40 or 50,000 years ago, we would have been without most of these trappings: subtropical hunters and gatherers. We would have looked remarkably like any group or troop of social primates; some kind of chimp. And no linguist I know of believes that these humans didn't have language in essentially the same form it exists in today. Human language has probably been around for a very long time — way before we did much more than hack out a few flakes from pieces of flint.

Well then, he could still observe our verbal behavior — or could he? **How** could he do that? What things would count or not ... as language?

Now, the first fact about verbal behavior is that we humans don't call all our verbal behavior **Language**. Only a little bit of our verbal output, the part we can write down like I'm doing now, we call Language. But there's a lot more verbal behavior we produce that an outsider would probably record right along with the **message**. And how is he going to separate his data into language, plus whatever's left over?

The second fact is that we don't have very good ideas about how we humans do just that; separate verbal behavior into its various 'parts'. But we do speak and understand, really quite well, all things considered. So what do we think language is? And what is it used for? Maybe we should just ask why a nonhuman would raise this question in the first place.

Without probing too deeply into the motivational structure of the outsider, let's consider what language **seems** to mean; which parts of verbal behavior are considered to be **linguistic**; what other parts are there; how do we decide?

Verbal behavior seems to be a pretty **continuous** kind of thing once it starts, rather a **process** without any very abrupt stops or starts or holes in it, at least within an utterance. It's a kind of **stream** of behavior, part of the normal activity of our bodies. It can be depicted like the wave it would be if portrayed on an **oscilloscope**. The **noise** or power of the sound wave varies in such a way that it causes an oscillating diaphragm in a microphone to vibrate analogously. This can be made visual on television (CRT) tubes which form this ongoing pathway: 〰〰〰 . And with electronic equipment, we can **sample** the smallest parts of a word, look at the 'outline' of an entire utterance, at parts, processes.

Offhand, we don't know how any nonhuman would sample an utterance. We aren't even sure how we do; because most instrumental studies of human speech have taken a **single** human ability — namely our ability to distinguish musical tones — and have devised instruments which utilize this ability to alter, 'operate on', and **analyze** the speech wave. Unfortunately, almost all of the human acoustic data comes to us in this form: one which nonhumans might not relate to very well. As in some other technical science endeavors, most of our data has been gathered and analyzed in some partial way, depending on which human ability appeared so striking to the observer who set the style in the field (in this case, it was one of the fathers of psychophysiology — Hermann Helmholtz — about a century ago).

Although we're fairly sure that the musical-tone ability is really quite important in our understanding of speech (particularly of vowel sounds), this doesn't necessarily help us to know very much about the whole sound stream, that thing or process the outside observer is **likely** to attend to. What other kind of 'information' is located in verbal behavior, in addition to the stuff we think of as the 'core', the message?

In any utterance, really in almost any single word said out of context, we get a lot of information **about** the speaker and his situation or setting. It seems reasonable that an observer of verbal behavior would also record this as part of his **primary** data.

Lest we think that this is a rather insignificant or smallish part of the signal, it appears that probably the greatest part of the amplitude, the loudness, is a function of the physical distance between speakers. In interactional contexts, where people are talking to (and understanding) one another, the loudness of speech reflects distance and size of the audience. (This can be tested anecdotally by trying to carry out a two-person 'private' conversation at its 'correct' level, in front of an audience of some size.)

On testing — by taking bits of tape out of a variety of contexts and playing them to an audience — it also appears that much more situational/contextual information occurs in the speech: relative age of speaker and audience, type of room, some aspects of the conversation (e.g., reading), telephone, relationship between speaker and listener (e.g., husband-wife, parent-child, friends, formal). Most of this information must be available pretty continuously in the speech stream, because we can get an audience to identify them fairly accurately from most parts of a tape of real situations.

So it looks as if our outsider may have a bit more trouble in finding out about our 'language' than we might have supposed.

Why do we humans believe we have language? (Conversely, why **don't** we believe that others have it?) How do we separate L from non-L?

We seem to believe, first of all, that there is a major or primary function of L: namely, to **convey meaning**. Second, we seem to believe that only some parts of our verbal behavior do this; namely, the parts we call language. While no one would want to strongly deny that non-H's do much the same things, if not verbally, then through gestures; if not through language, then through other aspects of verbal behavior (often called 'paralanguage' or 'tone-of-voice' phenomena); it still seems that we Humans do some 'special' H-things. These seem to be the ones we call Language.

It seems clear — if anything is exactly clear — that there are some funny games going on here. I won't pretend to try and straighten them out; but we should go back to our original question about Non-H. Could he discover these 'special' aspects of H-L? Does he actually **have** these as part of his verbal behavior? If he doesn't, he'll probably never be able to solve the problem.

All of us agree that verbal behavior is 'composed' of sound. H's have decided that some aspects of this sound stream are patterned, repetitious, limited, few in number; in short, we have figured out how to describe the language stream in a rather 'fixed' way: we can do it well enough that we can **recreate** much of our original verbal behavior simply by going through this descriptive shorthand. (We usually call this: writing, the alphabet, etc. We can also **understand** the messages, but how we do this will, as we'll see, continue to remain problematic.)

It thus turns out that H-L's are alphabetizable. But, would this appear obvious to a non-H? After all, the alphabet is a very recent invention — it dates approximately from just after prehistory (or maybe, just before). We 'spoke' L's for a long time before we observed ourselves to be describable in this way.

What is an alphabet, and why was something so obvious to us, so obscure to our L-speaking ancestors? Languages weren't, as far as we know, very different from their present forms, and there are still some preliterate people. An alphabet has to do with the notion that we break up our conceptual world of sound into a number of distinct parts, that we're very consistent in this, and that speakers of a given language (or dialect) all do (can do) this in just about the same way.

Linguists speak of language as being composed of phonemes — the sort of basic particle or atom of speech. Even more finely grained, the subatomic particles are called 'd.f.'s' — distinctive features: a set of oppositional elements by which we can generate all human sounds. These are **built up** into syllables, words, phrases, sentences. Presumably we have recording phoneme-synthesizers in our H-minds which take a domain of d.f.'s, select the proper ones, order them, give a directive to our speech-makers which translate these into muscular action upon an air stream emerging from our lungs, and we produce language. The listener then receives all of this — perhaps he empathetically moves his oral muscles — but the story says that his ear vibrates sympathetically, sending ordered phonemes and d.f.'s to his brain, and his 'interpretive cortex' then understands this utterance. At least he gets the sounds in order.

In this particular description, perhaps it's a theory, of sound production we have left out any notion of **meaning**. Everyone knows that words mean something; they refer to objects, tell us about things. So do sentences. Peculiarly enough, however, H-sounds are considered to be sort of independent of meaning. (But animal-behaviorists do not consider non-H, terrestrial animal sounds as independent of meaning — i.e., animal 'calls' are considered directly meaningful to animals. On this issue, particularly, H-L linguists and non-H linguists have very different views, although they seem scarcely aware of such differences.)

Phonemes keep 'words' apart! They 'tell' us the difference between *pin, pen — bit, pit — dig, Dick*. We can construct an alphabet for any H-language which consistently incorporates such distinctions.[33] Phonemic distinctions occur only in the contexts of **words**. It remains problematic as to whether phonemes are the only sound units of sentences or longer utterances. We do know that alphabetic symbols, essentially phonemic, can be used to write all utterances, so there are almost undoubtedly **some common factors** in phonemes; word contexts and phonemes; sentences. The sound $/t/$ is like itself in all contexts. We do not presently know much about what else happens in longer than word contexts, except that speech in context is a lot different sounding from words spoken in isolation. (Which would Non-H hear — could he distinguish between words and sentences? Not easily!)

Languages (and **dialects**) differ in their distinctions along a variety of lines: they have different numbers of phonemes, or they are distinguished somewhat differently; but a phonemic system, an alphabet, can be constructed for all H-languages. (A dialect example in American English: most dialects distinguish between the vowel sounds in *cot* and *caught* — some, particularly along the 40th parallel, Pittsburgh, do not. Children seem to accept the same sets of distinction as their parents, to 'hear' and speak in about the same way; thus there is continuity much as in any biological species or subspecies factor.)

This job, the 'discovery' or laying out of the phonemic system of any H-language, is a fairly easy one for H-linguists. They use a native speaker of a given H-language to set out a list of minimally different words; words like *bit* and *pit* which are different only in one variable: *b* vs. *p*; or *pit* and *pet*: *i* vs. *e*. Not all languages distinguish, say, between *b* and *p*. No native speakers of any language seem to carry around a very conscious or explicit awareness of this skill, this part of their being. Nonetheless they consistently make just these distinctions. Phonemics is a set of questions or a methodology by which we can control **our** observers' ways of hearing distinctions (and try not to impute them to others) and allow others to tell us about **their** sound systems. It is objective in the sense that it permits an **outsider** to get into the 'mind' of the insider.

In the non-H observer, the problems in discovering phonemic-type distinctions are: (1) in knowing about words; (2) the fact that only some very few words are minimally distinct; (3) and in **already** having a cross-species communication system by which he can ask somebody to match two words which differ in a single variable.

It seems unlikely that he could do any one of these, quite implausible that he could imagine doing all three, unless of course he has/had language in the same sense as we. But then we would have little reason to refer to him as non-H.

Consider these problems in greater detail:

(1) Knowing about **words**.

While we all seem to **believe in** words, it turns out that their existence lies more in our shared beliefs than demonstrably occurring in the sound stream. We hear, or think we hear, ourselves speaking words in some order; we can take any of these words in this sentence and say it 'in isolation', alone. We can say, aloud, such things as: *we, take, words, sentence* ... and think we believe that the spaces we leave between written words somehow also occur in speech. But they don't.

Speech is an essentially continuous function; the non-H observer would not be likely to note the spaces between 'words'. Perhaps we would say 'single words' to him – trying to make contact – but would single words appear very different from phrases or sentences to his oscilloscopic (or sound spectographic) type ears?

In fact, single words said in isolation are much like short sentences on an oscilloscope. They look quite different (but also quite similar) to the 'same' words said within sentence contexts!

(2) Minimally distinct words.

Our **words** – any particular word in any H-language – sound (and look on an oscilloscope) a little bit different in every different context. That is, the sounds which we call 'words' are also carrying other kinds of information, additional variables to those which minimally keep words apart. (If non-H had been lucky enough to use a sound spectroscope as his primary observational instrument, he could have eliminated or at least depressed the obviousness of the nonphonemic information. Again, it seems an unlikely choice for him to have made.)

One of the interesting differences between linguists and callists is precisely in the use of instrumentation. H-linguists **first** do an interpretive interview with a native speaker of some language in order to elicit words which contrast minimally. He must get his **informant** to both say words in isolation, to think up some contrastive cases (not a simple chore for most people), and to somehow communicate which parts of a word are different: English *pit* and *bed* would sound essentially identical to speakers of many human languages, yet **we** recognize **three** significant distinctions, so these are not a useful contrastive pair of words to a linguist.

After this job is done, H-linguists may put these phonemes on an instrument such as a sonograph in order to have another basis for differentiating them, or to make a voice synthesizer for that language (a necessity in making a voice translation machine). But the instrument contributes **nothing** to the phonemic analysis.

Callists – on the contrary – put the verbal output of their non-H subjects on some instrument early in their data analysis. Machine outputs are compared for similarities, and, if judged to be **similar enough**, they are included under the rubric of a single call. In general, only calls which occur in similar semantic-behavioral contexts would be compared. But the judgment of similarity is made by the observer, not by the informant of the H-linguist. The comparability of the results remain completely dubious. Calls and phonemes (or words) are not even approximately similar units.

The H-linguist is convinced that he cannot make judgments about the similarity/differences of sounds in languages other than his own. In his view, the would-be animal linguist has misapplied his instruments in making judgments about how animals differentiate sounds.

My impression is that non-H language investigators are either unaware of how H-linguists actually work, or they underestimate the possible complexity of non-H verbal behavior, or both. How could a non-H get some H to make minimal contrasts, out of context? Those of us who have tried doing this with other H's know full well that it's not easy to get people to play this contrastive game. We have to get them somehow to know **about** the game — by demonstration, example, interest, compassion, etc. But a lot of people either cannot or will not do it. Again, this seems to be an unlikely possibility for a non-H to even attempt to do; even if we **have** L's and phonemes, he'll not find that out, unless ...

(3) X-species communication system.

Most science fiction writers (the people who have been most concerned with this problem) have postulated nonterrestrial beings of similar or 'superior intelligence' to ours. Usually their form, their bodies and brains, differ from ours, but we relate to them in some mental or rational sense. Mathematics is seen as H at his most logical and universal; others who have developed civilization are too, so we'll use mathematics as our common 'language'. Implicit in this notion, of course, is the idea that mathematics is in some sense 'extra-human', an attribute of the universe, and not merely one which is particularly human or develops from how we H's particularize or abstract the world of objects. 'Objectivity' is a characteristic which is attainable by those of superior 'H' intelligences.

It's worth noting in passing that many of us seem to hold out greater hopes of communicating with nonterrestrial beings (or dead H's) than with porpoises or chimps. But note again that our direct ancestors of the not very remote past would have resembled these terrestrial non-H's more than we seem willing to admit.

Granted that our postulated non-H observer was 'smart' enough to get to Earth; granted that he is unlikely to find out about words, thus also unlikely to break up our sound stream into the phonemes we consider to be basic units; what can he do with all this sound we emit? How can he discover order, organization, code — whatever attributes we seem to think of as characterizing language?

We admit H's have not been able to 'break the code' of any non-H terrestrial 'language'. We're in no better position to do this for birds than an other-worldly creature would be in observing us. But why should this be so?

It hasn't been for lack of 'data'. A great deal of work, much admittedly recent, has been done on animal 'sounds'. But it hasn't been **comparative** in the sense we are likely to impute to the intelligent extra-terrestrial, non-H.

What has been done in comparing verbal output across species, and why?

The answer: almost nothing! Because they're **assumed** to be non-comparable.

Even for biologists, C. Darwin among them, man's language is just a little bit **special**, just as H's are just a wee bit 'outside of Nature'. Language is most always at the heart of the 'deep' explanation for our specialness. Whereas most former writers attributed this to our 'soul', to knowing God in a uniquely H-way, this practice has been replaced by omitting the term, **soul**, on grounds of scientism, one supposes.

Here we must speculate: how would a non-H conceptualize his own place in the universe, and what would he believe ours to be?

Why would he bother to compare himself with us? He could, if he felt we were like him in some bodily sense, use us to experiment on. We might be cheaper than his species of non-H. Whom would you use, an H or a non-H, etc.? (I think our first problem in meeting nonterrestrial intelligent beings on their ground would be political, to set up the grounds of vivisection, for self-protection, of course.)

But let us grant him some kind of Boy Scout creed, one no less honorable than our own, and assume he is well motivated toward us. If he's interested in the problem, we'll simply accept his faith at face value.

Is **he** in or out of nature? Is he a member of a species which has evolved in the same ecosphere as many others? Is he a social creature, tied for his survival to others?

If he is asocial, our antivivisection lobby is probably doomed; he's probably not a Boy Scout, and he's likely to be a mirage; i.e., we're talking about a social creature who's already learned about himself and others. Not only does he communicate in order to cooperate, he communicates in order to continue living. He's so deeply committed to others' existence that he can only imagine himself in their terms which he has to continually recreate and test.

But if he's not so social, has no imagination, he simply wouldn't be very concerned.

We believe that we have L, other terrestrial species have 'calls'. L vs. 'calls'. What's the difference? What would non-H have?

Actually there are several differences between H and non-H, but different sorts of differences:

(1) They **sound** different: H's sound different from chimps, bees, porpoises, crows; but consider that chimps sound different from H's, crows, etc., etc., – and, in fact, most species are probably 'fully aware' of this. Consider further that H's sound different from other H's, but often in very peculiar ways that have little to do with what we think of as Language; i.e., there's a tremendous amount of variation possible without crossing species lines. The range of variation across H-languages and language families has never been examined in any but the narrowest sense; e.g., the folklore of most descriptive linguists allows them to identify the areal family of a language previously unheard. How do they do this?

(2) 'Calls' are a burst or stream of sound which is temporally delimited; they also **have** meaning: H-language words are delimited like calls and have meaning, but they are not sound exactly, because sound is considered to be a (sensory) medium which **carries** words. There is a crucial difference here between what H-linguists and non-H 'callists' regard as 'sound data', and likely to be implied analytic differences which derive from this point.

(3) Meaning theories; what the data is about, what it symbolizes, or refers to, are quite different **in practice**. While there appear to be quite comparable H and non-H meaning data, H's and non-H's clearly share a large degree of commonality – the methods of both groups have somehow bypassed this common ground.

Animal sounds are assumed to be **about** fairly basic and general kinds of things: sex, food, danger, territory, aggression, etc. H-sounds which are considered to be **linguistic** refer to more specific things: they locate objects in space and time; they 'activate' or predicate these; they tell about what is, did, or will happen to what/whom. No one denies the 'animalistic' sounds that humans make, but these are usually considered to be **prelanguage**, para- or epilanguage, and remain virtually uninvestigated.

(4) **Context.** H-language studies are done essentially context-free. But most non-H language studies attempt to classify similar sound patterns both in terms of sound similarities, and the apparent contexts which provoke them, or in which they occur. H-language is assumed to be 'context-sensitive' in some vague, uninvestigable sense; but H-language exists 'independently'. Non-H is usually believed to be context-tied, if not context-fixed; i.e., context is **causal** for non-H's, but not for H's.

(5) **Communication.** While common 'common sense' would have it

that H-language or any non-H sound system has a primary function to communicate between members of any particular society, this notion has not entered into anyone's methodologies to any great extent.

How would our hypothetical non-H observer choose to look at this problem? How would his position affect any potential solution?

·If he decides to view us (our language) as we view our own language, I'm convinced that he could not possibly discover that we have language. He might come to believe it on other grounds (our technology, propensity for war, etc.), but he would have no means of putting questions to us about our words, phonemes, sentences, and no way to evaluate any answers we might give him. Nor could he even sense that we were **answering** anything, unless he already believed that we were. So we must impute a rather constant faith to him that very few H's have maintained *vis-a-vis* other terrestrial species.

On the other hand, he could have come to some other conclusions about viewing us which could, indeed, lead him to finding out a great deal about human behavior. He may even discover, perhaps rightly, that we don't have language in any of the senses, in any terms of which we're used to thinking.

First, he must believe that his problem is examinable and ultimately soluble. *Per contra*, most H-linguists regard H and non-H verbal behavior as sufficiently different so as to be essentially noncomparable.

Secondly, he's likely to view us as emanators of behavior, not just acoustic behavior. Even if he believed that language exists as a thing independent of our other behavior, it would seem an overly restricting place to start looking. To look at something called language, you already have to know what it is (and isn't) **before** you begin your observations. Non-H, being bright and loose-minded, would be unlikely to observe just verbal behavior.

Third, he's likely to assume that we H's **relate** to other H's. Now, if he viewed us from above, he might see that we relate to different H's in particular ways. This he'd have to learn from watching our bodies, since we're as likely — possibly more likely — to speak in public to nonfamily members than to our immediate family. But this, in turn, would depend on the situation: an old school reunion, or a cocktail party, a family on a journey or at home. But none of this social, contextual structure would be apparent or recorded if he merely used his non-H microphone analog device.

Non-H must, in other words, be committed to believing that all of our activity, particularly interactional activity, is investigable and ultimately explainable. He's likely to start big (social context, social structure), and go small gradually (sentences, phonemes). If he, at any point, starts believing that our behavior, verbal or not, is random or individual he can **never** arrive at a solution to the original problem.

He will, if at all careful, have ample data to support any position he finds comfortable to take; he will easily be able to believe that **we** have calls, and he'll be able to generate a methodology for comparing them. But the only way he'll ever discern that we might have language is to maintain his belief in its possible existence until he has been forced to abandon all other interpretive possibilities.

If he ever gets to know about our social matrix, how might he narrow his approach to our verbal behavior?

Let's assume that he is lucky enough to 'hear' and record a single person's voice, consistently, out of the maelstrom of noise which characterizes most social settings. His instruments would still show either an unbelievably great amount of variation or almost no variation, depending pretty much on what he **counts** as sameness/difference. Take the oscilloscopic output of anyone's speech, and you'll be so overwhelmed by sheer data, that you're likely to try to dampen some of the variation, hoping it won't be significant. Almost everything looks (sounds) different.

At this point, we must grant non-H at least a bit of faith and imagination; faith, that if H's do have a language, they must somehow act like his instruments, yet they must have created order out of this apparent chaos; imagination, that sounds can be about lots of things simultaneously. Non-H must believe that sounds carry many different kinds of information, and that most all H's have fancy interpretive equipment which lets them attend to many variables at about the same time.

(He might have thought about tingling our bodies or brains, to see how we're constructed. But he, being the astute observer he'll have to be, probably looked at little H's and figured that he and they were equally outside. He saw that they had no particular opportunity to diddle anyone else's hearing apparatus, and assumed that they had to operate in some other manner. Now if he could only find out how they do it.)

What apparent data will show up on his oscilloscope — how can he interpret it?

First of all, working as widely as possible, he may notice variation between speakers/movers. He'll note that interactors' bodies and voices are active together; listeners' bodies and voices are very quiet, relative to speakers' (obviously he'll have to figure out some way of judging which interactors are really communicating which ones merely in close proximity, but we'll neglect this issue here).

On observing a number of individuals, he'll note tendencies, ranges of pitch variation to be different for different speakers. Maybe he'll be able to separate males from females by this method, but this seems less certain now than I formerly thought. He'll note a great deal of variation in every individual's voice. Due to what?

Sheer overall loudness seems to have a lot to do with the distance between speaker and listener and with the number of listeners. Non-H will have trouble in cases where speaker's **intended** audience is out of sight, while others are closer; e.g., calling one's children while standing next to one's spouse.

Loudness will also have much to do with surrounding **noise**. This may be a severe problem to non-H, separating an H-voice from its surround. But H-voice amplitude is intelligible to H's if only a few decibels **over** the surrounding noise. Thus amplitude, so far, is a purely social variable – really, a set of variables – about the speaker's perception of the interactional situation. But this is overall amplitude; is there variation or change within the stream of speech?

Many, many! If non-H happened to get in on the 'beginning' of a dialogue, and kept track, he would have noted that the voices of the participants decreased as the thing went on. (At this point, my own data is remarkably thin!) That may imply to him, that amplitude also has something to do with the working out or delimitation of a social situation. It should recaution him that random sampling techniques in such social situations will lose this information.

In smaller, i.e., shorter segments (but we still presuppose our data located in **organized** segments) **relative** loudness also seems to be a feature of things. *Ceteris paribus*, the beginning of a sentence is the loudest thing around. This observation raises a couple of questions: (1) What is it loud about? E.g., does the amplitude carry any information about what's to come, besides being a kind of boundary phenomenon? (2) Why do ends of sentences 'seem' to sound louder than anything else?

We would assume that non-H is likely to record amplitudes and compare them. How is he to guess that we H's attend less to overall or absolute loudness, more to relative loudness in certain positions in a sentence? How does he separate the loudness which tells us about sentence organization from that which conveys information about relationships within that organization? More simply, what's the same and different? With respect to what systems?

If non-H is lucky, he might be asking questions of the kind like we've been asking: at some point in an utterance (say, T_1), which information is about T_1 and which about $T_0, T_2, ..., T_n$; which about the apparent entity $<T_0 ... T_n>$, say, a sentence; which about R_1 (a very similar event to T_1 – but located in $<R_0 ... R_n>$); which about T_1, an event with which T_2 is **contrasted** (e.g., /T_1/ we went vs. /T_2/ we **went**).

A major difficulty is that while non-H may record $<T_0, T_1, ..., T_n>$, the most patterned, similar events to T_1 don't occur **in that situation**. Non-H will only hear T_1, in contrast to $<T_0, ..., T_n>$; not in contrast to $T_1{}^x, T_1{}^y$. ...

In any ordinary human utterance, this is exactly the case. If we refer to plural objects, say, *horses*, we know that the singular is *horse*. The plural *iz* is but one of three regular English plurals. How is non-H to determine this, in any utterance which is **meaningful**; which is discussing the real world?

It appears that children are **corrected** in a pretty systematic fashion. If they say *dogziz* (a very characteristic error for most children I know of, during one short period of language development), their parents say: *No; dogz!* that is, parents respond to linguistic errors, but also with a theory of meaning in mind, precisely the theory that they're going to force their child to adopt as its own.

How do these demi-H's get to figure out that a 'dog' is even being talked about, when there are close to an infinite number of object-events in any eyeful? My guess is: through watching what the parents are watching. Translating that into their own bodies, they begin to focus on, to attend to the same objects as everyone else around them (they attend to lots of other things, too). But the critical languaging elements seem to be (1) knowledge about what others are/will attend(ing) to; (2) willingness to move into such a shared universe of eventing; (3) knowledge about when they are public and when private; (4) ...?

Where does this leave non-H? He's got to get some things which he can compare systematically: T_2, R_1, T_1, etc. He will note that they are quite similar (though how he'll think to compare them in the first place is not immediately obvious to me). His next problem is what to attribute the similarities and differences to; if he has figured out that *dog, dogz, doggie*, are about the same event, what are the differences about?

(Although I hesitate to point this out, even if non-H had these three words listed on a recorded tape, they still are more different than we would suspect; e.g., the presence of the *-z* in *dogz* doesn't just get added on to the 'end' of *dog* — it affects, to at least a limited extent, the -*g*, the vowel, and even the *d*-; if we have it in mind to say *dogz*, we'll start differently than if we are going to say *dog*. An illustration of this 'anticipatory feedback' can be noted in getting ready to say the word *h*ill and *h*ole; before the mouth opens, you can feel your lips forming the initial *h*'s in quite different ways — due to, or caused by, the vowel to follow. But note that we are already acting with a sound-image in mind **and** body, way before the different vowel sounds will occur. Serial order in the sound realm is more complicated than a phonemic model would suggest.)

Here, let's leave non-H for a moment and describe a study in Intelligibility, using the kind of methods I think might be appealing and obvious to non-H.

In this study I compared words which are phonemically identical, looking for nonphonemic patterned sound differences. Indeed, these occur and are probably as acoustically apparent as phonemic differences.

Are these differences, for example, between two instances of the 'same' word said as a phrase: (*a a*) phonemically written /*ey ey*/. Both are obviously the phonemic word /*ey*/ — e.g., not /*i, e*, or *bee*/. But they are clearly different from one another.

To check the consistency of the difference, try any other word: (*b b*), (*cat cat*), (*pencil, pencil*). However one describes the **differences** acoustically, they seem to be constant, regardless of the phonemic makeup of the examples. The first member of each phrase is higher in pitch, louder in amplitude, but in this type of example it is clear that within the duration of each word there is a lot of change, this type of change, too, seems to be very patterned.[34]

In longer phrases: (*a a a a a*) all the *a*'s are different in some nonphonemic manner. Again the differences are about the same in any phrase of this shape (*dog, dog, dog, dog, dog*).

Note that each one in order (except the last) becomes quieter, its amplitude drops rapidly **across** the phrase. Since these words are very much the same — i.e., each one is very much like the previous one — it may be that dynamic similarity is signaled by a diminution in amplitude.

In a similar phrase such as (*a a*) (*a a a*), the relationship between the amplitudes is very different.

Apparently such differences depend on **location** in the phrase, on the nature of the words preceding and following. There seems to be acoustic information about the organization and ongoingness of any phrase located in the sound stream, simultaneously with phonemic information. Granted that a spectrum analysis of sound probably enhances phonemic differences and depresses locational and organization differences, which is non-H's best strategy in trying to discover if we have language: to do, or to avoid phonemic analysis?

From the acoustic view of non-H, there are only three variables which characterize all sound data: amplitude, frequency, duration. The only question is what we can/do do with these which make us believe we have language. Expressed differently, what is the nature of the H-ear? Dynamically, vowel sounds are characterized by sound-wave reoccurrences; each vowel sound such as /ey/ is made up of about 30 or so of these. Double that figure for a female voice. Only in a few contexts is it difficult for a listener of a tape to decide that /ey/ is /ey/ (and not *i, e,* or *you*). It is also quite clear on hearing *a*'s taken out of context, that they **are** out of context. A sentence composed of a single word — e.g., a word spoken in isolation — does **not** sound like the same word in a different context, though both are recognizably the same word, to us.

Is there a particular organization to the stream of L-behavior, by which we can begin to understand this variation? Non-H must believe it.

A suggestion: words (and smaller or larger forms) contain information about themselves (*a* = *a*, in almost all contexts), but they also convey many things about other forms, the structure in which they're found (e.g., sentences), the context. ... In a few cases I've found that words taken from their original context are **not** understandable as that word; if they were understandable **in** context, then the information about that word had to be located **elsewhere**. Where?

As suggested earlier, words at the beginning are long and loud, partly to cue beginningness, but also to convey information about what's to come; and what's not to.

The kinds of information seem to be more about structure than about particular occurring events. That is, in a beginning word, information is conveyed that there will be several more words, at least, coming along in a tight string — don't interrupt!

It also conveys the notion that the next word or grouping is just like this one — or it isn't — e.g., the word *said* differs in the following contexts: "He *said*, 'oh,' and I *said* he should." Presumably the presence of the very high pitched 'oh' causes this anticipatory feedback. But note that this is similar, if not the same, to what happens to phonetic shapes within a given word. Similar mechanisms can be employed in quite different ways to do a number of jobs.

Words at the end tell us that something has preceded and may tell us more is to occur, but of the shape of a sentence, say, not just another word. It should be becoming clearer that the same word will always appear different in different contexts because it can convey many different kinds of information. Perhaps it is also clear that this problem is studiable, and further, that we speakers are good analyzers of all these systems, whether we know about it in any 'conscious' way, or not. There does, indeed, appear to be a potential acoustic semantics.

The discovery that the really, truly same word said in order — no brackets permitted — diminishes in amplitude, is a major clue perhaps. It would mean, in this informational sense, that any word has to convey minimal information about the next one — e.g., that it's the same. Thus, it can get very quiet indeed.

If this could be used as a base form, then any words of different shape from ◁▱ ▭ ◁ can be assumed to convey more information. Thus when, say, birds are chirping in apparently identical fashion, each individual chirp must be considered to convey **new** information; otherwise there would be a diminution of amplitude.

Obviously this theory depends on a kind of circular reasoning which builds on **our** H-perception, but it does illustrate that we cannot just listen with H-ears and assume that we can hear sameness even in our own languages. Our notions of sameness are constructed on a model of comparison which is perceptually altered from a purely acoustic description of the same events: namely, events that are perceptually the same become acoustically quieter in a sentence. How is non-H to guess this?

Every recurrence, every actualization of the 'same' word, is different. We've seen that such differences are due to noise and other social/contextual variables, place in the conversation; they are also due to different locations within smaller structures. Questions:

(1) What are the actual mechanisms for doing this? Do H- and non-H species have the same mechanisms employed in theme and variations?

(2) Can we find any very general notions about verbal behavior with respect to ...?

Sameness must be **specified** within particular social group boundaries. A table has **some common properties** to all speakers of English. Sameness can, however, only be specified if specifiable objects or actions are involved. This kind of clarity and exactness can only be shared among common language speakers. But it is one kind of shared meaning which many people claim to lie at the bottom of objectivity, rationality, etc.

However, there may also occur lots of other samenesses which are patterned and consistent. But they belong to other realms of behavior; e.g., the way we speak, the dialect. We just do it correctly; we never get to know **about** it. It never comes up in talk about things. Or our walking styles; all we do is get comments about how funny it is. There is no vocabulary for such processes. All we can do is work on them and try to satisfy a more-or-less well-defined image of how others would have us be. Interestingly, we do this about as well as we talk about objects. It may be clear by now that these factors also enter into our languaging, and non-H will believe that he'll have to understand them if he wants to discover if we have language.

Obviously we just take such things for granted as a common set of experiences, a shared experiential base on which, or out of which, we construct language. But why should we believe that non-H would have this experimental base? Is this a part of what we usually call 'higher intelligence', and which we usually attribute to language?

Even from before birth, we deviate from other species in our experiences. While we search for differences in purely L-variables, it should be clear that this is not a totally productive way of thinking about language, within or across species.

In case I'm wrong, however, and there is no potential H and non-H shared area of acoustic semantics, we should not give up hope. If **they** do not turn out to be sufficiently non-Human to be nonaggressive, we can pray for compassion.

(3) THE STUDY OF LANGUAGE AND COMMUNICATION ACROSS SPECIES

> "...the adaptation of the behavior patterns of an organism to its environment is achieved in exactly the same manner as that of its organs ... on the basis of information which the species has gained in the course of its evolution by the age-old method of mutation and selection" (Lorenz, 1965: xiii).

Among the recently emerging approaches to the study of man is one which can be titled **Communication**, and subtitled **Human Ethology**. It consists of an embryonic body of fact and calls for the observation of social behavior in the belief that the best theoretical statements will be closely related to the organized data. This area of study concerns the changing concepts of man's nature, particularly in relation to similarities and differences between social man and social animals. This paper will attempt (1) to present the field in its historical context and to point out some present trends, including assumptions, arguments, and shared interests among interested sub-disciplines; and (2) to outline a program of future study in which anthropology may, indeed, have a large stake.

The Historical Context of Ethology

This paper deals with present concepts and assumptions in **Communication** and demands that strategies of research and hypothesis be distinguished from methods which cite data to justify rather than to clarify.[35] In this case, the assumption addressed is that which declares that 'man is unique' and justifies this declaration by focusing on differences between man and animals, and rarely on similarities. The consequence has been to exaggerate the differences on a series of traditional grounds (e.g., language), and to attribute these differences to anatomical, physiological and behavioral variation. It seems timely to rethink and rephrase the arguments which make man's language central to his distinction, and to seek a more productive approach. This approach should address the question of the nature of human nature.

The field of ethology, which is rooted ultimately in Darwin's *Expression of the Emotions in Man and Animals* (1965), has gained currency during the past generation. The question of 'origins' deeply underlay Darwin's search and pervades much of the thinking of moderns who claim, at least, to be evolutionists. But evolution can be presumed to proceed along horizontal or vertical paths, and those who seek 'origins' of man often convert the concept of evolution (i.e., change) to a moral, vertical notion (i.e., progress) as they extrapolate from careful observations of animals to somewhat less objective questions about man.

The three-quarters of a century since Darwin have been anti-Darwinian in many ways, particularly with respect to the study of behavioral processes. Studies were concentrated, instead, within the arena of pathology. The underlying thinking was more clearly motivated by the desire to cure, rather than to understand. A rash of physiognomic studies (Wolff, 1943) followed in Darwin's wake, but the methodology was abandoned as it yielded no new insight. The behavior-study strategies employed during this period followed Darwin's still-photo techniques, but lacked his sensitivity and comprehensive mind which sought to include in the 'package' the study of infants, the 'insane', the aged, works of art, all the peoples in the world ("especially ... those who have associated but little with Europeans", Darwin, 1965), and animals. Instead, the behavioral sciences became concerned with lesser questions. The subject matter was divided into comfortable sections, and the major questions merged into the background as each discipline fostered its own parochial concerns and made claims to 'own' the correct methods and theories. Each has acted under the banner of 'professionalism'. However, with the recent development of ethology, some interest has been reborn in studying natural group processes (Schaffner, 1958) and not merely the observations of **individual** subjects taken out of their natural social contexts.

Many approaches to the general study of ethology are being taken. The scientific climate has changed since Darwin's time: new equipment has enlarged our ability to record and observe (e.g., audiovisual laboratories and video tapes), and his question has been refocused. Attention has shifted from the isolated individual to the 'interaction-expression' – a reflection and function of others', as well as of one's own internal state.

It is clear to ethologists that primates – and all social beings – exist not only in common surroundings, but also in constant communication with members of their own species (Frings, 1964). The evidence strongly suggests that to mature and mate successfully (even to be eligible for membership in the gene pool, as it were) some degree of organized communication and mediated learning takes place. At least among social animals, this appears to mean that various orders of **nonrandom** processes influence the makeup of the species. Some understanding of these processes – **learned** processes, by most definitions – is crucial to an understanding of the nature of man and of his evolution.

The majority of studies concerned with ethology move rapidly to arguments about the differences between human and animal nature (Washburn, 1959; Ervin, 1964). Differences of opinion occur along the axes of biological vs. social nature (as if these are different), and before vs. after birth (as if the trauma of crossing the birth channel suddenly transmutes the biological individual to a social interactor). These axes are being shown to be assumptive (Hamburg, 1963), traditional, and not necessarily about nature at all. Such an intellectual milieu prescribes both an open-minded view to the future and an environment in which we observe what is there. It precludes attempts to understand phenomena without artificially restricting and pigeon-holing the problems of nature into incomplete categories. It suggests that there is no compelling reason to question the fact that man is man or that he is a primate. Factors of structural development force the systematic biologist to classify man-chimp-gorilla as a first order trio, and the other primates as a more-or-less closely knit clan. Since the skeletal system is durable, it furnishes the best and sometimes only comparative palaeontological evidence and has dominated the taxonomies to the detriment of attention to soft tissues and behavior.

But in addition to being mainly descriptive, this taxonomic system has had the interesting effect of making primate behavior studies **appear** more significant to anthropologists than behavioral studies of other animals. As I was told a few years ago by a prominent scholar, in the context of an American Anthropological Association section meeting on primate behavior: "primates are not sons of bees." But this assumes the puristic view that certain evolutionary pressures, even those of behavior, are operative only within man's musculo-skeletal group. On the contrary, it may well be that communicative processes are more similar among, say, man and dolphins and jackdaws (or bees) than they are among man-chimp-gorilla. If so, the study of bees may lend as much understanding to the study of man as do studies of our anatomical cousins.[36]

Most recent discussions on man's nature of the 'how is man unique?' variety eventually attribute the difference to language (Simpson, 1966). George Gaylord Simpson claims that the older arguments, such as *homo erectus*, '*homo* opposable thumb', and 'man-the-tool-maker' are no longer regarded as adequate. This leaves the field open to the would-be animal linguist whose responsibility it is to discover the essence of man's nature, since that which distinguishes man is said to be his quality of having language.

The explanation of man as the animal-with-language is most unusual and curious. The other arguments of the difference between man and other animals suggest slow change through adaptation toward man — except the arguments involving language. Somehow a giant, qualitative, **behavioral** jump is supposed to have occurred, and man emerged. It is not surprising that studies of animal language and communication have been unsuccessful, and that "The more that is known about it (that is, communication in monkeys and apes), the less these systems seem to help in the understanding of human language" (Lancaster, 1965). As long as such a large jump between the language of men and the 'noise' of animals is assumed, we can rest assured that animal communication studies will continue to be considered defective human systems and will continue to be unrelatable to those human systems. The notion of a sudden leap emasculates the comparative study of verbal behavior.

To the curious this sudden-change type of explanation poses questions about the very nature of human language. Which of our present conceptions of human language are assumptions? Which of those assumptions are worth reviewing and reconsidering in the light, not merely of language, but of the processes of communication?[37]

In the traditions of modern descriptive linguistics, which derive from Saussure (1959) and Bloomfield (1933), language is generally taken to be the significant units of sound (phonemes), organized into larger units, which are themselves organized into syntactic sentences — according to discoverable and statable rules. These syntactically organized sets of sounds, morphemes, phrases, and sentences are called a **grammar**; those things which are grammatical are 'the language' — to most linguists (Chomsky, 1957). Linguistic schools argue about the primacy of different units or where analysis should begin, but not about the primacy of grammar. In other words, it is this aspect of verbal behavior — the grammar — which the linguist **declares** to be his domain; and it is this aspect which most linguists seem to believe constitutes the greatest bulk and most important part of human behavior.

In that interesting intellectual process of reification, language is then **given** various attributes; since 'it' exists, a multitude of properties can be imputed to it, or taken away from it. Language is, variously: meaning, sound, lexicon, structure, digital, symbolic, expressive, emotive; it is **not** culture, paralanguage, analogue, emotional, extralinguistic. Language as an entity changes systematically, or its superorganism changes; language is not primitive; it **does** guide our cognitive processes. Language is in great measure 'out-of-awareness'; if you want to know what someone thinks — ask him. And whatever language is, animals don't have it!

These are some of the assumptions that have been built into our notions about language. Many of these assumptions may be well-founded, but at least some have little foundation in fact and tend to lead us away from productive, truly comparable, problems.

Since it is questionable whether human and nonhuman verbal behavior are strictly comparable, it is useful to rephrase the general area of the problem, and to focus on a conceptual framework which will allow us to look for similarities. Whatever language is, it is not merely (or even mainly) grammar, especially in a comparison of cross-species behavior.

A number of animal studies have been made in the tradition of a 'digital' model — language as made up of ordered discrete units (Busnel, 1963). The phonemic model is usually taken over whole as a descriptive tool, and operations are performed much as they would be for human languages — with some startling exceptions from a linguist's point of view. For example, in human language studies, the sound spectrograph is always used after the interviewing and analysis is complete; in animal studies this technique precedes analysis.

In most studies of animal sounds or verbal behavior it is assumed that animal language is organized from a number of significant sounds — like phonemes. Lists of the number of sounds per species are available and show an increase up the phylogenetic tree (Busnel, 1963). Almost all human languages are claimed to have more sounds than do animal languages.

But the operations which lead to such judgments are done out of context and are *ad hoc*. The history of **phonetic** listening in language description is long, well documented, and exactly what we try to teach out and unlearn in introductory courses in linguistics. Phonetic listening can yield essentially any number of sounds for human languages and can increase a hundred fold with increased attention and sensitivity. The idea of discreteness, as is well known to those who have any acquaintance with psychoacoustics, is in the mind of the perceivers, not in the nature of language. Thus, the different operations which are performed on animal and human language yield entirely different and noncomparable kinds of units; phonemic for human language, phonetic for animal language.

A second group of animal sounds or acoustic signal lists are made up by trying to relate discrete sounds to repetitive, nonverbal behavior. Although such studies may be done on the basis of hard-headed observations, the traditional assumptions about the nature of animal communication may be difficult to overcome. Consider this article of faith (Busnel, 1963: 69):

Phonetic animal expressions convey, almost without exception, subjective situations and aspirations. They are affective sounds which seldom tend to become objective designations or denominations. They express the idea of immediate time only, of a present situation or one which will occur in the immediate future. They cannot express abstract ideas which are unconnected with organic behaviour.

In this study, presumed discrete sounds are broken down by Busnel into such categories as sexual relationship, family relationships, relationships with community life, and sound ranging (1963: 76). To retain our canon of comparability, what would happen if human acoustic behavior was observed and categorized in similar fashions?

It seems a far stronger and more useful assumption to say that the comparable processes of man and animals are communicative; i.e., that there is no basis on which to compare such apparent entities as sounds or words or grammars across species without considering the natural contexts in which they occur. It is not idle speculation to suggest that we can examine the limited aspects of **human** verbal behavior we traditionally call language because we can assume an implicitly known and relatively constant human **Umwelt**. But, of course, we cannot do so for the animal world. The linguist cannot ask an animal if two words differ by one sound; he cannot elicit responses to pointing, to pictures, to situational anecdotes. The highly interpretive games of linguistic elicitation and analysis are human games. It simply is not realistic to compare a highly restricted aspect of human language (grammar) with the pure verbal activity of animals which, if it has a grammar, we have no way of discovering except with recourse to context.

While the empirical bases for thinking that animals have a grammar are not very strong, there is strong evidence that all social animals do communicate; that is, they have a shared repertoire of behavior, well-developed cooperative abilities, a social structure, and the ability to pass on an adult standard to infants through parentally mediated experience (Kawamura, 1963). The ways in which such things are done obviously differ between species, but the structures and processes may be very similar.

What of the other presumed attributes of human language? The stream of sound, which is the raw data, is not completely or solely composed of discreta. Phonemes are not the major verbal units of language. There appear to be other kinds of units which have very interesting properties including nondigital, nonlineal ones. These are presently being discovered. The need for postulating them arose from a series of observations which are not explainable if the sound structure of language is assumed to be digital, that is, each event finishing before the next occurs, and the reaction occurring sometime after the end of the event. On the contrary, Pollack and Pickett (1964) show that there is a kind of preknowledge – that in the context of everyday speech, we know, within limits what is coming next. We know about where we are in a sentence and can fill in one of the few possible words when a speaker falters and gropes.

Given presently existing models of language, there is no theory which can begin to account for or explain how we communicate verbally. There has been no attempt to account either for the subtleties of speech or for ordinary speech in the context of interaction. Even among us hyperliterates, speech is usually lacking in grammatical, or even in ungrammatical, sentences.

Structure is among the most interesting and promising of any of the imputed properties of language. The evidence that language and communication are highly structured seems very strong; a belief in the existence of structure is a necessity even in beginning research. Nonetheless, the possible **forms** of structure are intriguing. Linguistically, it is assumed that answers to the formal characteristics of structures are located within the concept of the sentence (Chomsky, 1957). A knowledge of the structure of all sentences and of relationships between kinds of related sentences will presumably solve the problems of structure. But if structure has more general properties (and it certainly appears to from my vantage point), then a series of context problems arises.

For example, if unit-forms, such as sounds or words, are also located within structures other than sentences, then each such unit probably contains information about the **structure** and not merely information about itself. If this is true, then a pure natural history approach is not sufficient to handle data; for the exact recording of each piece of apparent behavior will not allow the separation of the structurally related data from the occurring data in the stream of behavior. The only approach to solving this type of problem is to **begin** with models which can account for structural regularities underlying apparently dissimilar forms.

The mandate is, then, for the investigator to concern himself with language in context as occurring, structured behavior; his job is to compare verbal communication, however apparently unstructured, with verbal communication of animals which is equally apparently unstructured and ungrammatical.

An Approach to Ethology

The study of language-as-communication is being reborn among anthropologists, and our biosocial heritage is rejuvenated by this approach. The connecting cross-species theme is that, through probably similar communication processes, infants in each species grow up to be very much like the present adults, their parents. Men — as do animals — occupy space; they move with respect to one another as their musculo-skeletal structures allow. The musculo-skeletal system, itself, can be seen in communicative contexts to develop through the mediation of social means: the pull of muscles affect the formation of bones; children tend to hold their muscles as their parents do. Whether we call 'muscle-sense' learned or innate, the fact remains that some assumptions lead to productive research possibilities and testable hypotheses, while others attribute the evidence to such agencies as tension release mechanisms.

Within Darwin's first focus (1965) — the study of infants — productive work is being done or planned.[38] Given the notion that each phase of the development is crucial in all species to the emergence of the adult, we know surprisingly little about infant movement (Peiper, 1963), and a surprisingly great amount about psychosexual (Spitz, 1965) and intellectual-rational development (Piaget, 1952). Not only have the interests in subjects been heavily influenced by a very few theorists, but the deductions have also been limited and narrowly focused.

In carefully observing a slow-motion film of movement in a sleeping four-day-old, it becomes clear that simple mechanical explanations should be exhaustively applied before appealing to higher-level, mental explanations. In the infant, all movements of the four proximal ball joints are synchronous with one another. The more distal elbow, knee, ankle, and wrist joints move at different times and vary in velocity, giving the movement sequence the gross *appearance* of being essentially uncontrolled and unorganized (the 'startle' or Moro reflex). The proximal coordination may well be the external manifestation of natural intra-uterine movement. Hip and shoulder joints are, at birth, organized movers; the distal joints are not organized, probably because they had no intra-uterine room in which to move about.

The contrast between these two types of explanation is extreme. One imputes an innate psychic energetic mechanism to the organism. The other demands that we examine static and dynamic differences between mother and child, and that we force ourselves to consider the problem of social communication in its own terms.

The study of the insane, because "they are liable to the strongest passions and give uncontrolled vent to them" appears to be almost as good an idea today as it did to Darwin (1965), but for quite different reasons. Many people consider that the vast array of disorders labelled schizophrenia are, in fact, problems in social communication (Ruesch and Bateson, 1951). Although Darwin merely took it for granted that the emotions were real categories of behavior, there is considerable heat generated today concerning the separation of affective-emotional aspects of behavior from other behavior (Hamburg, 1963). Our view is that ideas, concepts such as 'sadness' and 'anger' only gain their meaning in context.

One pragmatic problem is of the following sort: if any individual organism is observed for some period of time, it 'emits' behavior, not all of which it is possible to observe and note down. Now, what a given observer will note down as natural history varies according to many things, as will his later interpretation of his notes. Both variations are undoubtedly related. In my several years of work experience in a psychiatric setting,[39] I began to realize that psychiatrists, for example, tend to 'see' and stress aberrancies. In their view, the well-disciplined scholar tends to be 'compulsive', the student of esoteric subjects is a 'voyeur' (the study of primitives is, of course, the search for one's own preconscious), and the provocative mind is a *provocateur*. Since the control of the insane is in the hands of the trained, most recent work in observing the insane utilizes the expertise of the psychiatrist to label particular aspects of behavior as peculiar or not. Thus the trained psychiatric observer tends to report in terms of his particular training rather than as an unbiased observer. This prejudges the very nature of the problems and prematurely limits the findings.

The problems of observing the insane can be broadened to include, in a way, the observation of any human or animal. No observer has any way of knowing which of the characteristics he sees are attributable solely to the individual (how he feels that day, in that situation), and which have to do with his shared biography (ethnic-, class-, and species-wide behavior). While there is no point in denying individual traits, the most productive approach would dictate looking for similarities – in structure and process. For this reason it seems unwise to over-concentrate on those persons who are claimed to be aberrant and bizarre, but it is sensible to observe – as a bare minimum – a viable communication dyad. Rules of continuity must occur and be discoverable in these contexts of shared behavior, regardless of the claimed peculiarities of one or more interactors.

Related to studies of the insane, there is in any case a great deal of more general interest to be learned from the study of pathology. One of the values of studying any behavior different from one's own is the potential light it may shed on overlooked processes of ordinary human nature. For example, the study of space among humans was given great impetus by studies of territorial aspects of animal behavior,[40] which is more obvious to human observers. The study of ordinary movement gains importance when it illuminates such neurological disorders as intention tremor and the tremor of Parkinson's disease.

In the past few years, it has been demonstrated that movement in a continuing interactional situation is made up of a high degree of synchronous, shared behavior (Condon, 1964). On gross observation, the way we know that two people are indeed communicating – and not merely standing near each other – is that the interactional space is composed of related movement: shared starts, velocity, and changes. It is also demonstrable that what appears to be smooth movement is not as continuous and flowing as we tend to think;[41] much of what is meant by 'dance' has to do with evenness of, say, an arm movement through an arc. The control and variation of space by eyes and body appears to be a highly ordered sensitive sequence. The acquisition of this ability by the infant may be as important as – and may even presuppose – the use of language in communication. Pathology in the sharing of space is striking and devastating in its consequences for future normal development and potential mating.

Darwin's third and fourth areas of focus — both of which he dispensed with in some measure — are the study of the aged and of art. Their consideration of these topics may cause us to review and recast our thinking. In his discussion of expression, Darwin talks extensively about facial muscles. Except for a book first published some 40 years ago (Gregory, 1965), comparative studies of *facial* expression have only reemerged within the past several years (Andrew, 1966). There has been no systematic study of the human face; Gray's *Anatomy of the Human Body* — the standard anatomy text — talks about expression as if it were fact: "The Mentalis (muscle) raises and protrudes the lower lip and at the same time wrinkles the skin of the chin, expressing doubt or disdain" (Goss, 1954: 423). Without becoming deeply involved in judgmental decisions about the meaning of gestures, there does appear to be a field of study of anthropological, cross-cultural interest, which has to do with the investigation of expression.

There are two contrasting ways of viewing the problem of what adults 'look like' developmentally, both of which follow from the simple fact that children tend to look and act like their parents: (1) muscle development — especially of facial muscles — is an innate function of general growth; (2) the muscles of expression are as involved as, say, language in an interaction system. That is, the positions of the muscles are learned and, within limits, changeable.

The first, more innate-genetic, assumption is current; its primary intellectual result seems effectively to have been to dispense with this as a problem area, hence the lack of systematic study. The study of muscle action and pathology is relegated to the low-caste in organized medicine as elsewhere; the dynamics of movement are taught only by and to physical education students in most places (Rasch and Burke, 1963). On the other hand a number of productive questions arise if it is assumed that the study of expression is, in fact, part of the study of communication.

To assume that expression is a part of communication is to suppose a more complicated interactional world.[42] Part of our ability to communicate is related to internal muscular perceptions of how other people are feeling — a kind of empathy. For example, the mother moves her mouth as she feeds her child; when she holds the infant after feeding, she has 'knowledge' of how relaxed or close to sleep he is. The mother observes the muscular response and changes in the infant. She is in some sense providing an image of how and when to move; she demonstrates what she will do when certain 'proper' (for her) muscular conditions exist. Other family members provide partial patterns of what to touch, of what to look at, and of appearance. Certain body parts are touched; some are not touched, some are handled and regarded differently — orifices are inspected in different ways at different ages by different family members.

With respect to the study of old age and art, it may very well be that the expressive ability of the facial muscles is molded and enhanced through such familial mediation. In the aged, the lack of elastic tissue reveals what the expressive muscular development of a group will tend toward. We can study how it moves toward the pattern and how growth or change is mediated at each age. The art and caricatures of each society aid our observation by stressing certain of the facial characteristics which are notable in terms of the particular culture.

In effect, this line of reasoning calls for cross-cultural study of muscular dialectology from birth on. For example, is the amount of lip which 'shows', a reflection about how one learns to hold his circumoral muscles, or is this merely a descriptive population statistic? Personal observations of upper-lip mobility in two areas of the world where such movement is very limited show that some movement ability gets 'fixed' very early in life — ten months to a year.[43] Appearance is acquired as much through muscle activity enhancement as through the early loss of movement by imitation of parents.

As is readily noted, such a theory can as easily account for a population continuing to look alike and allow for change as parental patterns change generation-by-generation as can a purely genetic model. Strategic reasons alone dictate the acceptance of an image from which infants learn, purely on the grounds of its utility in producing testable hypotheses.

The world of cross-cultural, cross-species comparison lies open. It seems to fit best into the academic domain of anthropology where a basic biological-historical heritage lies close to the surface, even if occasionally obscured. Considering the apparent complexity of the subject matter, it seems doubtful that present theories will lend themselves directly to application in this area. Instead, new models will have to emerge from the studies themselves.

Comments

By Gregory Bateson (Waimanalo, Hawaii, U.S.A. 23 IX 68).
Of course Sarles is correct in stressing the wide scope and relevance

of communicational studies and the fact that the same scientific stance should be taken in looking at both the communication of men and of animals. However, we have today a number of ways of ordering our thought about this wide spectrum of phenomena. I suggest that Sarles might have made his statement both more informative and more cogent by considering some of these.

Having agreed to look at the wide spectrum, we must then look for differentiation within it. There are contrasts of coding, contrasts of Russellian logical typing, contrasts of function, and so forth. I will briefly consider some relations between coding and function:

First let me demarcate, with quite artificial criteria, that sort of communication which I will call language in the narrow sense. Let "language in the narrow sense" be that exchange of information which can survive the transformation of speech into ordinary script, even when the placement of script on the page is rendered non-significant and the reader is assumed to be insensitive to verbal cadence.

We now note a profound contrast between this language in the narrow sense and the communicative behavior of dogs or cats. This contrast is **not**, however, an evolutionary 'jump' any more than the contrast between a pig and a coconut palm is an evolutionary jump: the pig was not derived from the palm. If what dogs and cats do had evolved into 'language', then we would expect to find that men would do **less** of what cats and dogs do. If some of the functions of the prehuman communicative activity are taken over by language, then the prehuman activity should be reduced in an organism which uses language. But this is contrary to fact. It is clear that men use kinesics, intention movements, and paralanguage not less, but **more**, than other animals.

It appears probable, then, that language serves functions totally distinct from those of kinesics and intention movements and is not an evolutionary modification of these. It is therefore unlikely that the characteristics of animal behavior will throw much direct light on language or vice versa. Indeed it is, in a strict technical sense, **insane** to handle a coding system of one kind as though it were a coding system of another kind.

Sarles advocates a comparative study of the communicational processes in contrasting species, and I agree. But comparison always demands three categories of information: the description of A, the description of B, and a set of concepts in terms of which A and B are to be compared. Sometimes the mere inspection of A and B suggests an appropriate conceptual frame, but more usually this frame is derived from other sources, e.g., from theories of evolution, epistemology, normative preferences, etc. In the present case, I suggest that comparison between human and nonhuman species can profitably be mapped onto contrasts between the many modes of *coding* that can be recognized.

At the present time, at least six such systems can be recognized:

(1) The digital coding characteristic of 'pure' language as defined above.

(2) Analogic coding, as this term is strictly used in the computer business, in which actual magnitudes are fed into a machine and are there acted upon by physical processes to give other magnitudes which are the output. At no point does the machine operate upon the 'name' of a magnitude. Much of hormonal communication is probably of this nature.

(3) Ostensive communication, in which an actual object or event is used as its own referent. The object is pointed at and proposes itself.

(4) Iconic communication, in which a representation of the referent (or a representation of some part of it) is used to propose it. This is common in the communication of nonhuman animals and birds and in human intention movements, etc. Combat is mentioned by the showing of a fang or other representation of some part of combat.

(5) 'Transformation', in which the referent is represented only by instructions for coping with it. The adaptive information in the genome is probably coded in this manner.

(6) Communication through action (perhaps a special case of the ostensive). When mother goes to market and leaves baby in the playpen, this 'communicates'.

This is not the place to expand upon the implications of using one type of coding rather than another or to discuss how the types may be combined. There are surely many implications for learning theory in the fact that all mammals, including man, acquire information (i.e., learn) by the way of all these types of coding — with no doubt very different paradigms for the different types.

It is worth noting, however, that digital coding is the only method which permits a simple indicative negative and that, insofar as they lack this, animals must go through a process of *reductio ad absurdum* consisting of a fight which is not a fight in order to affirm that they are **not** enemies.

Nondigital coding of various kinds is used by mammals for the computation and discussion of the contextual structures which govern their relationships to other individuals and to the physical environment. Matters of love, hate, dependency, fear, confidence, and the like are the subjects of these computations, which are seemingly achieved in comparatively old parts of the brain. In these computations and discussions, man seems to resemble other primates.

The nature of music remains totally obscure.

By German Fernandez Guizzetti (Rosario de Santa Fe, Argentina 9 X 68).

Since the fact that I am not a biologist and have no experience with the data of animal communication limits my critical capacity on this subject, I shall confine myself to making a series of observations from the point of view of ethnosemantics, ethnography, and the theory and application of models in descriptive linguistics.

In the first place, Sarles is quite correct in beginning with a rejection of biological reductionism in the characterization of human nature in favor of a focus on behavior — provided that 'behavior' is understood in sociocultural terms and is divorced from behaviorist dogmas. As he rightly points out, the patterns of communication shared by man with other genera may be more instructive than those shared only with other primates. In man, evolution surpasses almost all biological limits; the field of the noosphere assumes an infinite range of possibilities.

It is evident that the structured nature of human language — whatever model may be used to describe it — is one of its principal characteristics. I believe, nevertheless, that what is fundamental is something that the author denies ("language is not culture"): the essential difference between human and animal communication is the cultural nature of human languages, in spite of the very special status of language as a cultural fact. On the other hand, it cannot be said that a language, as such, is a superorganism, for direct observation in the field shows quite clearly that the concrete real systems are idiolects; a language, although an objectified fact of culture, is nothing more than the logical product of idiolects. Finally, the structural nature of human language is not conclusive, for any code, human or nonhuman, presents some type of structure as a system of signs (in the broad sense).

Another fundamental difference is that the meanings of human significance must be sought in the cultural world of the speakers and not in psychobiological processes of a hereditary character, as they appear to be in all cases of the use of signs for spontaneous communication by animals. Conclusions based on the signs that an animal learns to use through practice are irrelevant, for these are simply a matter of conditioned reflexes.

The study of animal codes should not be based on an anthropocentric point of view; only when their intrinsic systems have been studied can fruitful comparisons between animal and human modes of communication be made. The fact that nothing like our phonemes — distinctive to human language as far as they are in the minds of the speakers, precisely because they are cultural facts — can be found among the sounds of animals, does not preclude the discovery of some criterion relevant to the code of each particular species. For this reason, I agree with the author·in his criticism of Busnel and in his insistence that communication is common to animals and men, although in animals it may have a very special kind of grammar. The study of communicative behavior **in its context** seems to me to be the method by which we can arrive at the constants we need for the investigation of animal languages.

The author ought to have dispensed with the dogmas of Chomskian transformationalism in his judgments as to the nature of human language, for Chomsky's model does not represent real processes of coding, and it was not even his intention that it should. If its application to languages other than English requires a good deal of *hocus pocus*, think what can come of its application to the comparison of human codes with those of animals. It will be necessary to construct a model of the code for each species to discover the 'universals of animal communication'. This will require a **comparative semantics** — which raises the problem of the sign and its nature and function (especially the 'situation') across species.

In the case of using comparatively the observation of the behavior of informants, it is important to keep in mind that they are not simply primates, but rather beings-within-culture. Such behavior is a result of enculturation.

With regard to the value of the study of the insane, one must recognize that their aberrations are such with reference to the cultural world and are not simply psychobiological. Only with this understanding will comparisons be fruitful.

Finally, I think, like the author, that there is much to be gained from a comparative study of communication, across cultures and across species — but only if we bear in mind that communication in the various cultures forms a unitary bloc, human communication, and that while the cultural worlds to which the process of human communication refer are different from one to another, they are not so different as to constitute closed systems. Two facts demonstrate this, the second a consequence of the first: the proven existence of linguistic and cultural universals and the existence of the capacity for intercultural communication on a world-wide scale. Nothing of the kind can be said about communication between man and animals or between different animals.

By A. G. Haudricourt (Paris, France. 30 IX 68).

Studies of communicative behaviour cannot be distinguished from the studies of general behaviour that Mauss (1936) has called *techniques du corps* (bodily technology). Carrying methods are influenced by manner of dress (Haudricourt, 1948). An especially clear case is that of the offspring of White planters brought up by native nurses in the Oceanic islands, who completely lack facial mimicry: their expression — muscles relaxed, mouth half open — is quite characteristic of Whites born abroad.

Another problem that needs study is the means of communication between man and domestic animals. The command *dia* to a horse means 'to the left' in some parts of France, 'to the right' in others — depending, I think, on whether the carter walks on the left or right side of the horse. In Limousin, the same command to oxen means 'turn'; here the carter walks before the oxen, and his position indicates the direction of the turn. The real meaning of *dia* would seem to be 'come'. Problems like this one must be studied at once, for the utilisation of domestic animals (at least in Europe) is dying out as rapidly as primitive peoples.

By Victor A. Litter (Ituzaingo, Argentina. 11 X 68).

The great complexity of the problem of communication can be judged by the number of fields that investigate it: biology, psychology, philosophy of language, ecology, anthropology, and semiotics. This last being the general science of signs, and language thereby constituting a semiotic fact (see Barrenechea and Rosetti, 1968), it ought to have been dealt with in Sarles' treatment. Ethology should be investigated as part of ecology, where, according to Carter (1957), "each class of organisms is distinct from the other classes." Thus we ought not to seek the reason for differences among the species in the skeletal system, in structural development, or in some difference in the roles of the biological and the social. If it is true that the 'birth trauma' can be detected in the psychological makeup of individuals with social organization, we cannot doubt that the same will be found of other species — perhaps, in some species, even more strikingly so, as their behavior would seem to suggest. Such considerations can never be a factor in the appearance of differences in behavior.

The views of Simpson (1966) must be accepted in their entirety: We cannot today sustain an Aristotelian view of man. It is impossible to believe that only man possesses language or even that it is his distinguishing characteristic. Still less can we argue for his greater intellectual capacity. The work of Kortlandt and Kooij (1963) permits us to entertain a hypothesis of 'dehumanization' in the primates; in their experiments, a four-year-old female chimpanzee showed greater skill in the manipulation of a simple instrument than a six-year-old child.

According to Lancaster (1965), while many mammals communicate by sounds and gestures, these are simply the products of emotional states. She maintains that while the prehuman primates can transmit complete messages about their emotional states on the basis of systems of signs, they communicate almost nothing about their situation in the environment. She adds that cries of alarm and of predation are produced in different animals by a chain reaction. Leakey, on the other hand (see discussion in Slobin, 1965), with a great deal of experience in the life of the forest, thinks that differences among these cries can be detected through close acquaintance with them. This seems to be the opinion of others who live with animals as well; and, as Tinbergen (1965: 129) has said:

... animal sociology owes much to the work of 'amateurs'. ... As a matter of fact, official zoology has long left animal sociology alone, and the early work has all been done either by amateurs or by zoologists who had no training in this type of work at all. ... It is obvious that the best contributions have come from people who have given years of their life to careful, patient observation of one species.

Pointing out that "animals themselves are always more important than the books that have been written about them" (p. 139), he argues (p. 136) that

The observational work has to be followed up by experimental study. ... The change from observation to experiment has to be a gradual one. The investigation of causal relationships has to begin with the utilization of 'natural experiments'.

In the study of language, we have detected greater ability in man to identify objects than to express emotions, and for some years it has been thought that this represents a difference in the organization of the cerebral cortex. Until a biological relationship at the molecular level between the cerebrums of nonhuman primates and of man has been established, it will be difficult if not impossible to determine differences in the connections of the areas of association and in the maps of the cerebral cortex. The tests of behavior used up to now for this purpose are altogether inadequate.

Slobin (1965) maintains that one cannot think in terms of grammar when dealing experimentally and comparatively with the language of nonhuman primates. For this reason, the experiments of Sir Richard Francis Burton (see Hartmann, 1886) and, in Argentina, those of Carlos A. Merti (1957) have been unsuccessful. The views of Busnel (1963) are subject to the same criticism. Up till now, we have used techniques designed for the study of human language in our studies of the language of animals. Just as in the study of facial expression and behavior, what has attracted our attention in the animal, as Bergson (1950) long ago pointed out, is its similarity to man. So true is this that studies of phonation have only been made among species that emit sound similar to the human voice: the 'singing fish' of the coast of California, certain laboratory rats, many species of birds, and, above all, the apes.

I cannot accept the author's opinion that "we can assume an implicitly known and relatively constant human *Umwelt*" in the study of human language. It is as difficult to determine by their sounds when two words differ in a primitive human being as in an animal, and the same is true of the most developed languages. It is a commonplace that "the translator is a traitor." The attitude of modern linguists towards the problem is reminiscent of the speculations of Euclid in mathematics, of Newton in physics, and of those who preceded Claude Bernard in medicine. If the anthropological sciences are to approach the truth, we must think in terms of models better suited to our present knowledge (Litter, 1957). Ashby (1956) has pointed out that many investigators in the biological sciences — physiologists, psychologists, sociologists — are becoming interested in cybernetics and the application of its methods and techniques to their particular sciences.

The language and the common techniques of different sciences can readily be combined to lead to fortunate discoveries. In this connection, the spectographic study of sound is very important, although, as the author points out, traditional assumptions make interpretation difficult. If we consider language as a means of communication, it is evident that this study will be easiest done among domestic animals. It is to them that we should direct our efforts, even though they show no apparent similarities in sounds, no phonemes, no similarities in the anatomical morphology of phonation. I have tape-recorded the sounds of such animals and analyzed the morphological units that can be identified when the tape is played back at a slower speed. By this operation, the sounds of animal 'speech' are transformed into phonemes and morphemes; and human sounds, played back at greater than normal speed, tend to sound like those of animals.

Since the investigations of Bolk, we have known that ontogenetically man shows some deficiencies in his anatomical and physiological organization. Psychoanalysis has confirmed these conclusions for the area of the mind. We can consider, then, that human phonation may be the result of the emission of sounds at lesser velocity and with less force (on the basis of some such criterion as size and weight) than in animals.

By L. Stein (Birmingham, U.K. 1 X 68).

The argumentation initiated by Sarles in this stimulating survey will perhaps be furthered by the following sketch of a unified theory of the proto- and palaeohistory of language:

Those who put exploration before treatment can utilize their prejudices and preconceived ideas in formulating axioms, concepts, and assumptions; some of the latter can be 'fictitious' and are stated in the form of 'as if' sentences for heuristic purposes (Vaihinger, 1924). According to Spinoza's theory of identity, body and mind are, axiomatically, different aspects of the same 'substance' (Spinoza, 1948: Prop. 7 Schol.), the Body-Mind. Its interacting structural elements are assumed to be *a priori* existent 'theoretical entities' (Mayo, 1954, 1956; Stein, 1958) manifest in genetically fixed patterns of behaviour. These theoretical entities are posited because, without them, certain phenomena remain paradoxical, inconceivable, or inexplicable. Interaction of elements on different levels changes the structure, and new patterns emerge. The theory of evolution (de Beer, 1940) and Spencer's (1867) and Jackson's (1958) theory of dissolution have proved their value in respect of conceptualization, formulation, and verification. Dissolution leads to the dominance of evolutionarily ancient functions. The comparative approach to language (de Saussure, 1949: 16-20, 299; Meillet, 1925: 10) allows the postulation and/or reconstruction of earlier linguistic patterns; their existence and power are often substantiated by hitherto unnoticed normal or pathological phenomena. Psychoanalytical interpretations postulate an indivisible state of fusion between mother and baby on the deepest psychosomatic level. 'Communication' through action is thus primarily given. One of the complex behavioural patterns on this level is sucking. Sucking noises are **rhythmical**, signifying genetically fixed oral-erotic sexual acts, kisses. They are phonetically termed 'clicks'. That some clicks are species-specific in the apes (Schwidetzky, 1931: 44, 48, 56, 71) corroborates their great evolutionary age. Clicks also occur in several languages in Africa and elsewhere (Stein, 1949). One of the modes of onset of the voice, the 'hard attack' or 'glottal stop' is an explosive noise produced by the taut closure of the glottis. In its excessive form it is a truly human, anatomically determined symptom of anxiety (Stein, 1942; 1949: 57-58; Negus, 1929). In its mitigated form it occurs in various languages.

In the second stage of speech development the two contrasting patterns, clicks (incorporation, tenderness) and voice (expulsion, aggressivity), are integrated into a rhythmical sequence known as 'babbling'. The ultimate penetration of the emitted airstream into clicks engenders a number of 'consonants'. These are true symbols, i.e., the union of polar opposites. They first appear in rhythmical sequences, erroneously called 'reduplicated' syllables (Stein, 1951). This raw material, which played a part in the palaeohistory of words, is paralleled by many standard reduplicated word forms in primitive languages. Rhythmical reiteration is used as a grammatical tool for the expression of magic, intensification, multitude, degree, duration, diminution, instrumentality, negation, and tense (Stein, 1949: 124-34; Schleicher, 1861: 392; Stokes, 1861: 396-97). Rhythmical forms may in course of time be shortened into monosyllables. This assumption helps to trace the common ancestor of words, as exemplified below. Speech pathology has confirmed what the theory of dissolution predicts. Rhythmical syllables reappear as the first symptom of speech disintegration in stuttering, and in aphasia. In severe cases of stuttering the ancestral clicks are produced (Stein, 1953). The tense patterns of hostility and anxiety (glottal stop) are conspicuously absent in babbling. They appear in more advanced stages of speech dissolution.

The emergence of the monosyllable should be viewed within the whole framework of culture. Weekley (1930: 88) has postulated that Greek *pater* is not a compound of *pa* and *ter*, but of the baby word *papa* and *ter*, wherein the rhythmical part was subsequently shortened to *pa*. On Weekley's assumption, it may be possible to reconstruct the etyma of many other words. Compare, e.g., *pater* with the semantically compatible Greek *pateomai* 'I eat', Latin *pascere* 'to feed, graze, tend a flock', *pastor* 'shepherd', *panis* 'bread'

(Stein, 1951; Pokorny, 1959: 787, 789). The dominance of single (nonrhythmical) syllables heralds the advent of a more differentiated cultural structure in which the immediate discharge of an impulse is abandoned in favour of the 'attitude'. Attitude here designates the first phase of an action in which the organs concerned remain in the initial position with a degree of tension appropriate to the aim of the action. In our example this first phase (*pa* in *pa-ter*) indicates the partial realization of the oral-erotic act of comprehending, literally 'grasping' the object (rhythmical babble *papapa* ...). In this way the object is enjoyed 'as if' the attitude toward it (i.e., the first phase of the act of comprehending it) *were* the object (Stein, 1962; Blanshard, 1938: 583-94; Fenichel, 1960; Bull, 1945, 1946 *a, b*).

Viewing language in this light, I reject, with Sarles, the phoneme as a primary entity. Rather is it an abstraction indicating the contrasting elements in the man-made model of more perfected communication. Neither can I accept that language was originally due to 'learning', though this operated when primordial patterns were utilized in the making of conventional language.

By Lionel Tiger (New Brunswick, N.J., U.S.A. 7 X 68).

Sarles is correct in asserting the value of ethological findings and theory for anthropologists. To the extent that ethology (1) is a method of studying social — hence social systematic — behavior of animals; and (2) seeks to do this in terms of natural scientific data, it provides a possible general model for using neurological, paleontological, physiological, etc. data in studying human social behavior. The distinction between the 'social' and 'natural' sciences is at best a nuisance and at worst a formidable barrier to multi-leveled understanding of living systems. Ethological procedure permits a good start to the business of trying to assimilate the various kinds of information about human behavior. That this is difficult is reason for beginning right away, not for waiting until that Baconian holiday when all the facts will be in.

It is greedy of Sarles to try to fit all this "best into the academic domain of anthropology"; other social sciences need it, too, because a view of man exists in all of them and such a view must be based on known facts which a comprehensive use of ethological information can help efficiently provide. At least in North America, it is probably sociologists and political scientists who would find most useful and challenging the introduction of biologically oriented material into their array of resources.

Reciprocally, if it is the case that social scientists have particular skill in comprehending social behavior, it becomes their responsibility to make at least some of their results available to ethologists. This implies that they take into account the kind of data that ethologists consider pertinent to understanding an animal's social action. One way of doing this is to use units of analysis which have some biological basis, for example, young-old (the life cycle as genetic program is poorly understood and little studied as such) or male-female. It would be very interesting to find out how males learn gestures, postures, movement rates, activity patterns, etc. that differ from females' or that are the same. This is a part of the communication system in which Sarles is especially interested. Again, what constitutes 'sex appeal' in females (or its possible male relative, 'leadership') is important to know. Obviously there are differences between cultures, but the biological fact of species-wide sexual difference offers a bench mark for trying to pin down the various hormonal, cultural, idiosyncratic, etc. inputs into a reproductive system. It is good ethology to regard men and women as males and females, as primatologists do rather than as people serving different functional prerequisites of the social system, as do too many sociologists.

It would be helpful to others concerned with developing graduate (and undergraduate) curricula which reflect these various interests to learn more about the 'practical-didactic training program' to which Sarles refers. The catechism of an anthropologist or sociologist is not much more likely to include math than ethology. Handling data is important to know what data to look for, and why; to this ethology can contribute the enhancement of sensitivity and sophistication of comparative skills.

By Ralph Gardner White (Punaauia, Tahiti. 13 X 68).

The multiple ambiguity of the title of this paper led me to expect discussion of such matters as: communication between dogs and men, a bird's warning of impending danger to a rather wide range of animal life in its area, or the compatibility of incompatible species at a salt lick or a water hole or in a barnyard community. The example that came most readily to my mind was the case of an orphaned wild pig we once had who grew up with a litter of kittens and became feline-wise acculturated in as far as his physiology permitted. It is very instructive to see a pig try to follow kittens up a tree, or to take long leaps in tall grass, the way a cat does when hunting.

Sarles' purpose would seem to be to bring studies of language and/or/as communication back down to earth and to reintroduce objective methodology. This is all to the good.

There is certainly a great deal of truth in Sarles' thesis that 'our' notions of language are bound by many covert assumptions. There are probably always assumptions; but one of the basic functions of scientific research is to weed them out and make them explicit or overt. Sarles himself accepts, apparently through Chomsky's conceptual eye, a number of assumptions about 'the traditions of modern linguistics' which seem to me to be unwarranted or at least to require more careful formulation.

Language and communication: The use of 'and' here is deceptive. As I reify it, language is a special kind of medium of communication; one of its most outstanding characteristics is the possibility of communicating through it in the absence of **external** context.

Phonemes + organization = syntax + sentences = grammar = language = the aspect of verbal behavior of greatest interest and importance to most linguists: If grammar be defined in this way, it covers only a very small portion of the linguist's interest in language. In practice, a grammar is simply a compendium of generalized statements about 'a' language, as the linguist is able to set them down on paper. Theoretical controversy is usually about how to formulate such statements and to what portions of language generalized statements are applicable.

Behavior: Leonard Bloomfield was a self-avowed behaviorist, as have been many other linguists. However, 'behavior' has come to be used in a slipshod way almost devoid of meaning, and needs careful redefinition. A paper should be written on just what its relevance in linguistics is; it would certainly seem to be much more pervasive in ethology.

Reification: Sarles alludes briefly and incidentally to this term as "an interesting intellectual process." It is much more than that; it is the basic process of vocabulary formation, and as such should be of prime interest to both linguists and ethologists.

I should also like to hypothesize that reification is the basic process by which the language continuum is broken down into discreta and that study of it might help solve some of the basic philosophical incongruities of this paper.

The assumption that discreta and continua contrast and are incompatible would seem to be untenable. This may also apply to lineal (? linear) ~ altera.

Differences ~ similarities between human and animal communication: Ordinarily this question never comes up for the linguist except perhaps in the introductory chapter of a general textbook. There are a number of ways of communicating, of which language is only one. These should be reified, classified, and checked to see which are applicable to which species.

It may be worth noting that when, for instance, a man and a dog are constant companions, the dog does not learn to talk, nor the man to bark, but they can learn to communicate fairly adequately.

Different and noncomparable kinds of units, phonemic for human language ~ phonetic for animal language: This would be hypothesis; but I find it impossible to conceptualize 'phoneme' in such a way that the statement could hold true or be meaningful. Adequate discussion, however, would be book-length.

In conclusion, I feel that ethological methodology should be elaborated independently; there is no present need of comparing or contrasting it with any alleged linguistic methodology.

Being a linguist (pure and simple), I feel incompetent to comment on the second part of the paper, *An Approach to Ethology*, except to say that it sounds well worked out and worth going on with. The following works may be useful for this purpose: for a general theory of ethos, Feibleman (1946); for human ethological description, Hall (1959); for a study of human communication on a behavioral plane, McLuhan (1964); for a review of mechanistic research, Rosenblith (1961); and for a linguist's view of ethological material, Sebeok (1963).

Reply

By Harvey B. Sarles.

This paper is concerned with **strategies** of posing questions and doing research. Its main thrust is that premature decisions, often based on incomplete observations or unsupported intuitions, may lead to the closing off of rich research territory. Such decisions are deeply embedded in the 'dualistic traditions' (of which the human-language and nonhuman-no-language dichotomy is but one case among several) which have plagued the critical study of human behavior, particularly human **social** behavior, throughout the history of Western thought.

Most of the commentators have **reacted** to the reopening of an area that they prefer to keep closed. This stance is epitomized by Chomsky (1968a) in a recent article:

The idea that human language is just a more complex variant of systems to be found in other organisms is one of a set of 'arguments by extrapolation' that I think can no longer be held by any rational person. ... All normal humans acquire language; whereas the acquisition of even its barest rudiments is quite beyond the capacities of an otherwise intelligent ape. ...

The present article argues that the rationalist position, from Descartes to Chomsky, is principally one of definition (often of 'defining out'), rather than one of grappling with issues.

The modern anthropologist-linguist is caught on the horns of a dilemma. On the one hand there are the generative grammarians, with a monolithic, preformed **theory**. On the other are the empiricists, the 'biologizing' and 'taxonomizing' linguists, who also present a monolithic view – one which encourages data-gathering and organizing as the 'ultimate good'. Given this situation, it is little wonder that most scholars find 'fence-sitting' their usual, though uncomfortable, position.

The dilemma is sharpened when one seriously asks which position he should take and why. One cannot accept the results of one without finding it incompatible with or contradictory to the methods or results of the other. Part I, therefore, merely pointed out that no one knows or could possibly know whether animals have 'language' – that the very notion of language as we believe it to be would preclude doing potentially productive research, as Chomsky correctly points out. Chomsky (1968) would quit entirely at this point, while Bateson continues to do research on animals, apparently for no reason since he accepts the notion of "language in the narrow sense". The present paper suggests that the problem of "language in the narrow sense" be left **open** until we do some very intensive and questioning observations of animal **behavior**, which even Chomsky (1957: 56) has claimed to be the primary job of linguistics.

Part II outlines a program of research in terms of which is formulated a set of productive procedures and questions. It raises the problem of why we should observe **social behavior**, and not just individuals communicating. It implies, but does not state explicitly, that inter-species communication study is probably to be investigated only after we have achieved some understanding of the 'independent' cognitive operations of two or more species. It presents, I think, a **testable** set of hypotheses about individual development as seen within the context of social structure, where it might usefully be assumed that communication is an ongoing process and not merely a concatenation of stimulus-response or other similar kinds of units.

If we are to reopen the question of 'language', it is essential that we come to recognize our presuppositions concerning its nature. We may very well discover that Chomsky, Bateson, *et al.* were 'right' about the uniqueness of human language – but their approaches preclude discovering the senses in which their theories might have utility.

Concerning the responses, it would appear that almost everyone has his own theory about the 'origin' of language; Litter's is one of the most ingenious. All the theories seem to appeal, however, to some type of prejudgment or definition.

White's response contains several interesting points, one of which is his claim that 'reification' is the 'basic process of vocabulary formation'. I agree. What I intended to point out is simply that scientific thought is likely to advance through questions and observations that are 'counter-intuitive' — that there is an extreme danger of doing 'science by consensus' if we uncritically judge an explanation in terms of how well it matches our intuitions.

The reason I stake claim to this area for anthropology is also pointed to by White. Being in any one closed discipline — e.g., being "a linguist (pure and simple)" — puts one in a very vulnerable, uncritical position. Since linguistics, for example, has limited itself to a very narrow study (usually the study of 'grammar'), it is always in danger of exhausting its subject matter, and has thus often made dubiously strong claims of 'owning' an area which is somehow extremely 'basic'. It also is likely to use 'functional' definitions to delimit or justify its existence as an independent area (e.g., "language is **used** to communicate") without ever bothering to examine these functional foundations ("that is not the business of linguistics"). Although the results of the proposed research should be made available to all behavioral scientists, anthropology seems to be the only discipline, pragmatically speaking, in which the necessary training and practice can be coordinated and carried out within existing academic settings. It has a biosocial tradition which may wane from time to time but can be resuscitated if an interesting subject matter is developed.

On Sarles' Views on Language and Communication

By George Gaylord Simpson (Tucson, Arizona, U.S.A. 25 VI 69).

I was not among those invited to comment on the recent article by Sarles (CA 10: 211-15) which has only now come to my attention in printed form. This article contains several misunderstandings or misstatements, some .of which are ascribed to me explicitly, citing Simpson (1966), or implicitly in continuing text. I therefore wish to make brief correction of the three most important of these errors.

(1) The view that man has language and other animals do not is misrepresented as "Somehow a giant, qualitative, *behavioral* jump is supposed to have occurred." It was once a fairly common error,

but is not now an excusable one, to suppose that because a qualitative difference *now* exists between species (or other taxa) it must have arisen by saltation. I did not state or imply and I do not believe that this is true of the *origin* of language. Nothing I have ever written can be reasonably so interpreted.

(2) In continuation of this misrepresentation and with further disapproving citation of Lancaster (1965), Sarles states that a contrast between the language of men and the 'noise' (his quotes) of animals is assumed and that animal communication is considered a defective human system but (with what logic?) unrelatable to the latter. I do not venture to speak for Miss Lancaster, an authority on animal communication, which she calls communication and not 'noise'. For myself, I am aware of the obvious fact that animals communicate. It seems equally obvious to me that they do not use language, as I and most others have defined that word. Over some span of time in some group of primates some form of communication did evolve into language. That does not make the surviving nonlinguistic forms of communication of other primates and other animals either primitive or defective forms of language, especially as man retains such forms of communication in addition to language. The fallacy that because all language is communication all communication is language is too obvious to argue.

(3) In a statement that is a confusion of taxonomy, diagnosis, and nomenclature, Sarles cites me as an example of those who consider man unique because he alone has language, language being "that which distinguishes man." What I actually wrote (1966: 476) was: "Language is also the most diagnostic single trait of man: all normal men have language; no other now-living organisms do." Until someone finds a normal man who cannot acquire a language or another now-living organism that can, I take that to be an acceptable provisional truth. I did not say that this single trait sufficiently characterizes or defines biological or social man. On the contrary, in the cited article I took pains to specify many other traits and to emphasize that these evolved in a unitary, organized way.

There is another misapprehension in Victor A Litter's discussion of Sarles' paper. He says (p. 216),

The views of Simpson (1966) must be accepted in their entirety: ... It is impossible to believe that only man possesses language or even that it is his distinguishing characteristic.

But I do believe, as stated in the cited paper, that among extant organisms only man possesses language, and therefore that it is (one of) his distinguishing characteristic(s).

Reply

By Harvey B. Sarles.

In the area of language studies, the definition of 'language' is a primary concern to the linguist and to those who claim a knowledge of what constitutes language. There is a traditional view that language is exclusive to man, but this notion is now open to question. One of the implicit points of my paper was that to define language as uniquely human also tends to define the nature of animal communication so as to preclude the notion that it is comparable to human language. The view that language belongs only to man is quite old and remains a part of the prevailing intellectual climate even today. It implies a notion of man's normality that must be reexamined.

As Simpson's other works indicate, he obviously is not a saltation theorist. He is, of course, a modern biologist of the first rank. I disagree with him only on the issue of his definition of language, because it implies a narrow, restricted notion of language behavior. I have elsewhere stated that our modern notions of what constitutes language and communication, even in humans, are far from complete or correct.

Simpson states above:

All normal men have language. ... Until someone finds a normal man who cannot acquire a language or another now-living organism that can, I take that to be an acceptable provisional truth.

There are, in fact, a number of successfully reproducing humans who are considered to be 'aphasic' or 'imperfect' in their language. Granted that these persons are medically 'abnormal', are they therefore biologically abnormal? (The medical model of normality is based to large extent on our **social-cultural** ideas of what constitutes health and pathology.)

Who is to say what constitutes 'normal language' and what, specifically, are its attributes? Are these scientific truths or 'social truths'? There is a great deal of evidence that members of minority groups in this country are discriminated against in school for having 'defective' language. Here the majority has defined its own language as normal and that of others (lower class, Black, Native American, etc.) as 'abnormal'. Although Simpson does not subscribe to the implications of this model, others who use essentially the same definitions have found it useful.

The relationship between language and communication remains unclear. Historically, most linguists have tied the two together by stating that language **functions** in communication. A few, particularly those, such as Chomsky (1966), who see themselves as deriving directly from the rationalist Cartesian tradition, view language as an independent system. Simpson says (1966: 476):

Human language is also a system of interpersonal communication and behavioral adaptation essential for the human form of socialization. Yet human language is absolutely distinct from any system of communication in other animals.

I understand Simpson to mean that language is an emergent system. Like most others who define language in the Cartesian tradition, Simpson separates the "systems of emotional signals" of "so-called (animal) language" from human "discourse" (1966: 476).

The basis of my disagreement with Simpson can be summed up by restating the title of his paper: *The **Biological** Nature of Man* (stress mine). It implies that we can separate the biological nature of man from his other aspects. I think it a far better and more open strategy to consider that man has/is his nature — and to avoid any premature definition of that nature — if we are ultimately to answer the question of mutual concern **What is man?**

(4) LANGUAGE AND COMMUNI-CATION ... II: THE VIEW FROM '74

The study of aggression is a most important facet of modern behavioral interests. Its understanding and control is necessary to ensure our very continuity. It is a part of our existence which has nonetheless eluded deep understanding in spite of its having attracted concern and attention in the political, psychological, and philosophical traditions to which we are heir.

In the context of the ethological and comparative studies which have surfaced in the recent past, it has gained a wider, perhaps newer, sense because it appears to be an attribute of social animals in addition to man. We hope that we can extrapolate from knowledge about other animals to some sorts of deeper, perhaps 'biological', insights into man's nature and behavior.

While I share these hopes, I remain concerned about a number of issues or ideas which an overzealous biologism can carry on its ideological wings. We are in a paradoxical period where hard tissue and bodily form seem to be more plastic than was suspected (Enlow, 1968) while behavior is claimed to be less susceptible to change and learning than we had thought. As a person who has come to these issues primarily as a behavioral field-oriented (human) linguist, I am aware that we are heirs to curious traditions of **human** nature which have made us appear extra-natural: 'language', 'mind', and 'rationality' being some terms which encapsulate the essence of the human uniqueness arguments. Lorenz, for example, defines 'natural' human behavior as preceding reason, language, and culture in his book, *On Aggression* (1966).

My approach to thinking about issues of human nature and behavior in a comparative framework has been through the metaphor of language. Some of the current ideas I have fought, others I've attempted to bypass. Some seem to be 'conceptual'; i.e., earlier ideas of language have seemed so overwhelmingly 'self-evident' that the only way to transcend them is to rethink them in some critical, historical context.

I believe that the so-called affective components of our nature are bound up in the same or similar conceptual traditions and are fraught with the same conceptual difficulties. To attempt to shed some light on the positions and ideas that I find myself occupying, fighting, abandoning, rethinking – let me review a paper I had published in *Current Anthropology* several years ago (II (3), this book).

In this article I responded to a *Science* paper written by G. G. Simpson: *On the Biological Nature of Man* (1966) in which his ultimate definition of Human Nature was directly linked to 'Language'.

I claimed, among other things, that not only was Simpson's position unnecessarily dualist, but that any definition of language was more suspect than he or linguists of that era were willing to admit. Language is not in my view either peculiarly human or peculiarly individual, but we are social interactional creatures just as our forebearers.

Since that time, linguists' definition of language has indeed become open to debate, the implicit issue of man's sole ownership of language has become explicit, pushed especially by the work of the Gardners on chimpanzees (1969) and by the increasing abandonment of linguists by psychologists (Salzinger, 1970).

The original paper was presented in two parts – the first being a critical description of how human linguists and animal communication experts (callists) have some similar and some surprisingly different ideas and methodologies, with but little awareness of their assumptions and with a rather blind application of these ideas to subjects that they may not fit at all. The second part was a modernized program of research based on Darwin's original outline for the study of expression and emotions.

During the past several years I have thought and written about the variety of subjects a good deal; some of my views have changed (especially on the nature of faces and of the 'insane'). In the area of emotional expression, the literature has developed considerably, pointing in two virtually contradictory directions. The field of Human Ethology has gained a literature, if not exactly a substance. In fact, there may be two fields splitting and emerging – one which is essentially psychological-individual, the other more anthropological-social – as they tend to approach the same apparent subject matter from two quite different perspectives.

In this essay I wish to mirror the earlier one and to consider the language issues first; then I will point to some research directions especially from the anthropological-social perspective in which language is some subset of communicational behaviors not easily separated into discretely reified entities.

On Language

The principal dilemma in raising the issue of the nature of language is that virtually everyone believes he knows what language is; that each of us is an instantiation of a normal human speaker and thus 'knows' in some deep sense what language is. In my personal experience, however, there seems to be little actual agreement about the very nature of language.

It is difficult to gain a critical sense for the underlying issues since most linguists and callists use the term as if there is universal, self-evident, and exhaustive insight and agreement into its very nature. People do tend to agree that language is in some sense unique to man — but in which senses remains unclear.

In my view, this belief about human language is strictly an 'insider's' picture. Our so-called knowledge about the 'talk' of other species is derived principally from the 'left-overs'. These views about man's uniqueness are based less on fact and evidence and more on a western theological assertion that man alone has a mind or soul. Since this position is based on some idealized conception of man, it also has a tendency to push us to distinguish normal man from nonnormal man in ways similar to how we distinguish man from animals. That is, this arena of thought and research intrinsically carries the very seeds of Social Darwinism.

What, then, is language? Where is its locus? What is its 'purpose'? The term 'language' remains little more than a metaphor which prejudges the observation and analysis of verbal behavior and arranges the data to fit whatever the prevailing view. That is, we still don't know in any deep sense beyond what we can perform and that we are unlikely to gain any insight into our performances unless we relook at language and linguistic ideology and sweep away some underlying brush.

It's not that we do not have theories about language. The history of western philosophy was and principally is predominated by inquiry into the nature of language.

There have been two main sorts of theories — one an 'object' or 'word' theory, the other an 'idea' or 'sentence' theory. But both have been linked intimately to theories of **human** nature and to **human** development. That is, our theories of language have always been **exclusive** theories of human nature. These theories have been based primarily on ideologies which related man not to nature but to western conceptions of the diety.

Consider how language has been conceptualized as human nature: Man has a soul, psyche, or mind — this makes him unique. Attributes of mind include intentionality, will, consciousness, rationality, creativity ... (the lexicon varies in the hands of different writers). The body is a residual phenomenon — what the mind **is not**! (And the 'emotions' are thrown in on one side or the other and occasionally even disappear. They tend to be sort of intermediate, occasionally intermediary, between mind and body.)

One important thing to note in mind theories is that bodies curiously do tend to disappear. As our soul (the real me) 'leaves' the body after death (Aristotle's metaphor), it has some sort of existence of its own — the mind, *per se*. As we are able to conceptualize minds without bodies, we are able to construct verbal behavior as an attribute of mind. This, in turn, seems to legitimatize the notion of language, *per se* — also disembodied in peculiar ways. (Later, we will note how these thought constructions also have enabled us to create studies of facial expression which, in my mind, are also essentially disembodied!)

The dualist thought construction, which sanctions us to disembody the mind, also contributes to the disembodiment of language and has helped legitimate certain other notions, as well. For example, it is usual in the context of language to mention the term communication. Language, it is said, 'functions' to enable us to communicate. Not having a very clear idea of what language is — except that *it* exists *per se*, and it's what other animals cannot do — we heighten this 'house of cards' by speaking of a function of language.

To extend the bodiless metaphor a bit further, consider our prevailing notions of communication — as the passage of new information called messages. It is a configuration of 'symbolic' interaction, the meeting of minds. In fact, the literature, which is admittedly science fiction, carries the ability of humans to interact with other sorts of bodies (like your favorite Martian) and is willing to admit that mutual intelligibility doesn't require human bodies or even human existence. 'Intelligent life' — another metaphorical extension of our concepts of language — exists 'out there' in the same sense as our primordial ancestors finally discovered or were given intelligence, as if logic, etc. was sitting around waiting for man to develop into it. May I suggest that some missing links are not merely in Olduvai Gorge, but also in our pictorial theories of the development of man.

Since there seems to be little actual doubt that we have bodies, or that we are bodies, we might reasonably ask what these bodies are doing while we speak, if indeed they are doing anything. Is it possible that they contribute something to language? Or are they purely epiphenomenal, a place in which our minds accidentally reside (and a 'dirty' place, for some of us!)?

Well, bodies may have disappeared from theories of mind and language, but they haven't been entirely neglected. In any full library shelf of books on the mind, there are one or two about the body. And it is important to note what has happened to it, because its historical treatment has figured heavily in our conceptualization of language, especially as justifying support for the particular views of language to which we are heir.

The body is the place where the mind resides. In Western thought it seems inconsequential that our bodies are shaped or formed as they are. Rather, the essential person is one whose development is toward understanding, rationality. He gets language first **in order to** communicate later. I think it is worth pointing out that our stories about human development are parallel to or the same for the development of man and for each individual man. Our theories of learning also run parallel and tend to exclude the body from view and from analysis as part of language or intelligent behavior.

This theoretical stance pushes us toward a theory of communication which is very troublesome because it appears to require communication to be a meeting of the 'minds'. Messages or information flow from one metaphorical telegraph system to another, **using** the body or facial expression as the transmission device. But, as in telegraphy, this sort of thinking suggests that the face and body are as passive as the telegraph line in the transmission of messages. Facial expressions have no 'being', but are some sort of surface reflex of deeper structures. Language theories are the same, inasmuch as the behavior or sound is the vehicle for message transfer, not the message itself. In other words, the observable behavior of language in current linguistic theories has very little to do with the meaning of the messages.

This leaves the empiricist in the very uncomfortable position of either having to find some other nonempirical way into his data (the meaning), or virtually having to deny that interactors can **really** communicate or understand one another.

This is one of the disjunctions of theory and method which separate linguists from callists. Callists only have sound behavior to observe and have inferred, or imbued their subjects with, a semantic — albeit a simple one. Human linguists have been unwilling to do this, and semantics continues to be problematic; callists have been overly willing (in my opinion) to impute meaning to verbal noise and have been extremely naive in making judgments about the similarity and differences of animal sounds as they strike the human ear or are 'run through' a sonograph. Events of the sort which callists are willing to call 'the same' can literally make human languages unintelligible.

But even here, the human uniqueness theorem has apparently substantiated the callists' moves, since other animals can be chauvinistically assumed to be much simpler than we are. For example, the notion that other animals are locked in to a stimulus-bound present 'here and now' has permitted callists to act as if the observed behavior has no history or context. If two animals' speech was directed toward or about a third conspecific out-of-sight of the observer, no one would ever know with present methods, and we could continue to 'analyze' our observed data without fear of gaining any deeper insight into other species' cognitive ways. Given the variety of species on earth, we could continue to taxonomize and compare our apparent data far into any foreseeable future. And in the prevailing mood of biologism, I can even imagine that such nondata can be extrapolated to man, as part or parcel of his so-called innate/genetic linguistic endowment. I suspect that this is more truly science fiction than any of our stories about 'intelligent' life on other planets.

In many ways the era which promulgated these ideas is rapidly passing. But without any apparent theoretical underpinnings I fear that we are likely to carry these notions with us — under our breaths as it were — while observing such obviously communicative events as facial expressions seem to be. Perhaps it is worth pursuing the underlying model further.

The major difficulty, as I see it, is encapsulated in ideas about the nature of communication and of the presumed nature and role of the individual organism. In the traditional notions of mind, it is the individual who gets or learns language and is **then** enabled to communicate with others. In the beginning is the squalling, dumb organism. Only gradually does he begin to be able to 'speak his mind'. Maturity in Piagetian ideology (Piaget, 1963) has principally to do with increasing rationality or problem solving ability. It continues the linguistic philosophers' view that logic or rationality has some sort of overarching existence — we 'grow into it', as it were.

This picture of man carries with it an 'origin story' of man which focuses on how man is different from his predecessors. Instead of looking at all of the uniquenesses of man, including our very special eyes, mouths, and faces, these stories make it appear that we are special in extra-natural ways which exclude our bodies. Language, mind, consciousness, will, rationality, soul – all are terms which encapsulate these human differences.

Without making any strong claims that other species have language precisely in the human sense, let me point out that the data base for these claims is nonexistent. The methods used by callists is derived from prior ideas of human uniqueness; that is, that we have **human** minds, and other species do not. No one has, for example, seriously suggested that we observe humans speaking in the same ways as we observe other animals – by **calls** related to their behavior – because we have already assumed that we know what the differences are about.

Not only have these theories of human uniqueness affected our observation, analysis, and interpretation of the communication of other species, but it has also strongly affected the very formulation of theories of human language. Indeed, the current theories of linguistics are based on a dualism which parallels the mind-body, human-animal distinctions which come to us from long theological traditions.

Our very ideas about human thought derive from progressive evolutionary assumptions about the mind of man being created or formed in order to understand the deity. It is just those aspects of our thought and speech which tend to be called 'language'. They are said to be 'free'. 'creative', 'nonstimulus bound', 'the message', *langue*. Hardly any linguist (except possibly myself) has been willing so far to observe human verbal behavior in the same sense as callists must observe nonhuman verbal behavior. Linguists preselect from the stream of speech what they believe and agree to be language – no one seems to know if this represents about 90% of the total amplitude of ongoing speech, or, say, as little as 10%. In order to get intelligible speech over a background noise, speech needs to exceed noise by only several percent. So it may well be that linguists attend to only a small portion of the speech signal, while callists are stuck with observing 100% and believe that they must relate the total animal speech stream with its co-occurring behavior. If any other species did, in fact, have language in any sense, the possibilities of our discovering it appear to be nil with present methods. We are fully into an era of descriptive taxonomy based on a very partial, if not totally inaccurate, theory about nonhuman language.

Where does this leave human language theory? In my view, it must be unsound. And the ideas derived from it are equally suspect, as are those which parallel it. That is, I am suspicious of any ideas about human behavior which are like our mind-body dualistic theories, in which the individual is the repository of mechanisms which stimulate others to respond. Theories of individuality smack of the same sort of theology which says that the individual is where the soul is, and that each of us is unique because we have unique minds. By focusing on the presumed uniquenesses of man and individual man, we risk not seeing that each individual exists in and is dependent for his survival in a variety of interactional networks. He must always, in my view, know how to communicate — before and after birth. Language, as I conceive of it, comes much later. It appears, in other words, that communication is prior to language, not the reverse as our human uniqueness stories would make it appear. And the recent ethology bolsters this communication view in the sense of showing that man **derives** from social species — he did not become social and communicative after he 'stumbled' upon language.

Each of us must in some sense already **know** about himself *vis-à-vis* others; he is likely to derive his own view of himself as he interacts with others. While not wishing to deny the mind as the 'hard' behaviorists do, I suggest that the individual is not merely a thing which grows, develops, and becomes more and more rational by essentially preformed stages. He is a dynamic, processual thing who is observed and molded within the cognitive structures of those around him. In this sense, rationality and logic are statements about the ways adults think. They don't exist in any sense independently of human thought and being — as tempted as we may be to believe that they do, and in spite of the attempts of modern logicians and linguists to market their view exclusively.

Consider that part of our existence which seems to be the most sturdy and continuous and nonplastic: our bony structure. Let me contrast two ways of thinking about, for example, 'how we get to look like we do'. I believe that these are parallel to a developmental-stage vs. a dynamic view of interaction and communication.

The first story is, of course, the one we all believe: that we look like our parents in some sort of genetic mix. Whether we favor our mother or father more is explained away, rather than explained, except that we do! We get bigger and look more and more like ourselves. The great changes in our faces are attributed to age and gravity, as if these imply natural processes which are independent of other aspects of our being.

The other story — which is gaining substance in the developing field of functional anatomy -- is quite different (Enlow, 1968). We come to look like we do in complex interactional fashions. Our very bony structure is in constant flux and is determined to a very large degree by constant soft tissue interactions. The soft tissue — mainly muscle tissue — I see as amenable to the same 'habits' as our tongues in forming dialects. Dialects, we know, are an individual's muscular adjustments which are very much like those around him. We speak like our families do, and we are highly susceptible to change, particularly when we are young. As orthodontists have pointed out, the thrusting of the tongue is a great mouth shaping force, and most of us native speakers of English sit and think with our tongues on upper teeth or alveolar ridge, pressing with some degree of force. The very form of our face, our bony tissue, is molded in the interactional dynamic in which children respond to how their parents believe that they look.

In communicational-linguistic terms, this implies that expression is very much part of an interactional nexus. What shows up on an individual face is susceptible to interpretation by those around him, and those facets of expression which are interpreted consistently are the ones which the individual tends to use consistently. Whatever preformed expressive abilities are manifested by the infant, for example, it is those which are meaningful and sensible to its mother which are acted upon and reinforced. The individual becomes, in my view, the expressive instantiation of that person to whom his family responds. It is tricky to separate that person who is 'one's family's child' from that 'child-as-a-person'; one way of stating the existential dilemma that all of us find ourselves in. (It is tempting to suggest that the traditional dualism between mind and body be recast as the dualism in oneself between the interactional self as defined by others and the 'essential' self.)

This sort of interactional notion also implies a quite different view of normality and abnormality than a stage-developmental one. The recent history of psychometrics pushes us toward the notion that any factor of form or behavior has a population distribution and that popularity and normality are kinsmen if not twins, conceptually. This type of notion cannot help but seem persuasive particularly when it is bolstered by bio-political notions such as 'success'.

In a reply to the article on which this paper is based, G. G. Simpson (p. 84) chided me for criticizing those animal communication specialists whose work had only confirmed their beliefs about nonhumans and language. His critical tone confirmed for me the fact that animal behaviorists and some other biologists have a view of nature which makes man appear to be not merely unique (as are all species), but to be just a bit extra-natural, outside of nature. His notion of language is the metaphorical vehicle by which he justifies this claim. But note also that he elected to appeal to a particular normative sense to convey his ideas and that this appeal carries a greater intellectual load than it appears at first glance.

In Simpson's words (p. 85):

For myself, I am aware of the obvious fact that animals communicate. It seems equally obvious to me that they do not use language, as I and most others have defined that word. Over some span of time in some group of primates some form of communication did evolve into language. That does not make the surviving nonlinguistic forms of communication of other primates and other animals either primitive or defective forms of language, especially as man retains such forms of communication *in addition to* language. (Italics mine.)

Clearly man has what other animals have, plus he has more; namely language. Whatever Simpson has in mind by his definition, I believe that very little agreement is around on what language means. Even for linguists, the definition is in flux. The important point, in my view, is that Simpson's view is a mind-body dualism in which mind and human become coterminous through the appeal to a reified something called language. I find this totally circular.

Simpson went on to quote himself and to explain himself:

What I actually wrote was,
    "Language is also the most diagnostic single trait of man: all normal men
    have language; no other now living organisms do."
Until someone finds a normal man who cannot acquire language or another now-living organism that can, I take this to be an acceptable provisional truth.

In casting about for some reasonable way to characterize human uniqueness, Simpson uses a method that modern linguistics has called 'the clear-case' (Chomsky, 1965: 19). That is, while one's total definition is really quite fuzzy, one can make it appear reasonable, correct, and even popular by appealing only to those aspects of it about which everyone seems to agree. (In my experience, it turns out that if you disagree, you get called either 'incompetent' or 'crazy'!)

Underlying the method, and justifying its provisional nature, is some sort of promise that it will eventually elucidate some essential aspects of its subject matter; in this case, human nature.

But what about the notion of normality — of some sense of the 'ideal' man who lurks beneath the observable behavior — that Simpson claims we all agree to be language. I suggest that 'normal' and 'ideal' are terms which carry along a great deal more than the mere concepts of 'provisional definition' or 'working hypothesis' appear to imply.

My reply to Simpson's remarks pointed out (p. 86) that there are indeed a number of now existing human beings who are adjudged to be **abnormal** in form and behavior. I suggest that our ideologies which seem to imply an extra-natural status for ordinary-normal men also shield a potential implication for those whom we claim to be abnormal: namely, we tend to think of them in ways similar to those in which we think of animals. What else could a 'lack' of language, defective or deficient language, imply in a world view where the very definition of man depends on his having language?

What is really wrong with those people who speak peculiarly? Abnormally? Again, as in other aspects of theories of development, there seem to be two very different views. In the unfolding notion of normal development, there is something intrinsically 'wrong' with those who are abnormal. Within the context of a dynamic, interactional view, the problem is seen to be much more complex.

Keep in mind the fact that the recent recipients of the label of 'abnormal and deficient language' have been, increasingly, persons from minority backgrounds, and that the locus of their 'problem' has increasingly been claimed to be in their central nervous systems or brains (critically reviewed in Baratz and Baratz, 1972). 'Minimal brain damage' is a label by which we can trick ourselves into justifying these essentially political social judgments of abnormality-with-respect-to-the-majority, by claiming that such people had the sort of genetic endowment which limits the possibilities of their speaking (and thinking) normally.

In the *Realpolitik* of speech pathology, it turns out that the story is more involved. If the person 'looks right', then the pathology is generally considered to be small. So, as far as I can tell, one's face **and** language both affect how he will be judged.

Consider the population which seems to provide our very facial stereotype of stupidity: namely, Down's Syndrome/mongoloid children. Their mouths tend to remain open and their tongues to hang out. We interpret this look to mean that 'not too much of interest is going on in their heads'. As a population they are considered to be 'retarded' in thought and language.

Are they really retarded? What is their problem?

The question of Down's children may very well be a social-perceptual problem of adult-child relationship. In my personal observations of very young (two to four-month old) Down's infants, the clearest fact about them is that their external facial movements are extremely limited: very 'sharp' eyes moving against a relatively blank background; little hint of a smile or other affective expression. I surmise that their external facial muscles are not working properly, whether due to an intrinsically muscular or nervous innervation problem.

Now, without us making any strong assumptions about the nature and quality of their minds (which might indeed be 'peculiar' in some sense), it seems reasonable that the very **definition** of them as 'retarded' will suffice to produce the typically retarded person. That is, if parental perceptions of them is that they are very 'limited' intellectually, that's how they will turn out.

There is obviously much more to this story: part of it being that the mothers of such children get less affective response/feedback from their children than they seem to know how to deal with and tend to alter by very slight steps the quality and type of interaction. These children are, in other words, not terribly 'interesting'. But this may have only to do with how we adults conceptualize faces — it may not have very much to do with intellectual capacity in any deep sense; except that a child who is treated peculiarly is likely to respond to such a treatment in kind.

Consider how any child 'gets into' others' faces as part of the general problem of how any body knows about others' bodies. Consider further that the Downs' children appear to operate in this venture starting with a muscular endowment which is undoubtedly different from that of the ordinary infant. Not only is this a problem in adult perception, but let us assume that the child himself will attempt to 'model' others' faces — however infants do this. That his face turns out to 'look stupid' is probably just as surprising to him as the 'intelligent' child's face which turns out to look 'smart' is, to him.

What I'm suggesting is that the questions of thought, language, intelligence, and all that these terms imply should be considered in their conceptual and behavioral interactional dynamic. Our theories of normality may lead us to believe that such attributes of individuals such as I.Q. are really 'fixed' in some nonplastic sense, but I believe it is fascinating to attempt to reconceptualize these problems in other terms.

Some of the ramifications of these moves point to a new understanding of what it may mean to look or be stupid; but just slightly stupid. Teachers seem to get a great deal of their feedback about what's going on in their students' 'heads' from watching their faces.

Teachers must make rapid judgments about whether a point is understood, and by whom. Their data is primarily facial expressions. So a student who either looks stupid in some static overarching sense, or one whose look is interpreted as confused or stupid, will have some effect on the conduct of any class. Depending on the teacher, his or her mood, 'patience', etc., that stupid-looking student may get a lot of teaching energy — or more likely, apparently, he will begin to be treated differently from the 'bright' looking students.

All of this, I believe, does go on rapidly and subtlely in classrooms. One must be quite careful in college teaching, for example, to choose 'good' students for feedback. If one is trapped into using a student who is mainly attracted to the teacher for other than purely intellectual reasons, it may create long term havoc in that class, that course, and in the personal lives of teacher and student.

All of us seem to have pretty well-formed pictures of what we mean by intelligent looks and operate in terms of our own pictures. Surely they tend to become our prevailing operating truths, in some cases, irrespective of what may really be going on in the minds of our students.

I believe further that many of us are highly susceptible to 'reading' faces of various people in particular manners, similar to how we react to different forms of speaking. It is very easy to believe — along class lines — that people who use forms like 'ain't', and 'he don't' are not merely lower class, but also uneducated and probably stupid. To the extent that educators can 'spot' poor people, we must remember that we are reacting to bodies and particularly to faces. I believe — with only a bit of tongue-in-cheek — that the junior college movement is a mechanism whereby many students who do not look like proper university students somehow learn to look proper enough so that we university teachers will not merely dismiss them out of hand.

Beyond Language

To return to our earlier discussion, this excursion was prompted by G. G. Simpson's claim that only 'normal humans' **have** language. My claim, to the contrary, is that concepts like 'normal' and 'language' are much more complicated than a comparative framework would make them appear, and that these notions, in particular, are based on a tautological definition of humans being human **because** they have mind and language. Simpson, Chomsky, and essentially all dualists simply deny the possibility of comparing so-called animal speech and human language.

In the context of a model of human normality or ideal behavior, these concepts also carry the possibility of labeling any person who is considered to have abnormal or less-than-normal language as animal-like. In Simpson's formulation, normal humans have what animals have — plus we have language. Therefore, animals have *less* than humans. It is tempting to apply such a deficit model to those humans who, like animals, have peculiarities or abnormalities of language. It is apparently more tempting and easier to believe our own judgments of this sort when the 'retarded' also 'look different'.

How can the human uniqueness formulation be bypassed or somehow transcended in the search for variables which may lend new insight into the natural condition of man and other social animals? Using language variables as an exemplary area of relationship, I suggest that it will be more immediately useful to reexamine the nature and definition of (human) language, rather than merely extrapolating from the verbal output of other animals to man. Not only are they presently noncomparable, but many of our very notions of other animals' behavior are derived from these definitions of human uniqueness.

In the remainder of this essay, several ideas will be explored which will point toward some redefinitional aspects of language which are more likely shared by other species. Included in these are alternative perspectives of viewing human language: e.g., how could other species discover that we have language — how do developing humans discover that fact? Second, we should carefully study the history of linguistic thought, to discover the underlying issues and assumptions which govern our very conceptualization of human language — and which may then lead to postulating alternative lines of thought. Another line is to observe language not as a *ding an sich,* but as behavior: movement, vibrations, and tensions which characterize the stream of speech. The nature of intelligibility in real time remains obscure. What is the nature of **context**? Language study has always moved from structure to context; yet contextual studies remain a promise in the putative future. Lastly, what are 'tone-of voice' phenomena, often called paralanguage? Affect, emotion, etc. are considered to be epiphenomenal to human language. In order to be potentially comparable to animal languaging, can we reconceptualize paralanguage and show that it has some part in the actual semantics of the interaction?

Considering language as behavior, it becomes less clear that human language is as unique as our assumptions would lead us to believe. Languaging is a set of muscular phenomena involving the usual parts of the 'vocal apparatus'. But, from an interactional dynamic perspective, there is much more to it.

For example, language behavior is not only hearable — musical tones impinging on auditory nerves as Helmholtz (1954) characterized it — but it is excitingly *visual*. Young children's poetry is a visual 'trip'. "Baa, baa, black sheep" may sound good, but it also involves major visual lip changes in each syllable; and in speaking 'baby talk', parents virtually explode their lips apart, dealing in tension and distances far outside the ordinary interactional parameters of facial movement. Every time the low vowel *aah* is sounded, the mouth is wide open and the visual mask as it might appear to the infant is increasingly intricate as the teeth and rapidly moving tongue are exposed. Considering that humans are involved with faces more than any other interactional surface, and that parental faces likely loom very, very large to infants, the visual aspects of speech and language production should not be underestimated. Yet the linguistic literature virtually omits the fact that external faces are involved in language production.

Parenthetically, it may be noted that saliva is also a major factor in human speech at least. We must have and manage proper sorts and amounts of saliva to be able to speak at all. (I suspect it is also involved in hearing and intelligibility since it is presently forming on the upper tips of tensioned tongues of most listeners and readers.)

Thinking about language from a behavioral point of view also forces one to consider the fact that speaking and listening take place largely in interactional settings. Modern linguistics acts as if this fact is inconsequential to linguistic theory. That is, our theories of grammar imply that language is in each person's individual mind, that the presence and active participation of other people in speaking and hearing has essentially nothing to do with language (Chomsky, 1968).

The assumption that human language is only or even principally a grammar consisting of all sentences is to me merely an assumption. I believe that language is not even 'learned' in any direct, straightforward manner, but that verbal and other behavior occur in dialogues in which linguistic 'correctness' is quite secondary to linguistic, cognitive, and behavioral **sensibility**. Children, in my view, do not produce or generate phrases and sentences and then somehow learn semantics; rather, the mother-child relationship is a dialogue of questions and responses through which the parental picture of the world is constantly imparted to the developing child. This approach has, I believe, not only interesting implications for studying normal language development, but it suggests that abnormal language is a relational, not just an individual, phenomenon.

From this perspective, the fact that speakers have and use their faces and bodies becomes an obvious and interesting fact. The proverbial 'outsider' — the Martian observing humans or us observing nonhumans — is more likely to note that speech does not occur in the sorts of vacuums that the rationalist linguist creates in his mono-chromatic ideations.

In considering the question of whether any nonhuman could possibly discover that we have language (if, indeed, we do), it is clear that most of us have in mind the nonterrestrial creature who is somehow 'intelligent'. Considering the sorts of science fiction about, we might note that the bodily form of the creatures is incon-sequential to the 'fact' of their intelligence. Mathematics and logic transcend nature in those intergalactic fantasies which will ultimately have only computers left trying to manipulate one another.

I sincerely doubt that even the most well-meaning nonhuman could discover that we have language unless he already believed that we did before he began his study. If we wipe out the civilizations that have cropped up in the past 30,000 years or so, we would have appeared as Desmond Morris' vision of the *Naked Ape* (1967). Using the methods — and assumptions — that we apply to the so-called speech of other terrestrial creatures, there is no way in which the observer could separate the stream of speech into 'message' or 'grammar' and all the tone-of-voice stuff which is in speech quite constantly. If the outsider was an honest hard-nosed naturalist empiricist, he could not even tell when a 'loud' message was directed to the contiguous body or to the errant child behind yonder tree. How could any outsider distinguish, say, loudness from 'anger'? Even if a fight ensued, no one could say why, with any degree of certitude. A well-directed whispered insult, on top of a history of bad relations, can be more provocative than the loudest verbal assault!

I believe that present conceptualizations of (human) language, drawing on the origin myths of human uniqueness, do not permit any way out of our dilemmas. That is, much more of the same sorts of linguistic or paralinguistic studies will not possibly lend any new insight into the nature of language — human or any other. Are there any ways around or out of our conceptual dead-ends?

In the history of dualist thought, which is essentially the history of our linguistic and human nature ideology, the mind has reigned supreme; the human body has disappeared. It is the happenstance locus for the mind and soul (Vesey, 1965). In science fiction, and in much of the current fiction called science, the dualist is subtlely at work in indirect and insidious ways.

Linguistic theory has throughout this century posited two sorts of speech. In different eras they are called 'deep vs. surface' (Chomsky, 1965), *langue* vs. *parole* (Saussure, 1959), or 'competence vs. performance'. Behavior and body are either passive vehicles for the transmission of the real or deep language, or they virtually disappear. Our language theories are disembodied. The body is little more than the telegraph line which transmits the message. The body is not the message; paralanguage is not the message. ...

On the contrary, I suggest that the human form has a lot to do with human language, cognition, logic and rationality. Not only do children's auditory nerves get titillated by speech, but they seem to like their speech 'face on'. Speech pressure hits the entire face and body. It may well be that the stuff of language, which effectively gets to the auditory nerves and interpretation centers, is censored and shaped by those rather unique and special shapes which we all recognize as humanoid. It may well be that the listener who is passive in some of our communication theory mythologies is 'holding' his facies in the sort of tensioned fashions which deliver his 'favorite' sorts of sounds. The more active appearing speaker 'reads' the tension and variation in the listener and relates the message to what he thinks he sees; and feels, as well, in my estimation. It is worth recalling that the sound spectrographic techniques which are widely used in animal speech studies seem to presume that auditory nerves are essentially panspecific. It seems, to me, a curious presumption.

More optimistically, I believe there are ways around these dilemmas. But they require some commitments to rethinking and reconceptualization. Why, for example, not study contextual variables **directly** in human language?

I had noted years ago in a study among Tzotzil-speaking Mayan Indians in southern Mexico that I could usually tell what 'sort of person' was speaking to another, well before I comprehended the language in the ordinary sense; e.g., man and older women – adult with child. This was also observable while working at a psychiatric institute – I could usually tell from the hall what sort of person my medical colleagues were speaking to without hearing what was being said – wife, colleague, patient. And in my own household I can tell from upstairs whom my wife is talking to – often the specific person – just by the vague tones which drift up through floors, around hallways, and up the stairs. What sorts of things in those voices did I respond to – what do they represent – how might they affect the comparative study of language?

One of my students conducted a study which examined what she calls the 'nonlinguistic' content of speech in English and Japanese (Benjamin, 1974). She took short (half second or so) excerpts from ordinary speech in different contexts. The fact is that other people do know, with a fairly high degree of agreement and certitude from the voice of the speaker alone, a good deal about the situation, the speaker, the hearer, their relationship. The stream of speech carries our age as a constant message, for example, although we Westerners seem to be more in tune with this than the Japanese. We can tell if a person is speaking to one person, or to lots of people, even in another language.

While this muddies the waters of cross-species linguistics, it is one suggestive example of how thinking ethologically may force us to reexamine our presuppositions about human language. Benjamin and Creider have done a parallel video-tape study of the human face in different contexts, which showed that an audience was also sensitive to the contextual changes as they are revealed on an individual face (Benjamin and Creider, 1973).

I suggest that a method which proceeds by these sorts of methods of 'peeling off' the contextual and relational elements in speech first will ultimately yield more insight into the nature of human (or other) language, rather than proceeding by assuming that we know *a priori* what the nature of the deep or message aspects of language are.

The difficulties in any such study – intra or interspecies – is that the behavior is likely to be much more complex than we have thought. By reducing, or attempting to reduce, the actual complexity, we are likely to obscure as much as we can elucidate. Again consider human language. Unless we are only tonal or phoneme-formant analyzers as all of our acoustic theory suggests, it remains unclear how we understand each other, especially in real time. It turns out, for example, that entire words can be cut out, literally excised from actual conversation, with little or no loss of intelligibility (Pollack and Pickett, 1964). This means, to me, that information which **we** think of as a given word is more than that. If words can be cut out with no loss in intelligibility, information **about** that word must be present at other points in a given sentence. This presents a real dilemma for the naturalist-descriptivist since, no matter how careful and accurate he is, the data which occurs at a given instant may convey information about other instants, and not merely about themselves. Animal communication scholars have tried to get around this problem by claiming that nonhumans are stimulus-bound and tied into the 'present here and now' (Busnel, 1963: 69). In other words, our view of history and context for other animals is extremely simplex.

We should remain dubious that simplex observations, even carefully done, can yield insight into more complicated worlds. All the scientist need do is discount some of his observations, or make his simplex pigeonholes wide enough to accommodate apparent aberrancies, to keep his science 'pure'.

Consider this example — eliminated from linguistic purview on the ground that it is 'extralinguistic'. There is an old Stan Freberg record called *John and Marcia*. The record, the acoustic behavior, consists phonemically of just two words, repeated several times: she says, "John," he says "Marcia" — nothing else. But they simultaneously 'tell' a long story: meeting, greeting, loving, lovemaking, departing. Where is all this information — on the record, only in our minds? The fact that there is continuity in speech, that there is a story, a mutual history, is not part of linguistic theory. And its possibility has apparently been eliminated from the study of other animals' speech as well.

In other studies, always attempting to keep in mind a cross-species perspective, I have found that we are very context-bound, or context-congruent observers. By cutting a film in pieces to compare similar gestures, I noted several years ago that the accompanying speech sounded much different than I had noted it when listening in the ongoingness of the original film. It may well be that an immediate task of understanding other species and ourselves is to get some more insight into the sorts of observers we are. One method for doing this is to 'break context' and match what we observed 'in context' with the differences that show up out of context.

To conclude, studies of verbal behavior in different species have not been very directly comparable. While very few of us may believe that others share all of the features of human languages, there seems to be whole landscapes which have not yet been explored.

Reasons for this include the exclusive, theological preorientation of the human linguist in his proclamation that human language is coterminous with human being. If one believes that things are intrinsically noncomparable, he has every right to suspect his own motives in trying to compare them.

Animal callists – professed comparativists – have not been sufficiently demanding of themselves or of human linguists, either to proceed in similar fashion, or to force themselves and linguists to gain each other's perspectives. In my experience, many biologists have overly accepted the extra-natural definition of man contained in current linguistic formulations and have not yet demanded the same rigor of themselves in looking at humans that they apply in observing other species. If we desire more real knowledge about man, the comparative approach is crucial. But if we all begin with fictions about man, I am afraid that we'll end up with the kind of novel, biologized myths that have sold so well in the past few years.

I have tried to suggest a potentially rich direction for doing comparative work in verbal behavior. This is to reexamine and rethink the ideas which have led to the current theories about human language, to show that a very narrow, restrictive set of variables has been thought to characterize all of human language. I am convinced that human speech is a much more intricate process than it has been thought to be; and one which is potentially studiable. I think the comparison of human language and animal communication suffers from misconception, not from discontinuity!

I am leery of current extrapolations from nonhumans to humans, not because it is difficult, but because we have often defined nonhumans more as deficient humans than as rich interactors in their own social-cognitive terms. In trying to find some primary essence of humans or other, which would seemingly allow us to cut through or bypass the complexities of life, we may have impoverished our theories about the human condition. If, as I suspect, the study of aggression runs in any way parallel to the history and traditions of linguistic thought, we should continue to be as critical and careful of how we **think** about the problems of comparison as we are about the observations we make.

(5) TOWARD A DYNAMIC LINGUISTICS

In a review article Charles Hockett (1967) accused Eric Lenneberg of using a nonempirical linguist as his only linguistic consultant. Noam Chomsky, he said, is a neomedieval non-Bloomfieldian rationalist philosopher. This paper agrees with Hockett but will point out that Hockett's incomplete empiricism **also** rests in great measure on rationalist arguments and Platonic substance. The antidote in both cases is a critical naturalism – a tough-minded, hard-nosed look at the stream of speech in the context of the stream of behavior to attempt to see completely what's going on in the real world.

It is necessary to read both Hockett (Hockett and Ascher, 1964) and Chomsky (1966) in wider perspective – to trace the Bloomfieldian (Bloomfield, 1933) heritage to its clear antecedant, Saussure (1959) – in order to see that both are Cartesian dualists; that both assume a language made up of a series of **basic units** (call them phonemes or distinctive features, they are the stuff of substance and appearance). They both apparently believe that language is a distinct **entity**; that its grammar consists of mostly **novel** sentences; that sound 'carries' messages, but that the sound itself is not the message.

The split between the more pure rationalists and the 'soft' empiricists occurs early in the game. One uses what a philosopher-of-science colleague calls a 'downward seepage model'; while the other takes essentially the opposite approach, an 'upward seepage model'.[44]

The more pure Cartesian downward seepage model requires a beginning set of assumptions about the nature of the subject matter – a **theory** – before actual work is begun. It must be a theory which attempts to cover the subject in umbrella-like fashion and will tend to proceed from larger to smaller parts with no necessary use of different levels.

The upward approach, on the other hand, proceeds from empirical observation and plays-it-by-ear with no necessary preconceptions. The incomplete empiricism to which Chomsky reacted (1967) was the postulation of Platonic entities much too early in the game. The stream of sound was split in Cartesian fashion into language: non-language parts as if, in fact, a rationalist was sitting on top with his preformed theory.[45]

It is worth examining the enterprise laid down by Saussure in the attempt to see where the present movements got their initial thrust; to point out the assumptive bases and traditions of descriptive linguistics; and to suggest other possibly more holistic and productive assumptive and procedural foundations for the field.

Saussure, like Bloomfield, was primarily an 'act psychologist': a statement of the form: "... we distinguished three successive events in an act of speech," is typical[46] (Bloomfield, 1933: 74). One effect of this form of thinking is to prelimit the world to be observed by throwing away part of occurring behavior as 'not being part of linguistics, *per se*'. Another effect is to strongly limit the kinds of theories which will 'handle' the material. Language is thus reified; a kind of Cartesian dualism which splits the world in two and leaves us with the feeling that what we choose to observe somehow is more 'essential', more real even than behavior. The basic ploy of Cartesian (hard or soft) is to claim that only part of the stream of behavior is observable, while some other part is not amenable to observation. The hard rationalist feels that the part not observed is 'deeper', more real; while his half-brother seems to regard the part he selected to observe as the 'stuff' of language.

The decision concerning what to look at or consider and what to throw out is usually made on *a priori* grounds which happen to fit into a given tradition − in this case extending back into the dim Sans-kritist past. Thus to say that language exists *sui generis* − as a 'thing' − must be assumptive, and the workers in the area need only agree on where its boundaries lie. As long as this is somehow productive, or promises to be productive, the rest of the field will usually go along. What we have witnessed in the past decade in linguistics is the substitution of one type of *a priorism* which gives us such a promise, replacing another brand which had, in effect, shown signs of becoming unproductive.

While Cartesian rationalism *à la Saussure* and his descendants may lead to many interesting and productive ideas, insights, and method-ologies, it seems to restrict and mold thought, as well as open up new areas of investigation. It has already led to the belief in 'basic units' making up 'sentences'; to the notion of grammar, the set of all sentences; the postulation of an ideal language, which, if we under-stand how it works, will give us insight into the real world. The idea is based on the belief that traditional definitions, *a priori* boundaries and all, are truly an analog to their behavioral counterparts; a wholly doubtful conclusion which is usually dodged by the promise that it will be checked for predictive value with the real world at some point in a putative future. Thus has the field of linguistics been based, except for a few brief forays by Sapir (Mandelbaum, 1949) and his students (Whorf, 1956; Trager, 1958) within a fairly purely Cartesian dualistic tradition.

The other aspect of *a priorism* does not, in most respects, belong to linguistics, but has been part of the psychological tradition which everyone has merely held to be true. It rests on the sensation psychologists attempt at a construction of a model of mind to either justify the dualism or to call attention away from it. Helmholtz states, again on *a priori* grounds, that: "... musical tones are the simpler and more regular elements of the sensations of hearing, and that we have consequently first to study the laws and peculiarities of this class of sensations" (Helmholtz, 1954: 8).[47] That is, sound is made up of basic units, tones, each carried by a single nerve or nerve bundle. The ear, in Helmholtz' view, is made up of some 15,000 or so nerve fibers, each of which responds to a particular musical note and is, in effect, a Fourier analyzer.

Within the act model, the listener is a passive decoder of lineally ordered units, and does his decoding by taking these sounds singly in order and breaking them down into their component frequencies — or rather into the relatively wide bands of frequencies dubbed 'formants' which the ear is purported to respond to instead.

This belief is underlain by the belief that verbal behavior relates **only** to sound and leads to the belief that the ear is **only** a Fourier or spectrum analyzer. But those of us who have been trained in the field[48] and have been taught to observe and interview carefully within the Sapirian tradition, intuitively feel that this is an overly simply model of the world, if this is to be the only model. From observation we already have the feeling that communication — the wider context in which Bloomfield implicitly places speech (Bloomfield, 1933: Chapter 2) — is really not just a buildup of particles or basic units, but has, in addition, some element of **organization** which is not necessarily located in the sound stream at all. In fact, however, the brilliance of Helmholtz has been so great and enduring that his audiological and visual work have been taken as gospel until the past few years, when we have begun to allow ourselves to begin observing again.[49]

The most productive part of the Saussurian story, and the most reified, has been the notion of contrast. From the simple idea that contrasts reveal a good deal about the native speakers' cognitive worlds, which relates to a set of phonological ordering phenomena, we are asked to jump to the belief that sound **only** keeps utterances apart (Hockett, 1958: 15); that opposition of sounds is their **natural** state, and that this is the only **linguistic** function of sound.

But if I may return to an earlier portion of the essay, this point has already been presignalled and predetermined by the original Cartesian assumption. What we have witnessed since is the 'playing out', the operationalizing and classifying of the phenomena which have been traditionally packaged as linguistic. The moves we have seen in the past generation, including those of the past decade, have been made within this narrow context. Each change has been forced — usually sensibly **within** the tradition — by the more and more clear approach to the limits of fully played-out methodologies which could produce no new insight into the nature of language.

The latest, and perhaps cleverest move, gets around most of the earlier difficulties and even gives us the 'promise' of being quite productive. What Chomsky does is to posit an ideal, formal language in the Platonic sense (1957); to give us the feeling that this somehow relates to real behavior; to posit a small number of 'clear cases' and 'intuitive transforms' which have the status of Platonic essence; and to hold out the promise that at some point in the future, if we work within his form of the Saussurian enterprise, we will be able to make very general statements about the very nature of language, and even about behavior and the mind. This is tantamount to saying, within the very similar Talmudic tradition, that if you have sufficient and enduring belief and faith in the 'word' — in this case the **sentence** — the truth will become known.

One way out of this self-fulfilling dilemma, the Cartesian at bottom, the Bloomfieldian to us, is to begin by denying this assumptive framework and going back to refresh our observational approach. If we are able to forget momentarily that sound is said to 'carry' language and attempt to examine the stream of sound in new terms, it is clear — as most field linguists have intuitively known from their experience in the world — that much more subtle things are occurring than we know how to account for. If these factors are not preattributed to extra-language status, they must be handled as ongoing behavior; we have no preknowledge that speech is one kind of act within a 'confusion' of nonverbal acts other than the shared security of heart-felt tradition.

We must find new ways to understand dynamic data. We already know that scientific traditions for handling ongoing behavior have essentially all been atomistic: phoneme-like. Analog data is handled as if digital, with little notion of history, context, or organization. And for most purposes in the physical sciences, this still remains productive. That clearly leaves it up to us, then, to produce our own observations, data, theories, models, and to constantly check our models with actual behavior. I strongly doubt that other disciplines have any prepackaged theories to borrow, and there is strong evidence that psychology, for example, is now hanging on to our coattails rather than the reverse (Fodor, Jenkins, and Saporta, 1967).

The problems of observation are not simple to solve, but do not seem at all insurmountable, if the reconceptualization in stream of behavior terms is made. We must first realize that the stream of sound is a single, dynamic acoustic phenomenon. As speakers we have agreed to treat some aspects of the continually varying signal as if they are the same; that we regard different acoustic phenomena as the same by calling them the same word is a fact of the cognitive world in which we grow up. It has no apparent perceptual status outside of its relevance to that world. Facts of similarity and of difference are, then, conventionalizations which have their basis for being outside of the stream of sound itself. Children have no choice but to find out what the speakers regard as the same and to adopt that procedure as their own, or be labelled as defective. And we have no good reason to believe that children choose contrastive situations within which to discover how adults treat the transient sound stream. For the fact is that no sounds or sentences occur out of context, and we may as well start from that point rather than looking for an idealized situation which has never led back to context.

Given the graceless state of the art of observation, there appear to be two general ways of proceeding: call them 'forward' and 'backward'. Since the first or forward procedure (which is how my thinking has actually developed) requires a major shift of thinking based on really believing that the acoustic world is constantly transient yet ordered, let us first consider the backward or 'engineering' approach.

I recently proposed to a Twin Cities' electronics firm that we attempt to build a voice simulator which would speak 'real language'. This is based on extensive personal work with stored oscilloscope photos of dynamic speech signals. We would work from the actual speech signal rather than from speech which had been 'operated on', such as through filter bank or spectrum analyzer. Given this approach it is really unnecessary to make any deep assumptions about the nature of speech or language, since we will attempt to use aspects of the signal itself to remake speech at all points; and the check will be a reconstituted speech signal. Its measure of goodness will be whether it sounds natural to us and gives us back what we thought it would: a self-correcting system of analysis and synthesis.

To attempt to do this with no good idea of what is contained in the speech signal is possible, but given the actual **asymmetrical** nature of the speech signal,[50] the number of variables to deal with would be essentially infinite. A concept of language made up of sentences made up, in turn, of phonemes does not seem to reduce the number of variables in dynamic speech to anything handleable either, so it will not do for a starting point.

So what I proposed proceeds from situational nonverbal variables, in essence, and goes from there to contextual verbal variables and approaches the usual linguistic 'units' very late in the game. We have every reason to believe that the ongoing speech signal contains information about the speaker, the situation, the listener, as well as information which is often considered to be 'linguistic'. That is, the 'message', as we usually think of it, is 'hidden' somewhere in this other mess, but since we don't know where or how, it is better strategy to begin to peel off the other. It really makes no difference to us whether sentences do or do not occur, since we are taking what comes and seeing what we can do with it.[51]

The forward approach developed from the insistence, principally of George L. Trager, that careful and continual observation is crucial to good theory: that disputes will be settled by relistening as well as by rethinking.

While it is difficult to be an unjudging, objective observer, practice, experience, and expertise are no less important in a behavioral science than in any other form of scientific venture. In this sense, a major criticism of the non-Sapirian linguist is the *ad hoc* use of empiricism at relatively arbitrary points in the analytic procedure, i.e., once a deductive linguistics has been given its substance, most work is descriptive and leads to few, if any, new questions about the very nature of this subject matter.

The forward approach in this instance comes from the attempt to fully describe the verbal portion of a filmed interaction. Trager and Smith had earlier[52] attempted to do just this in conjunction with Ray Birdwhistell. Part of the difficulty with this attempt was, in my experience,[53] that the descriptive system outlined by Trager and Smith (1951), while very useful for pedagogy, was incomplete, as it attempted to deal with language as independent from other aspects of communicational behavior.

Instead I was soon convinced that more was going on than could be described. This all occurred during a period when it was becoming unfashionable to deal with phonetic-acoustic data as having any substance apart from the phrase structure it 'carried'. Since that move seemed at best to be exchanging one myth for another – and since Trager further insisted on the necessity to be an anthropologist – "speech occurs in **context**, but give priority of analysis to speech", I saw no very good reason to believe that the verbal part of communication had become uninteresting. But it seemed to me that perhaps there was more to the story than had already been told; that people could understand one another even in cases where there is a great deal of noise.

Trager always thought the 'ambiguity' argument to be a great deal of **nonsense**, that 'clear cases' were another form of 'linguistics by consensus', ambiguities are rare in real life, and the ultimate concern of the anthropologist-linguist should be with what really happens.

My route has been through a reexamination of phonetic data to see if it is fruitful to try to conceptualize some other parts of the story. The first step was based on a very hard relook at the Smith-Trager System. I found that most judgments of stress and pitch seemed to be based on a comparison of each morpheme relative to those which immediately precede it in order, in a phrase or sentence.

Given a 4-stress, 4-pitch system, the analyst tends to assume that any relatively ordinary sounding sentence begins on pitch 2 and goes up, down, or stays essentially the same (varying allophonically). Similarly, the loudest stress is defined as primary, etc.

I discovered that pitch 2 was a widely varying, but **orderly**, phenomenon as soon as I began to 'break the context'. That is, by comparing the same or similar words taken from different phrases – out of their original context by recording them together on a separate tape – the sound system appears to be much more complicated and interesting than a purely phonemic approach would suggest. This opens up, it seems to me, a new way of proceeding to analyze sound in context. Minimally, it reopens the world of Sapir and Trager to new questions and allows us to change as we understand more, rather than to engage in the kind of polemic in which a marvelously broad field work-conceptual tradition was almost lost.

PART III

(6) A PHENOMENOLOGY
OF NORMATIVE THINKING

Many people, 'looking out', visualize a world in which they usually see a mix of what is and what ought to be. What is unusual is not only different in their comparative visions but often peculiar. The range of views, close and far, in the nooks and crannies of 'world-fill' is dominated by the dualist comparator. How it actually works out, where it goes, differs depending on a number of ancillary thought habits, interests, foci; who one is **not!**

This essay explores some of the paths of thought which an habitual dualist might take. Let's start at the beginning. Most of us have a history of common sense and 'reasonableness', and this often persuades us to take certain directions rather than others. Linguists are just like us and have considered that language has a kind of **ideal** structure and that the traveler is an "idealized speaker-hearer who is unaffected by [such] grammatically irrelevant factors" (Chomsky and Halle, 1968). Let us then travel the linguists' path of relevance and see where it may lead us.

We'll begin with the notion of **ideal** as a sort of descriptive adjective in the context: (Ideal + type); and proceed to think of its possible synonyms. When there are synonym groups which seem to share a bit more with one another, let's keep them separate, as a tentative arrangement. We can put in arrows or equal signs and such if we see some kinds of relationship emerging.

From this list as our 'home base', we'll begin to travel to 'anti-land', 'correction' land, to 'unit land', to 'causal land' in no particular order, but as our fancy leads us. Some of these will seem to be connected by 'natural bridges'. If there is method in our meandering, perhaps we'll find it on our way.

Ideal, in the best of commonsense-science, usually begins at path (a_1). It means a **typical** kind of thing which is much like, for example, an idealized missile. If we wish to understand the basic (b_1) aerodynamics, we first examine the system as if it functions ideally according to Newton's 1st law — once in motion, it tends to remain

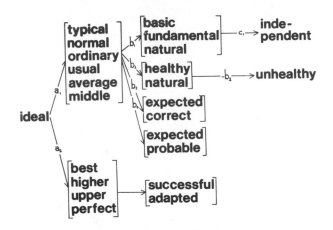

in motion, etc. **Then**, we calculate all of the forces which we impose on it, or which act on it naturally; implying an ordered procedure.

This is a very useful way of thinking about some physical objects in some settings since it permits us to examine the interaction of forces **as if** they exist 'independently' (c_1). But it depends on knowing or at least having a very good idea of what the (physical) object **is**. Do we know what language **is** in the same sense?

Ideal in its (a_1) set also might mean 'normal' or 'ordinary'. While these terms overlap in the sense of 'usual' or 'expected', the term 'normal' has a number of other 'meaning sets' — an interesting one being the (b_2) group, 'healthy'. There is no question that the ideal state for any of us to be in is good health — to be healthy is **better** than to be sick.

So far, so good. All normal people are in good health, and we can easily define a healthy state; but what about an **unhealthy** state? Do synonym sets automatically imply their opposites? When are the opposites or antonymic sets 'invoked' in our thoughts? When we think that someone is unhealthy? (I guess that we've slipped from machines to language to people.)

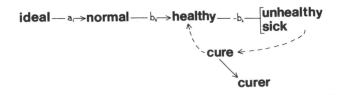

Now one of the curious properties of the 'anti-ideal' set seems to be that it attempts to undo itself, to 'correct' itself. Just as an

unstable dynamic system must be corrected to maintain it in its 'desired' state, so the unhealthy person must be 'cured'. Thus, the implied antidote to '**un** health' is a **cure**.

Again we might have a pretty good idea of who is sick, and we're able to get at least a fair amount of agreement on certain illnesses. But this, in turn, implies a sort of subset of unhealth — what **causes** the problem? Because we might know how to cure it better if we know the cause — at least the 'effective' cause.

But who has **unhealthy** language? Certainly the people who go to speech pathologists! That's their business — to cure speech. But what's bad or sick speech? There's no question that variation is a rule of life. And that different means different. But it also means **deviant** in normal-land. I've always puzzled over how **different** becomes **defective** via **deviant**.

Let's expand our ideal ($a_1 \rightarrow b_2$) healthy trip and see where it may take us, first in health terms — then, almost by coincidence, in language terms (—means an antonym set).

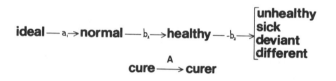

Consider the area (A) alone for a moment. Sickness implies (to us, at least) a cure, a curer, and by extrapolation, **health**.

Depending on where we enter into the people process, we may desire to **precure** to **prevent** disease 'before it starts' (Public Health and Preventive Medicine). Or, we may decide to intercede only after a disease entity rears its ugly head. The latter is most usual, but the Public Health Service is not a small operation either.

Most, if not all, societies sanction certain people to spend much of their time being 'curers'. (Mothers do this as part of their ordinary tasks.) Call them physicians, shamans, witch doctors, dentists, chiropractors, helpers — all of them are committed, in very interesting ways, to help 'return' people to 'health'. (A few modern specialists actually spend most of their energies trying to help people — particularly older people — to **adjust** somewhat better to a 'chronic bad health' situation.) But we must return to 'sick language'.

We might agree that anything which differs from ideal language is sick or pathological.

For example, all native speakers of 'English' might decide that all foreign languages are somehow sick. Much of the American reaction to immigrant languages of the first half of this century was of this sort. But, historically, it was German which usually came out on top in the 19th century. The 'classical language' was revered by many as the only 'pure' one, those being cited most often being Greek, Latin, Hebrew, and Sanscrit, depending on one's persuasion. It would, however, be hard to convince many readers now that English is the best of all languages. Besides, there are native English dialects which at least some of us have a very difficult time understanding – these seem to differ depending on where we're from!

If one is willing to accept the likelihood that English is no better than some other languages, are there some which are sick or unhealthy compared to English?

(Does one feel that the word 'primitive' might be more appropriate here? What antonymic path is that on our map?)

There is little question in most of our minds that some people do 'have' pathological speech, or that they do speak 'peculiarly' at least. We take some language development difficulties for granted in our children and include them under the category of 'baby talk'. (Actually, 'baby talk' is more likely an adult 'dialect' which is used in talking to children, often in making love – in various languages – perhaps in other circumstances!) Children have 'trouble' pronouncing /r/, or /l/ – often /s/ or /š/, and a few other very usual sounds. They get 'tested' in kindergarten or first grade and are asked (forced?) to take 'special' classes if they have one of these 'defects'. They have to speak within fairly well-circumscribed 'normal' limits by the time they're five or six. In effect, the teachers or testers are our society's agents for making these children 'public' and trying to 'help' them. In smaller, less anonymous societies, the children are, in fact, much more public much earlier, and neighbors' and relatives' comments and criticisms are likely to be reacted to by parents, if not by the children, much earlier than age 5.

But we'd better pick up our map again lest we seem to wander off the beaten track and take a reading on where we are and how we got here.

Ideal a_1 typical b_2 health is the basic path. But remember that the (a_1) path also leads us to words like 'ordinary' and 'normal'. Perhaps they also have a (b) path to 'health'.

A notion like 'ordinary' doesn't seem to want to make this trip, but 'normal' clearly does. In addition to 'health' it also seems to imply, in a similar way, the idea of 'natural'.

Thus, if health is a normal or natural state, it is abnormal to be

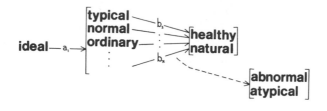

sick. And people who are sick are both abnormal and atypical, possibly 'unnatural' as well.

It turns out that there are, indeed, a number of people who might fit these categories. If we continue this train of thought, we must add a few 'facts'. There are a number of people who **never** get to talk – either not at all, or very peculiarly. These are called, most generally, 'aphasics'. Many of these unfortunates are called 'retarded' (formerly: idiots or imbeciles), some 'autistic' (formerly: insane or crazy), depending on whether the curers **believe** that potential change toward health is **possible**. Western curers seem to believe that retardation is an absolutely permanent state, whose causes are basically in the organism and which cannot be 'undone' (e.g., 'brain damage' is presumably irreparable.) Autism, being more of a 'social disease' with causes 'unknown', but at least 'undoable', **could** be cured later in life.

Now in our mapping we must have left out a few 'dimensions'; they're not exactly words or places that we can go, but they're there in any case. The 'historical dimension' is one of these. Can people be cured – or are they labeled for life?

In historical terms, anyone who is not healthy as part of his physiological development prior to birth, is a kind of cripple, a defective who must learn to function as well as he can; or if he finds someone to take care of him as well as he can become accustomed to. Many severely retarded people find themselves in very difficult, but unaccustomed, straits when a loving parent or relative passes away. They may be institutionalized if they have very little effective control over their own destinies, whether or not they are 'competent' to have any. On the basis of the thinking characterized here, some citizens are thought to be inherently incompetent and may easily be deprived of various civil rights.

To move from the more strictly medical model of pathology and cure, back to language; do we use the same kind of thinking in picking out language 'defectives' who are in some sense impossible or at least very difficult to 'cure'? How do we make such judgments?

Clearly the judgments are made about people who differ from **us**.

Any 'ideal' model implies just that — an 'ideal' against which all is measured. If we are dealing with Russian, we might say, as many Russians do, that all Russian except Moscow Russian is not quite as good. Moscow Russian is the 'ideal' in case you're a Muscovite or would like to be one.

Pathological speech disturbance of a central nature provide the only opportunity that we have to observe language in *dissolution*. For the linguist, who is concerned with the *fully developed structure* of language its acquisition and dissolution cannot fail to provide much that is instructive (Jakobson, 1968). (Italics mine.)

Abstracting from this quote we can fill in our map a bit more.

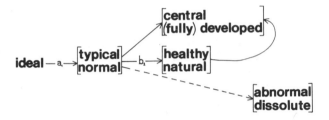

Not only does unhealth refer to abnormal, but there is a strong hint that one can 'fall back', regress from the ideal state toward 'dissolution'. Perhaps this is why the feeling earlier that 'primitive' people have or 'are had by' primitive languages — maybe they are abnormal — in the regressive direction. At least one popular, often serious, author takes this position very forthrightly in a rather devastating criticism of 'earlier anthropologists', by which he means most modern anthropologists:

The earlier anthropologists rushed off to all kinds of unlikely corners of the world to unravel the *basic truth* about our *nature*, scattering to remote cultural backwaters so *atypical* and unsuccessful that they are nearly extinct. ... The work done by these investigators ... revealed just how *far from normal* our behaviour patterns can stray without a complete social collapse. ... What it did not tell us was anything about the *typical behaviour* of *typical* naked apes. This can only be done by examining the *common* behaviour patterns that are *shared* by all the *ordinary*, successful members of the major culture (Morris, 1967). (Italics mine.)

Later in the same book, Morris also refers to the "rule" of "biological morality" which "ceases to apply under conditions of population overcrowding" (1967: 99).

Since this book was the number one best seller for many weeks in 1968, we can assume that much of the American population, at least, is familiar with this position — whether they believe it or not. It is, at any rate, a short well-traveled path from abnormal to primitive and **unsuccessful**. The fascinating part, to me, is the reverse use of the path — that unsuccessful people **are** primitive, 'therefore' they have 'dissolute' language. Morris doesn't make this trip, but many others do. Let's add a 'success' dimension in its proper setting.

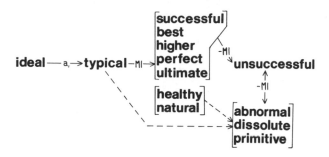

The path is (MI) (Making It), and the associated (-MI) sphere of ideas. This happens to be a path high in social value, because rather than traveling down it, we **want** to travel up it. We have the habit of picking out unsuccessful people and attributing to them all of the features of the set characterized by the term abnormal. We have a strong tendency to believe that (socially) unsuccessful people are also primitive and dissolute and that their attributes, such as language, are part and parcel of their problem. Some of us equate unsuccessful with uncivilized — the direction of causality being irrelevant.

Now our 'ideal' map can only account for differences (from the ideal) as being antonyms to ideal or one of its synonyms — to be different is to be atypical, unhealthy, abnormal, unsuccessful. It so happens that in the American population there are not simply unsuccessful **people** (individuals); but there are also unsuccessful groups of people (... at least they appear to be unsuccessful-as-groups — witness Whitebacklash, Polish jokes, etc.).

And it also happens that most of the members of these groups do **differ** from the 'successful' members of society along a number of lines — physical, linguistic, etc. Just as most Black and Native American people are physically recognized by the White majority, their voices or dialects are also **recognizable** to many nongroup people. Apparently we respond at a very deep level to 'contrast' — whether we can be explicit about what we're attending to, or not!

Our map suggests, however, that because these groups are unsuccessful, their other attributes are somehow abnormal, primitive, or dissolute. We must **cure** them! (Is it possible to conceive of an outside observer and an ideal model in the same terms? Isn't an 'ideal model' exactly an **insider's model**?)

We seem to have fallen into a complex labyrinth of thought. Yet the processes of common logic regard this as an apparently reasonable way to think! Witness a current spate of articles on differences between different 'racial groups' — lower class people come out lower on practically all tests (I.Q. and others) which depended on their original calibrations, of course, for prediction of **social** success. How surprising is it that a model which assumes an ideal tends to study deviance from that ideal, and that deviants show up as deviant on all of our ideal-based tests? This should cause us to pause and consider our travels so far — we might reflect on how we got here, if it was a reasonable path, and, if so, reasonable to whom? How would an outside observer feel about this? Or one of those judged to be deviant? (Would one's willingness to grant that these thoughts are reasonable depend on his 'ability' to become and remain typical?)

Since we are somewhat refreshed we might backtrack a little and consider another potential path. Just above, it was mentioned that ideal models lend themselves to the study of 'deviance'; that is, difference from the ideal or typical. In other words there is another negative-antonym path from typical or ordinary which represents differences. One might ask, what kinds of differences?

$$\textbf{ideal} \overset{a}{\relbar\joinrel\longrightarrow} \textbf{typical} \dashrightarrow \boxed{\begin{array}{l}\textbf{different}\\ \textbf{deviant}\end{array}}$$

And we might answer — any difference. Thus we could count physical differences, social differences, or any others that we can observe and/or which come to mind (size of cigar, hair color, height, etc.).

One way of characterizing the models we fall into is in terms of college course grades. Most of us have become accustomed to being graded on a 'curve'. The usual curve is a 'normal' curve — the measure of our goodness or success as students is how well we do in comparison to how other students do. The mark we get depends on how far, and in what direction, we deviate from a 'mean': positive deviation means A or B — negative deviation D or F (failure). Our measure is taken with reference to the bulge in the center — in effect, the **ideal** population. Woe to the 90+% student in a class of 95%'s!

We also tend to put people on such curves and measure them against the mean. We give marks, and often for features of being, not just of performance. Deviation is often failure. However, modern biology tells us that variation is a very natural state of affairs.

The 'professionalisation' of deviancy study has come to characterize much of what is current in behavioral science. Much of what passes for good methodology is the examination of features of traits of people examined from the point of view of typical-ideal model, with deviance seen as being relatively far from the mean-average-typical. Many of the problems these scholars concern themselves with relate to the likelihood that two or more such features are **related** to one another!

In a slight extension – hardly a detour – of our model, which brings the time dimension a little closer to the surface, it is easy to see that most of these ideal features are rather long-lived. In this topographically complex region, it seems as if we have a choice of maps: we can 'jump off' the ideal plane, or we can look at these domains of 'typicality' as rather **natural** to our being. If we stop and get off, we might get confused and lost, and probably become lonely as well. If we stay on, it might also require a kind of jump, one which seems to become shorter with practice. Since (we might observe) practically everyone has a particular trait, we might assume that this is part and parcel of our being.

Remember the quotation from Morris (1967) which claimed that **success** was the 'measure' of the (evolutionary) survival of typical traits of normal people. Now, on this rose-strewn bridge from observation to 'knowledge', it is easy to imagine that most of our important (successful) traits are **inherently** human. They are, in some sense, innate, inborn and natural to us.

If we, as Morris, are interested in interspecies differences, we may readily accept the 'apparent differences' between man and other animals as being more important, basic, or fundamental than some other features. We are likely to say, as many behavioral biologists, that these features, being part of our success, must be genetic. That is, they are part of our **biological** endowment, part of our evolutionary history, and essentially **unchangeable** within the context of a lifetime at least.

Granted this, our intellectual-observational enterprise might concentrate on just these differences which are **judged** to be fundamental to humans. Much of our current interest in science is motivated by our caring about the nature of man, so why not look for man's (unique) nature in those features of his which he alone has?

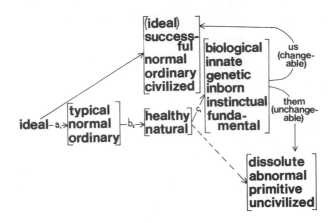

In the antonym set of genetic-natural, there seems to be another implied set — perhaps a possible path from ideal-typical, but one which is somehow obscured. This is the set of features which are **not** genetic, instinctual or unchangeable. It has many terms — some of them are environment, learned, social-cultural, nurture.

We ought to ask why this set is obscure unless we take the path from typical to innate (b_1-c_1). All we seem to have done is to build in a short bridge; yet it implies its own antonymic set. This was not at all obvious when we began our trip.

One possible answer is that each path opens up its own 'new' world of meaning sets and that we should expect it to happen.

Others might argue that the domain of ideal, etc., simply does not 'contain' the antonymic set of natural-genetic. Yet many social scientists use these models as part of their initial intellectual baggage. Would the outside observer see something wrong in this? For them (i.e., us) or for him?

Of the schools of people who use this model for the study of language, one seems able to study language as a purely innate function of man (i.e., all men have the innate 'capacity' to have language — no animals do); and another group who accept this and make another trip on our map, which seems to be enticing even to the most careful thinkers. This is the short jump to the 'health' set and all of its sub- and antonymic sets.

The above argument concerning the innate capacity of man for language always (in my experience) is juxtaposed with the inability of animals to 'achieve' language. Does this have some scientific basis, or is it simply implied in our common-logic mapping procedures? Which kind of people (following the thinking in the ideal map) 'have' deviant language? Are they more like animals in our thinking — i.e., 'primitive', less able to achieve? Granted that any other wordly observers would be assumed to be rather 'incomplete' humans, how might they feel about this entire 'scientific' enterprise?

There are an astonishing number of scholars who seem to forget the path that took them from typical — healthy — natural, and who operate in medical pathological terms on social issues. While health is an easily agreed-on ideal model, and one which few of us would reject on personal-familial grounds, even if it turned out to be scientifically nonuseful for understanding how a 'normal' organism functions, it seems to be quite a jump to apply a **sickness** model to people or groups who appear less socially successful than some others. Yet it is popular, easy, and self-justifying for those who are able to live their lives as ideal-typical persons, for their 'curers', and for those others who would enjoy being among them in some indefinite future.

PART IV

(7) THE STUDY OF INTELLIGIBILITY

Although language is usually studied and described as a static kind of structure, the dynamic language of everyday interaction is also of interest to linguists. Interactional language is a rapidly changing, transient series of phenomena, and is extremely complex. Yet it is understood; it is intelligible to any normal speaker of the language! And to the extent that it is intelligible, it ought to be structured and studiable, just as are any other shared human phenomena![54]

The problem is how to conduct such a study. The general approach has been to employ a model derived from other structural considerations and to apply this to interactional speech.[55] Although this is a natural and useful solution, it may tend to obscure and delay certain kinds of questions which are particularly pertinent to the dynamics of speech and which contribute directly to its study. These have to do with context, information, relationships, and canons for the measure of sameness and difference.

Since moment-to-moment phenomena are tremendously numerous, even from a simple observational frame, one of the first questions to be asked must concern the nature of units. Are there things like units of intelligibility? If there are, what kind of structure might such units have? Can they be demonstrated, and how?

If there are units of intelligibility (and research strategy would dictate making this assumption), it is possible that they somehow involve more than a single phoneme or morpheme. As interactors, we often know, for example, just what a person is about to say. This is particularly clear when a speaker hesitates and gropes; the audience is often ready to provide just the right word. So it appears that there might be presignalled information. That is, a given word or phrase not only contains information about its own shape, but may simultaneously signal something concerning the structure of what is about to come. And in the light of earlier work on juncture, it appears that words contain information about the shape of structure of what has just occurred — whether an utterance was a word, or a phrase, or an entire sentence. Therefore, the duration of any given word, taken from any context, may very well include multiple kinds of information (Trager, 1958).

To whatever extent this is true, it will mask the search for particular kinds of units, since it is difficult to decide which information pertains to which functions. The search for units is tied intimately, then, to the study of all those environmental and contextual characteristics which comprise differences between sounds, position in a structure, different individuals, age, sex, and general information on the one hand; and room shape, echoes, and general noise, on the other.

The problem outline having been set, this paper will proceed to give an account of my attempts at handling various aspects of the problem, and is, in effect, a progress report.

There appears to be no methodology or instrumentation which seems to be suitable in an unrefined state, for direct application to examining interactional speech. This poses two sorts of problems: that of instrumentation; and, more fundamentally, the search for comparable kinds of data, which point up those aspects of language having to do with intelligibility.

With this problem more-or-less well in mind, several observations were made which have subsequently led to a more general type of approach. These had to do with very particular aspects of stress, of pitch, and of time **relationships**.

With respect to **stress**, it appears that certain semantically related items have special stress relationships to one another. Items which are contained or included in others seem to have a relatively stronger stress than the word which is the more generic and inclusive term. Examples are: *days* in the *week, leaves* on the *tree — days* is normally louder than *week*, and *leaves* is louder than *tree*.

In ordered sets, the **pitch** of each item seems to vary with position in the set. Numbers or letters in order, go down in pitch over the set; except for the last member. This becomes clearer if a normally ordered set is said out of order: one, three, two, four. The pitches also seem to be out of order.

A combination of pitch and stress relationships is noted in certain **contrast sets**. These often occur in two separate sentences, or in a question and response, and thereby imply a sense of historicity which is nonlineal. Examples are: *the big boy*, contrasted with *the big bóy*, where *boy* is the thing in question; or contrasted with *the bíg boy*, where size is the problem.

More generally, this can be shown in contrasting similar words which have no specific meaning, such as letter names. For example: a b c : a b c. The two b's are in contrast with each other in some way which has nothing to do with the fact that they are b's, or that they occur second in each phrase. Rather, some other characteristic imputed to b, must be contrasted in this pair. It is the characteristic of a common semologic set to which they both belong.

Some curious **time relationships** also show up clearly, in sentences which express mathematical relationships as formulae. In this case, those things written as plus or minus symbols, and numbers or letters, are the words. But parenthesis or contrastive divisions are expressed partially in terms of time. In a formula like this: $a \cdot \dfrac{b-1}{2}$; the a and the pause following it are quite long compared to the other words. If the pause before *over* were longer than it usually is, then the pause after a must be **very** long in order for the sentence to be the one described. If this situation is reversed, then it is an entirely different formula: $\dfrac{a \cdot b - 1}{2}$. In other words, the length of pause at one point in a sentence may very well be related to another somewhere else in the sentence. In this case, if one changes, the other must change, or the meaning of the **entire** sentence is altered.

More curious, perhaps, is the following: if durations of sound are **measured**, it turns out that the duration of the same words in different phrase groupings is not linear. A group of three words does not take one and a half times as long to say as a group of two words; e.g., in a sentence, (xx) (xxx), the group (xxx) takes only about 5/4 the time it takes to say (xx). This suggests even more strongly that contextual relationships may determine parts of the grammatical structure. These relationships may be independent of lineal order or of specific meaning.

Assuming that the problem of interactive speech may be at least as complicated as is being suggested here, an instrument which yields a dynamic readout seems desirable. This points directly to some form of oscillograph, which is today available in the form of cathode ray tube oscilloscopes with storage and filming facilities.

The use of oscillographic techniques for investigating speech has a fairly long and quite **un**distinguished history. As Pierce and David (1948: 93) point out: "The trouble is that these records contain too much information even for a sophisticated sense such as sight to comprehend." The problem, again, is how to separate out the various factors going into speech, since they are all present in unknown quantities in any dynamic speech display.

In order to move from a theoretical to a practical level, it must first be shown that words do, in fact, differ considerably as a function of their context. However, since any two words might differ according to many variables simultaneously, how can purely contextual differences be demonstrated? How can one be even relatively sure that what is observed is related to some **particular** function?

The approach used here is the comparison of the **same word** throughout variously structured 'formulaic' sentences: e.g., (aa) (aaa) as opposed to (aaa) (aa). Phonemic **quality** is therefore a constant. In this case, all words are clearly, a/ey/.[56] Presumably, variation is a function of context, location, and function within these. Any things which are very similar in oscilloscopic display ought to function and be located similarly — compared to different, contrasting forms.

Figure I is a set of five such sentences; recorded by the investigator, and then fed through the oscilloscope and photographed.[57] The pictures shown are directly analogous to the sound pressure and were made at a constant speed and gain. The structure of the sentences is noted after each set of photos. Each sentence consists of five a's for easy comparison.

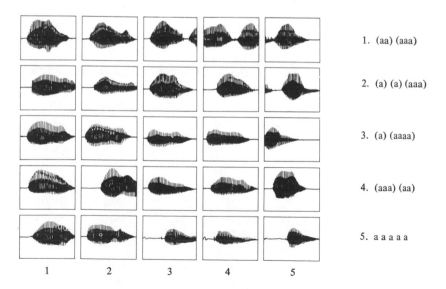

1. (aa) (aaa)

2. (a) (a) (aaa)

3. (a) (aaaa)

4. (aaa) (aa)

5. a a a a a

Fig. I. Drawings of photographs of differently phrased sentences each composed of 5 a's: Read and recorded, then displayed through oscilloscope as separate words and photographed. Speed per single drawing about 3 cs.

In these pictures, made at about 30 cs. per photo, not much more than the external shapes or outer envelopes of the words can be seen. The outer envelope is most directly related to what we hear as stress. Note the amount of variation in shapes. And note, particularly, that the finals are, in all cases, more like one another than any of them is like anything else. They all have the appearance of being essentially round; this is the result of their having most of their amplitude concentrated in roughly the first half of their durations.

There is a great deal of variation in form, even though these are all the same word. The procedure has been done for all the vowels in English with several speakers. Such variation as is seen in these photos is the rule and not the exception. This suggests that a great deal of care must be taken in comparing forms extracted from different contexts. Further, a comparison of words taken from similar contexts may not be completely representative of the spectrum of actual differences, since there is such wide variation as a function of location.

In the same photographs, several other things can be seen. First, the amplitude of the sentence-final words is not the highest in each sentence. Rather, it appears that the perception of final strong stress might be a complicated matter. The finals increase rapidly to a maximum and decrease about as rapidly. The rapid changes may give the impression of heavy stress.

Secondly, in the long sets such as in the third and fifth sentences, note that the amplitude is quite reduced and diminishes over the set until the final word. This suggests that it may be redundant to keep each word at the same level in situations where each succeeding word is very much like its predecessor. This may be a way of judging levels of sameness and difference in situations where similarity is not as obvious as it is here (e.g., animal speech).

The words which generally have the largest amplitude, both positive and negative, are the initial words in the sentence. But note that phrase initials are also higher than the words which precede and follow them. Initiality, on various levels, seems to be a significant contextual factor.

Lastly, in these pictures, the phrase finals have two characteristics common to them, but not generally shared by the other words: length and a tendency to increased amplitude just before the end of the word. The phrase-finals are longer than any other words including the sentence finals. The rise before the end can be seen best in the first sentence, second word.

Before going to finer data, it must be pointed out that a general problem, reset in terms of the oscilloscope, is that of interpretation: how to relate what is seen to what the linguist hears and knows. The lines of the photos are analogous to speech. The conception of what they represent and how to examine them is problematic. The lines are continuous mathematical functions and can be examined as such. But they also reflect what the linguistic investigator perceives as many different kinds of data.

Measurement of displays can be done in various ways; some quite automatically with an increasingly sophisticated array of automata, and others quite laboriously. The raw data can now be operated on before or after it is displayed. In any case, a great deal of thought and basic spadework, the posing of salient questions, should be done first, in order to determine what to measure and count.

The fact that words do, indeed, vary considerably in their different locations has been demonstrated. The second problem involves the kinds of different contexts which may be significant. In this case, it becomes necessary to look a bit more closely at what goes on through the duration of a word and to approach the problem of quality differences among different phonemes.

The photos in Figure IIa include some of the same words as those used earlier.[58] Each picture consists of two lines, spoken by the same person. The top line in each photo is a_1 of a group of two, and the lower line is a_2 from the sentence (aa) (aaa). The top line is then both sentence initial and phrase initial, while the lower can be said to be phrase final.

The up and down movements of the line correspond to sound pressure changes across these small time periods.

Initial probes into the interpretation of what the photos might represent is now in order. Here the comparative method is used carefully. One of the most obvious differences is that between male and female voices. The female voices, in the photos on the left, have more frequent cyclical peaks. Since the speed here is 1 cs. per division, the lowest, or fundamental, or "basic frequency"[59] can be calculated. A distance of one division between peaks would be a frequency of 100 cps.

In other dimensions, however, there is nothing obviously apparent in the photos. In terms of general appearance, they are far from identical. Even the two lines spoken by the same person differ considerably. Compare these as a group, however, to the entire group in Figure IIb (all u's [uw − phonemically] and all corresponding person-wise and positionally to the respective a's), and it is quite

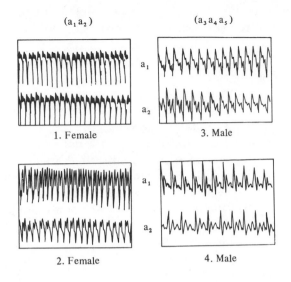

Fig. IIa. Central portions of 4 person's a's /ey/ from a_1 and a_2 in the sentence: $(a_1 a_2)$ $(a_3 a_4 a_5)$ a_1 is above a_2 in each drawing. Speakers same as in Figure IIb.

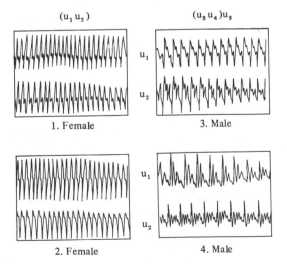

Fig IIb. Central portions of 4 person's u's /uw/ from u_1 and u_2 in the sentence: $(u_1 u_2)$ $(u_3 u_4 u_5)$ u_1 is above u_2 in each drawing. Speakers same as in Figure IIa. Speed 1/2 cs per drawing.

clear that the a's are more like one another than they are like u.

Are there any other similarities or differences which can be seen in these photographs? Consider the bottom line vs. the top line of any single picture; the peaks are further apart on the bottom line than on the top. On checking each other photo, this is seen to be shared by all. This means essentially that the phrase final is lower in pitch than the phrase initial. The consistency of this observation for several speakers and various vowels strongly suggests that this interpretation is correct.

There is also a considerable amount of other information present in these displays. How do individuals' voices differ from one another as far as the oscilloscope displays them? What are the differences between those things we recognize as phonemes? Suggestive attempts at answering these sorts of questions can be made now with some sense of my thinking process.

Although the two female voices seem to be very similar to one another, the male voices differ considerably. Taking the a's as a group, while they are similar compared to u sounds, they still differ from speaker to speaker. One of the solutions to this problem is a function of the 'basic frequency'. As the basic frequency increases, the large spikes get closer together. As this happens, the small spikes, internal to each cyclical peak, do not merely move closer together. They actually disappear. In the photos this can be seen best in the top line of speaker 4. His a and u go from four peaks to three.

The evidence for this was gathered not only through measuring such very tiny changes, but over a pretty wide range. This was done by sustaining a given vowel and singing it up the scale. Continuous photographs of this show the condensation of the large peaks and the disappearance of the minor peaks, as the voice goes up the scale, and still retains a given sound. A male voice shows a progression from 4 or 5 peaks, to 3 and then to the 2 which is generally seen in the female voices here. The number of minor peaks is, therefore, a partial artifact of the base frequency.

This fact is important for still another reason. Since the measurement of minute instantaneous change is difficult even with sophisticated instruments, the appearance or disappearance of the minor spikes seems to be related directly to perceived pitch change. Compare any a_1 to its corresponding a_2, or any of the u_1's and u_2's. In all cases there are more minor peaks in the bottom than in the top lines. In the a_1 of speaker (4), Figure IIa for example, there is a fairly rapid change over the line from 4 to almost 2 peaks. This correlates with the closing up of the base peaks and indicates a moment-to-moment rise in pitch.

As useful as this notion may be, it may be valid only within a single person's speech. That is, a *u* with three well-defined peaks in one person's speech may be at a different frequency than the same picture in another's voice. This may be related to the no-man's-land of 'voice quality'. Granted that a single person's speech is almost constant in quality, it may yet be very valuable to trace momentary changes within one person's speech.

Another more general comparison can be made between different vowels. How is it that speakers differentiate among different sounds; what is constant about *a* or *u*, regardless of the highly variant forms they each take?

With respect to frequency, each photo can be matched with its corresponding one in Figures IIa and IIb. With careful observation it is clear that *a* is consistently a little lower in frequency than *u*. Care must be taken in selecting comparable material for such a study, however. If, for example, an initial *a* were compared to a phrase-final *u*, the conclusion would be reached that *a* is inherently higher in pitch than *u*. And this is a likely occurrence if two sounds are matched in an ordered pair: the first will be higher than it would otherwise be, purely in terms of its position in a phrase.

In more comprehensive observations, various of the vowels in English are characteristically different, while there is a considerable overlap in others. For example, /i/ and /u/ are very similar in appearance, while all the low vowels are quite different from these. Consistent differences among them has not yet been established, but it is already clear that most of them **develop** or **change** in characteristic ways through their durations.

The relationships between vowels, consonants, syllables, and words should also be investigated in future studies. The study of position has preceded this, since location in a context seems to be fundamental to any more comprehensive investigation using this methodology. Hopefully, data gathered in this way, and the rules of change and relationship discovered thereby, will be carried over into actual interactional speech with little difficulty.

In summary, it might be asked: Where does this lead? Clearly this paper is not concerned merely with groupings of *a*'s or of any other word. What it does suggest is that there are discoverable rules which have to do with dynamic language: how units are connected or organized in structures like sentences. Any rule of relationship would add to our knowledge of how it may be that people communicate.

The extremely wide variation among the a's in Figure I suggests that simple measures of phoneme quality are not the complete answer to the dynamics of speech. Instead it appears that a great deal of information is available to both the speaker and listener — from moment-to-moment — about the past, present, and future within the duration of any given utterance.

It appears clear that the structure within which a word appears contributes considerably to the acoustic properties of that word. The shape of a given word may be affected by: (1) the length of the sentence to come, (2) the location within a substructure such as a phrase or sentence, (3) the location within a conversation or discourse, where, for example, a question and answer are related in particular manners, and (4) in spite of our ability as speakers to act as if words are the same entities throughout this broad variation, there is no good reason to retain the belief that words retain the identical structure either with respect to source or meaning in all contexts. It is, on the contrary, suggested here that a positional substructure underlies this variation and must be 'peeled away' before this wide variation can be understood.

The use of the oscilloscope is not magical. It is a versatile instrument if used sensibly and is particularly suited to dynamic studies. However, measures of sensibility and significance are not built into any machine, but occupy some niche in the investigators' minds.

We should **not** be wed to the instrumentation, but to the area of problem. The dynamics of speech is linguistic, is structured, worthy of investigation and worth continuing as a problem area which deserves increasing attention as extremely interesting, if not fundamental to human behavior.

(8) LANGUAGE PERCEPTION AND BREAKING CONTEXT

Social animals, including man, seem to operate in a number of sensory modalities simultaneously. We do not operate as hearers, **then** as see-ers, feelers, tasters, or smellers; we do what we do, use what we've 'got', what we 'are' as physical beings, as bodies. Traditions of sensory study have tended, however, to be analytic; to take our body and divide it up into component chunks to be treated as if they were independent. The traditional study of the senses and the traditions of the study of language are mirror images.

These traditions are based on a number of assumptions — some of which we must question. Like bodies, the senses are assumed to reside in **individuals** — they are 'private'. Until very recently (Gibson, 1966), the body was assumed to be a **passive** receiver of stimuli; the major percipient activity was/is presumed to be in the brain — the 'place' where we 'construct' the cognitive world. Historically, most of the arguments about our perceptual functioning had to do with where the real world 'really' is — outside or inside of our brains. The individual was assumed, in his growing up, to become both more **complex** and more rational.

In this assumptive web, thought and thinking were seen to be filtered by language in some indirect sense. The task of language study was to get at the rules of language, 'filter-free'.

In this sensory component world, speech is observed as if it were a function of each individual, which depends ultimately on the kind of instrument our **ear** is — the kind of receiver, the kind of information which it gets and which it allows through, can be the subject or study for a perceptual/acoustic linguistics.

We might, as ethologists, worry less about the nature of the instrument and consider variables such as information flow in a social group: the maintenance or boundary conditions of a social situation; the relationship between what verbal messages occur and how they occur; what the listener does as the speaker is speaking. Until very recently, however, the relationship between speaker and hearer was considered only as (new) information exchange, not as communicational maintenance, so we ought to prepare an account based on an individual-oriented sensory acoustic model.

The trouble began over a century ago. The great psycho-physiologist, Helmholtz (1954: 8), was struck with a particular property of hearing which he thought was primary or central to all else:

... musical tones are the *simpler* and more *regular* elements of the sensations of hearing, and that we have consequently *first* to study the laws and peculiarities of this class of sensations. (Italics mine.)

While his work tells us a great deal about music, sound transmission, and reception, it places great constraints on the ways we might think about sound in speech.

Helmholtz thought of the ear as a bundle of fibres each of which responded to a different musical tone – a sound which vibrates at some particular frequency. By this account, our ear somehow puts these all together to form a total **spectrum** of sound; sound is composed of different loudnesses at different frequencies. If we look at, say, a word by breaking it down into its **component** frequencies, this will characterize the sounds in the word. And this can be displayed visually in the form of a sound **spectrograph.**

This model, as it is applied today, also assumes that phonemes (or their component parts, 'distinctive features') are **the** units which make up the sound stream. Phonemes come along in linear order, and we hear and 'interpret' them by **analyzing** each phoneme's spectrum one-at-a-time. Putting this together, somehow, we 'hear' words, phrases, sentences. The analogy of the telegraph sending and receiving letters characterizes this perfectly.

In order to analyze speech using these instrumental methods (sound spectroscope), we must **already** have a phonemic analysis of a given language by some **other** method; e.g., interpretive interviewing. Phonemes (and d.f.'s) are the units of sound which exist in **word** contexts (CVCVC) – they keep the words distinct. Instrumental methods assume that we can take as given these word-units, phonemes, and build them up into longer utterances. Perhaps we can. Possibly we do.

There appears to be more to the sound stream than a phonemic picture alone suggests. And there is good reason to believe that the ear is more than simply a spectrum analyzer. The Helmholtz tradition has provided us with **minimal** and incomplete pictures of sound. These pictures have been used, however, as if they fully characterized our sound behavior. We accepted Helmholtz' picture and his priorities as if they were totally exhaustive.

Apparently the 'ear' can do much more than distinguish sounds-as-phonemes. By taking speech recordings and altering them in various ways, psychoacousticians have found that we can 'construct' (or 'reconstruct') the words, very often, even if they have been substantially altered – sometimes, even if they're 'missing'. In other words, 'context' provides enough information about other words in, say, a sentence, that we need only 'minimal' sound information in the duration of the word itself.

This is clearly not true of single words in 'isolation' – out of context. They are what they are: words provide the context for sounds. Do words themselves exist in larger contexts? And do these affect phonemes' sound qualities? In effect, linguistics has said: 'no', to this question. Distinctive features are the basic features – they, and they alone, (can) characterize all sounds.

But what of psychoacoustics? We've been shown that sound, even whole words, can be missing in larger contexts – yet we know what they are. What does that tell us about sound perception?

First, that there's more to the story of sound! But how about us ... as ears, as sound analyzing instruments?

The location of words in sentences is in my view an important factor in sound. But location can't have much to do with "d.f.'s" or with sound spectra. True! – in fact, it suggests that part of the sound information available in the stream is not about phonemes, but about location. Where a word is – what's coming next – and in what relationship. (Locational information, being omni-present, might be much more apparent to outside observers than phonemic information! Perhaps the 'call systems' of animals – the ones that we attend to – are mostly about message information – not 'information' itself!)

And the psychological aspects of psychoacoustics? Sounds do not really exist in isolation – yet we recognize constancy. Some features must stay the 'same' for us; e.g., the fact that a word such as pat is heard consistently as that word, and not pet, or pot. Linguists have elevated these features to being central features of language.

How about the boundaries of phonemes? Phonemic analysis is a kind of 'timeless' method. Any method which seeks for the units of a phenomenon tends to be this way. Yet sound is spoken and understood in 'real time' – in fact, in extremely fast real time. I doubt that the human ear could possibly decode and understand at the rate it ought to if it merely decodes phonemes. At any given point in an utterance, we listeners already have a great deal of information **about** what's coming.

(This, it seems to me, throws great doubt on the methods of animal sound analysts. They tend to believe that animal calls are distinct — much like phonemes are thought to be. But no would-be animal linguist could possibly do a phonemic-type analysis because he can't get animals to tell him about any **minimal** contrasts (to them). All he can do is set up his own **outsider's** taxonomy in relation to similarities he hears — or sees, if he 'analyzes' the sound on a sound spectroscope. This, alone, makes animal language data noncomparable to human language data — all that can be said is that animals sound different — one species from another, and from man. That's not news! As we will see, those parts of human verbal production which might be comparable with other species have gotten almost no attention from linguists, since they are **assumed** to be 'nonlinguistic' as linguists **define** their subject matter.)

Given that we hear phonemic-type constancies and distinctions — what else can we hear? Apparently we **attend** to relationships within some kinds of structures. But all of those structures are not necessarily in the same situational context that we happen to observe. For example, if I say to someone: *I'm going!* — with lots of stress, high pitch, and other things on the *I'm* — we all recognize that *I'm* is contrasted with *he's* or *she's* or *you're*. This *I'm* may be accompanied by a flushing of the face, hand gestures, mouth tightening, and strange eye movements — loads of **affect**, or perhaps a 'special' lack of affect — in any case, lots of behavior to observe. Yet the discussion, leading to this one, might have happened yesterday or last week. The purely naturalistic observer, looking for contrasts or merely seeking to describe as exactly as he can, is in real difficulty. He could never possibly discover the contrast, no matter how careful he is, how exact his recordings and video tapes. To get around this difficulty, he may claim that animals have no 'memories', but, again, there's no evidence for that statement. He is not even likely to find out that *he's* and *hé's* are different actualizations of the 'same thing' or event, since they probably sound quite different to an outside observer, and he is not even likely to compare their sound spectra.

This is the dilemma of the would-be animal linguist and why it is that he is unlikely to discover animal language, even if there is such an entity. We couldn't possibly discover it without first believing it might exist — even then, we can't simply take humanly derived linguistics which 'defines out' so much of verbal behavior and is really based on minimal contrasts — and discover animal contrasts. So we need new methods, based quite probably on gaining more insight into the full variety of systems which we have gathered under a single name, Language.

What else is there to language? How do the features of language relate to the way we hear? Better phrased, perhaps, how does the way we hear (perceive) relate to those phenomena we call Language?

We hear **constancies** — like *pit* and *pet* — and the implied differences. We hear locational variables — we hear loudness and frequency — actually relative loudness (stress) and relative frequency (pitch). How do we know **where** we are in, say, a sentence? That is, can we attempt to move from a static set of units, to a dynamic, sound-stream picture? Will that help us to examine animal language? Can we get at animal language without such a dynamic analysis of language? I don't think so.

We'll consider a few conjectures — speculations — based on my work on the problem of Intelligibility; then ask how that animal, the human infant might see language. What is his perspective, what **is** he *vis-à-vis* language?

Within the context of intelligibility — what is a truly 'same' occurrence — what are its properties? Contrast these **(say them out loud)**:

(1) a a a a a . [a_1, a_2, a_3, a_4, a_5]

(2) (a a) (a a a) . [(a_1, a_2) (a_3, a_4, a_5)]

Let's consider the *a's* in (1) as essentially the **same**: that is, they contain a **minimal** amount of information about what's occurred previously or will follow — that the 'same' word will follow and has preceded — or about the whole sentence. (Note in (2) that each *a* is really pretty different in this sense!) In oscilloscopic (real time) photos of such sentences, the minimal information *a's* in (1) always become relatively reduced in amplitude — they literally become **quieter**. How do we hear or perceive them; as **about the same**. That means that we are geared to perceive diminished amplitude as the same, thus we're pretty peculiar observers even of our own speech. And the **loudest** point in (1)? — we think it's at the end, on the last or final *a*. But it's not — it's on the first *a*. The last one is a lot louder than the second last (a_4 — the penultimate) — so the last one **sounds loud** to us, by **contrast**, but it's not very loud compared to a_1.

Such factors as these are only discoverable if we already know about structures like sentences — organizations of sounds and words.

Do animals have such organized structures? No one knows. Some oscilloscopic photos of animal sound look remarkably like human sentences – displayed the same way – the amount of similarity we see obviously depends on what we select to compare, and we can't even do that very well. But if **sameness** does mean something like minimal structural information, and there is some systematic variation across a structure (e.g., declining amplitude), then perhaps we can rethink about the possibility of examining animal language.

And our closer relatives – our own infants? How do they come to recognize the **same** constancies, structure, and organization as we?

We really don't know what an infant hears except that we can recognize that he does hear (from 'startle reactions' to loud noises) or how he comes to differentiate the same features as we do. Clearly, the infant's problem is to hear the **same** way we do – not simply to hear and to recognize more-or-less similar/different sounds. A Spanish-speaking child comes to make five vowel differences, to **not** distinguish between *sin* and *sing* or between *bit* and *beet*. The child's 'job' is to treat or respond to sound in about the same way as those around him.

Offhand, we don't know what his strategic problems are. A way of thinking about it from an acoustic (really, psychoacoustic) point of view is this: an infant (we'll conjecture) can 'hear' very well. This means that he responds to air waves, changing frequencies, amplitudes. The infant's first problem is that he doesn't know what ones 'count', and for what. He's faced with several creatures whose acoustic output is quite different; mother's voice being 'higher' than father's in terms of greater frequency (and probably in other things as well, such as 'voice quality', manner of addressing infants, and in what state they find themselves when talking to or around him). So it may well be that an infant regards the 'same' word emanating from mother and father as quite different acoustical events (which they are in part). His job is to attend to the features which are the same – to the parents – and come to regard them as the same, himself. (This, of course, would be a dilemma for a nonhuman examining language – which features should he regard as significant?)

The task of hearing/sensing similar and constant features is probably a simple one for humans (and others) since almost everyone seems to do it with little difficulty. (An audiologist colleague has suggested to me, however, that many of the 'hearing impaired' are **not** acoustically deaf or nonreceiving of sound exactly – some of them don't seem to be able to 'straighten out' significant sounds from noise.)[60]

How does an infant figure out that these constant features are to be considered the same, while other very similar features are to be considered different (e.g., the difference between the vowels in *bit, beat, bet, bait, bat*)? Is this similar to the problems of infants of other species? If so, how can we devise a strategy which will enable us to guess the constant/different features of nonhuman infant sound systems?

Consider the infant-as-observer, not just of sound, but of social activity as well. We could think of the infant as a 'generalizing machine' — one which tends to generalize on most observations, and one which proceeds from the general to the specific. (Other perspectives might also be taken, e.g., that they go from specific events to general characterizations. I think the one proposed here is potentially the most interesting to an ethologist because it presumes that the infant is already social at birth. The second seems to beg this problem and usually leads to a study of how individuals grow up — **as individuals**.)

The child sees and hears the male parent, female parent, siblings. The differences (in most families) are fairly large and quite consistent. In fact, sex differences are pretty constant **messages** in the sound stream, regardless of what's being said or talked about — it occurs in the higher or lower frequencies which characterize female and male speech. At first, the infant might well distinguish male and female voices, and not much more. It seems likely that he detected such gross differences even while in the womb. But the other 'social' information was either missing or, more likely, mediated through the mother's body. To get some sense of what this might sound like, turn a radio down till it's just barely audible, and see if you can tell the sex, age, topic, etc. Or listen to two people speaking, but through a closed door, or some other muffling device. Amplitude and distance from the speaker are also clearly related and perhaps the clearest aspect of speech to the outside observer and to an infant.

It also seems likely that an infant can begin to relate such things as his 'state' (e.g., alert or sleepy) with the occurrence and amplitude of speech, in what fashion and how much he gets handled. Slightly older infants cue in on their parents' faces, apparent as the richest source of information, whenever there's a big change (from the infant's point of view) in the environment, e.g., when someone new comes in a room. So he learns to watch eyes and mouths to see how they change — to see if a situation has altered for the parent or not. Perhaps this is part of the problem of teaching a child what to be scared about and what not to be. (A large proportion of 6-9 month old children go through a 'shy' stage with 'strangers' — we might wonder where the information concerning who is a stranger, is located. And why some infants are 'bolder' than others. That is, is this due primarily to the infant's perception and evaluation of the situation, or to his interpretation of how his mother perceives it? In species where predation is quite real, this ability is, of course, a matter of pure survival. We also have to wonder why it is that children come to 'trust' their mothers, and to use them as interpretive mirrors. Perhaps some children don't and/or won't!)

Thus it is probable that a child has already learned **about** a number of (social) constancies in features of speech before he 'learns to speak'. And thus it is that a purely instrumental approach to acoustic (or other 'sensory modalities') is such a confusing problem area. These approaches seem to ignore other percipient or social behavior, and regard their area (e.g., language) as 'independent'.

When does a child say his 'first' word? Gradually infants begin to vocalize — i.e., to use their vocal muscles and articulators and to make noise as they 'exercise'. It's often said that they are in some sense trying to 'mimic' adults, but they are some distance from this in the so-called 'babbling' stage. What's been happening during this period?

Part of the mimic routine begins with feeding — close one-to-one interaction with the infant. All parents I've ever seen, open **their** mouths as they want the infant to open his, to get fed. This ingesting being is not regarded simply as a passive food-intaker, but as a potentially **powerful** person who can exert great control simply by refusing to open his mouth. Moving one's face is not simply an activity, but part of the politicization-socialization process into family structure.

As parents speak to children from close distances, the child **sees** as well as **hears**. In saying many poems which are most popular in this youngest age group, there are a very large number of facial contrasts, changes in the mouth or teeth (or surrounding muscles) which are visible at this distance. Not only visible, but highly **contrastive** — mouth opening and closing is a great change — probably also to the infant. *Bah, bah, black sheep* has a change on every syllable which involves major lip changes. Even the /š/ initial sound in *sheep* is made with **pursed** lips — and most people talking directly to infants exaggerate all of these movements, apparently enhancing the contrasts. So the information available to the infant is both visual and auditory (not to mention breath and other odors at this distance!).

Similarly much of the information about the infant's state is located in his face. Whatever 'emotional' state the infant is in, it is usually reflected through a smile, a lower lip projection, puffed-up eyes from crying. The problem of whether such states are the infant's 'own', or are in some sense defined into being by the parents, is an interesting question here. In many animals-can't-symbol-theories of language origin, we (humans) are said to have the same emotions as animals; i.e., emotions are part of our animal nature; basic and innate to our being. Opposed to this idea is an ethological one; that infants do what they **do** — parents **impute** the parents' view of its state, and he comes to make it his own. In this notion, parents and children kind of share a domain of understanding; parents react to the child in terms of what they **believe** his needs to be. He comes to share these beliefs as he does their other ways of looking at the world.

A test case for this is that certain children, e.g., those with Down's Syndrome, whom some call mongoloids, have little control over their external facial muscles — they can move 'deeper' ones such as tongue and eyes. This lack of movement appears to be related to, perhaps responsible for, their facial configuration; a 'flat' face much like some oriental populations — thus 'mongoloid'. Many of these children do not become apt speakers and are not intellectually successful as most of us define this term. We now call them **retarded** ('idiots' or 'imbeciles', formerly) and assume that their brains were somehow 'damaged' in prenatal development. An ethologically-oriented suggestion: part of the language and intellective difficulty is that the grounds for 'reading' the mongoloid infant's state is lacking. Parents get very little information from his face — it remains 'placid' — thus they are unlikely to enculturate him and to 'make' him have the full range of 'feelings' which he is supposed to have as a social being. He also seems to lack a kind of feedback from his external muscles (i.e., lip or circumoral muscles); the major sound-forming muscle, the tongue, doesn't seem to 'know' what to do with itself. Thus, in many older mongoloids, we see a fairly characteristic tongue, hanging out of the mouth in a particular manner.

While these ideas haven't been investigated in any real sense as yet, the difference in approach is interesting. In one, we tend to 'condemn' the child — the other looks to the social setting for a developmental dynamic.[61]

At some point in the babbling stage, the parents become increasingly observant waiting for the first word. This will demonstrate to them that the child is more human, growing up. Meanwhile the child is vocalizing — his tongue spends a fair amount of time lying on the bottom of his mouth, and the sound emitted in this state is a fairly clear *ah*. His anxious parents keep saying to his face, *bay-biii*, and *maa-maa* and *paa-paa* or *dae-dii*; each of which requires a large, contrastive facial change such as mouth opening and closing — while the child vocalizes with his tongue kind of lying there, and sooner or later he gets to say *ma-ma* or *ba-ba* or *pa-pa* — mouth contrast with vocalization. If the sound is released nasally, it sounds to the parents like *ma-ma*; if orally with lip tension, *pa-pa*; less tension, *ba-ba*.

The child has merely gotten two or three things working together with his mouth, tongue, lips, air release — but the parents are over-joyed! Here we have two very different points of view about the same event. If the child repeats his new skill several times, the parents claim for him a new **kind** of knowledge and ability. The child, who seems to thrive on making his parents happy, has figured out how to make several parts work together in some way which is obviously interesting to his parents. He can do lots of other things as well, but they don't get nearly the same payoff. And it seems likely that he'll work harder on those things which are more game-like to other people. (I think that the same dynamics occur in animals; usually domestic pets, for whom we claim speech, the ones I've seen vocalize while they're opening and closing their mouths. Saying *ma-ma* to a dog's mommy is a very rewarding thing — for dog and mistress.)

A colleague[62] made a similar suggestion on watching his year-old son who is so 'friendly'. This child had just begun walking and liked to be picked up by almost everyone — thus, he's adjudged friendly. His father — a Human Biologist — observed that when someone 'new' approaches, the child stops walking, looks up to the parent's face (as he's done for several months when anyone new is around), has to raise his arms up and forward (or else he'll fall down, because kids have such large heads, etc.), and smiles (his way of testing the 'surround' — his mouth is a sort of 'center' for examining the world at this point.) So this child who is 'really' trying to keep upright, loves walking, is tolerant of other persons, is **perceived** by adults as a very friendly, delightful, fun child, and keeps getting picked up, and fondled. He wants to be let down right away, of course, but meanwhile he has enriched the life of these people. Or we could simply say that he's a friendly child; just as we say that some dogs are friendly — our reasons are probably just as confused/correct.

Whether or not this is a correct interpretation of the event, it does portray a *via media* by which a child whose 'life strategies' are unknown to us, can be acculturated. We don't have to impute unchanging qualities to him as a completely independent being who is endowed with (human) reason.

To return to our examination of 'acoustics', it still remains unclear as to the nature of our receiving instrument (ear, *et al.*) and the interpretation instrument ('the brain'). Is there any other approach, any other sorts of problems which might yield insight into how we process auditory sensory information? What is it that people do? How do they **understand** one another? (What do animals do?)

As discussed earlier, it has been assumed, since Helmholtz, that we understand by hearing **sounds** — one at a time, slightly after they are said — and we somehow 'remake' these into words and sentences. When this process is done, a message signaled, we get a kind of whole picture of what was said. And by some sort of secondary process, it is then interpreted by the brain. If I say *bat*, you (the listener) hear sequentially /b/, then /ae/, then /t/. Then you add this all up to *bat*.

In addition to this being purely a phonemic approach, this model of hearing-understanding is not very satisfactory on other grounds: first, it implies that all the information present in speech is in the sound stream — the face doesn't contribute anything to it, nor does the context: it assumes that /b/, /ae/, /t/ are separate, individual, equivalent entities and that the speech signal is composed only of ordered phonemes. From an ethological standpoint, it seems to concentrate on information transfer, rather than pointing toward the contribution of both listener and speaker. We ask, instead: how do people understand **one another**?

Some observations: in informal conversation, speech (and phonemes) come along at a very rapid rate — yet misunderstanding seems **rare**. In fact, at the 'beginning' of a conversation, it is relatively slower, but speeds up considerably as people get into the conversation.

Some psychoacousticians have taken recorded messages and 'cut off' high frequencies, or low frequencies; they've even removed whole words in some cases, and comprehension remains very high. This suggests that the information **about** the message comes along in serial order in the speech stream, but it also gets 'carried' in a number of other ways.

But what do I mean by saying **information about the message**?

Think about the listener's problems in a real interaction! What does he have to know and/or do in order to be 'polite'?

(1) He has to know when **not** to break into a conversation! He must know when something is continuous or when it's about to end;

or he is **interrupting**. How does he know, where is the information, which tells him when he should speak his turn? When is he breaking in? The information in this must be in the same sound stream as the 'message'. Perhaps it's also in the speaker's face! (Note that children, probably [of] other animals, too, get special treatment here. Perhaps they don't know all the signals yet, but there may also be other reasons.)

(2) He has to put in 'continuers'; at certain points in most conversations, the listener has to 'nod' or to say *um-hm* ... right? Even while reading this past sentence, you can **imagine** doing it, whether or not you actually move your head — correct?

(3) If and when he speaks, he has to say something **sensible** — not just **sane**, but also **sensible**. He must demonstrate to the exspeaker credit for being what he thinks he is and make sense in that context. A diabolical spirit-listener can reduce most speakers to nothing (e.g., silence or simple fury) by acting as if the speaker is not to be taken seriously. (Also a favorite ploy of 'insiders' against an 'outsider'.)

It seems plausible, then, that the speaker also has a fair amount of knowledge about the listener's problems and gambits. And words and sentences and sounds occur within this contextual framework.

What other kinds of information are present in the context? Which of these are also part of the stream of sound?

The loudness (amplitude) of speech is called 'stress' in language — but the actual loudness in conversation is related overwhelmingly to the physical distance between speaker and listener. We must speak at a level several decibels above the surrounding noise — think of how a speaker sounds so loud just as a fan or air conditioner goes off. (And these are the loudness variables which a different species observer would probably attend to as his **primary** data because they are much greater in amplitude than the relative amplitudes of ordinary speaking.)

In the speech stream there is a great deal of variation in one's voice depending on the situation (talking to a class, to a person, over the telephone) and the type of audience (someone older, a child, a class, a congregation). A test group given excerpts of tapes in different situations can, indeed, tell most of these contextual variables apart — regardless of the message (Benjamin, 1969).

To test this, you might attend to the 'situational shifts' that you or others make. You'll soon find that they are there, but that you hadn't been aware of them in any conscious sense. Actually I first became aware of these social-situational differences while working among Tzotzil speakers. After a while I could tell what kind of people (e.g., young man and older woman) were talking to each other — well before I had any real comprehension of what was being talked about. It seemed quite probable that infants and pets might be in about the same position as I was then. Once you become aware of them, such differences do not appear at all subtle.

(This experience suggested to me that there are probably many aspects of behavior in which situational differences exist, but since the behavior is consistent or congruent with that situation, it simply doesn't stand out. This is similar to the problem of the fish discovering the fact that it's in water, and one good reason to do field work among other peoples or species, and begin to observe from their perspectives.)

What other **strong** acoustic signals exist in the sound stream? What do they have to do with? Several years ago I became interested in the speed of speech. I had been working on a filmed interview of a woman and her therapist. My job was to **describe** the sound as completely as possible. Eventually we were going to correlate sound and movement — the eventual goal to learn more about The Interview as a cultural form, and possibly how 'curing' took place in this context.

Well, for complicated reasons having much to do with bureaucratic difficulties, we didn't learn much about curing. It turned out that we (I, several physicians, psychoanalysts, and a philosopher) all had come to the situation with well-developed ideas about what curing means, and no one was very willing to change; so any potential data was inconsequential (unless one is intrigued with how people from different disciplines approach various issues and why interdisciplinary studies are usually doomed!).

At any rate, I did note a few things about a particular lady's speech (we called her Doris) which hadn't occurred to most linguists — since they don't spend much time listening to chunks larger than sentences usually. The data occurred in a sound film of about 33 minutes' duration — a short therapeutic 'hour', due to the film setting up.

After listening to the tape some large number of times — often with the film, sometimes not — I about knew the 'script' by heart. Because we were interested in looking for movement (gestural) patterns, we kept breaking into the tape at odd places, and even split and spliced the film (and sound) to compare more easily some of the similar gestures.

We didn't learn much about gestures, as far as I've been able to tell in retrospect, but I heard some interesting things in this 'context-breaking' process, that I had not noted listening to the tape serially as it was said. There was great variety in Doris' loudness and pitch of voice which was really striking out of context, though it went unnoticed **in** context. Apparently we are so well attuned to these characteristics of sound which are usually called 'tone-of-voice' or paralinguistic phenomena, that we are **not aware** of the immense variation which occurs in ordinary speech. Linguists are accustomed to making comparisons, but only within or between short, contiguous utterances. It suggested that what goes on in speech, and what we **perceive** to go on, are at variance.

Several other vocal phenomena showed up in Doris' speech as well. She was in a foul mood – at least said she was – hubby was away; the 'hour' to be short; and she started off: "Gee, of all the days in the year when I wanted my full hour, too; today would be it." I spent a ton of hours examining this 'thing' (I am not sure what it might be, grammatically – it does not 'mean' anything unless one knows a lot about the scene!). For all this effort, a couple of ideas suggested themselves, serendipitously, I suppose.

The words *all ... days ... year* seemed to have some relationships to one another in addition to their meaning relationships. They sounded 'clipped', fairly 'fast', 'raspy'. And they had a loudness relationship (or a pitch relationship – I had, by this time, 'lost my ability' to 'hear' the difference. The same thing happened in working in Tzotzil, at first I was **sure** of pitch and stress differences, and gradually lost confidence in my ability to judge them.) The word *all* was loudest, *year* in the middle and *days* least loud, as displayed on a meter which was supposed to measure amplitude. In and of itself, that wasn't very interesting, but it occurred to me (as I was losing interest in Doris' problems – it was a poorly made film anyway) that other, similar phrases have the same kind of pitch-stress relationship: *all* the *leaves* of the *tree, all* the *trees* in the *forest, many men* in the *army*. There seemed to be 'families' of relationships.

Whatever the actual psychoacoustic variables are, they are essentially the same for the same **kinds** of words in all these phrases. That meant that a potential 'phonological semantics' was on the horizon – at least it was possible. Whereas linguists have always said 'study structure first', then 'meaning'; this observation said that *sound* and *meaning* are related if not coterminous – we only had to figure out how to examine them.

Clearly linguists had been comparing things 'too narrowly'. There are a fair number of differences and relationships from one word to the next, and linguists had concentrated on these, to the exclusion of comparisons between separated words in a sentence, and it soon became clear that there are interesting relationships – similarities and differences in sound – which occur in separate utterances. This indicated, to me, that words in sentences do not relate merely to the particular sentences they occur in, but they must occupy some kind of **slot** or **location** in families of sentences. And they might even perform some kind of function; e.g., 'beginningness' or 'introduction', 'endedness', 'continuity', etc. It began to appear that the very complex appearing thing called language might be quite simple in part; only we had been looking at the wrong parts and in the wrong way. And, ethologically speaking, it is very desirable to seek simple systems, for a number of reasons; for comparative purposes, it is impossible to compare a language of infinite form with an animal 'call system', by definition; for 'esthetic' reasons, we do not want human language to be more complex than animals languages. It can **appear** complex without really being so; and since almost all children learn their language, we are forced to assume that it is either an innate ability, or that language learning is a relatively **simple** task. Only the latter view seems potentially comparative.

One potentially comparative approach is by this problem of Intelligibility – how do people understand one another; where is the information which is the message, 'carried' in some particular person's voice? How do we distinguish them, or can we find a method so we do not have to separate message and vehicle?

In addition to phrasing this as the Problem of Intelligibility, a way to think about it is to reverse the linguist's procedure preference: the Problem of Context. Instead of proceeding from structure (sentence, phrase, word) to context, take the reverse view: context to structure. This is appealing on various grounds. It seems likely that infants, of whatever species, operate in this manner. They work from some sense or feeling for 'the scene' – to ways of communicating about scenes as the mature beings in that society regard them to be (actually, this is not an unreasonable definition of language in cross-species perspective).

And so some students and I devised a kind of 'maximal' test to determine what ordinary people could tell about the social situational context merely from the 'sound' of a **speaker's** voice. Rather than attempt to see how many people could tell if the **listener** was much younger than speaker, or a female or a friend – a correlational method – we asked them what they 'knew' about the listener and the speaker and their relationship. Because we were afraid that the 'message' (the words) might reveal something about the situation, we took very short (¼ – ½ second) bits extracted from in-context tapes and used a bad tape recorder (albeit an expensive one).

It turns out that we social interactors 'know' a great deal about what's going on; not just from the message, but from the 'paralinguistic' or tone of voice phenomena which are unnoticed in context, because they are so context-congruent.

We can tell, from a speaker's voice, if he is talking to a good friend or not, the relative age between listener and speaker, a lot about some contexts (e.g., story reading to a young child), sex of the listener, over the telephone or not, etc.

We seem to be able to get an increasingly good picture of any situation more as a process of 'ruling out' possibilities, rather than being absolutely precise in the first 'n-th' of a second. That is, if we know the approximate age of speaker, and relative age to him of the listener, we know a tremendous amount about what is **not** going on. And this knowledge increases rapidly. Most of us can enter into an ongoing discussion after a few minutes, but we sometimes enter prematurely. If we were part of a conversation and left for a moment, we can usually return in context in a few moments. Obviously 'all' situational information is not present in the speech stream; just watch a television program with the sound turned all the way down. But we can extract a great deal from speech alone. And it is most intriguing to become aware of how most of us can carry on extended phone conversations.

A rethinking of this essay from the point of view of the behavioral comparator – the ethologist – may help us to get some sense of the difficulties inherent in doing studies in other species' communication or linguistic ability. In adopting the fiction that we alone have language, we have been overly content to examine and contrast those characteristics which differentiate human languages from one another. We can only speculate – given the experience of these 'context-breaking' studies – that many features of human verbal behavior remain to be observed.

(9) AN EXAMINATION OF THE QUESTION–RESPONSE SYSTEM IN LANGUAGE

Introduction

The weight of tradition in linguistics has opted for the definition and study of a central, more systematic part of verbal behavior — Saussure's *la langue* (1959). In its current phase, linguistic study considers its central concerns with the grammar, made up of all (grammatical) **sentences**. Complete analysis of the grammar will presumably yield insight into linguistic rules and possibly into extralinguistic considerations as well, and deserves priority over 'behavior' approaches (Chomsky, 1959: 57).

While this approach is apparently quite attractive to linguists and psychologists, there are other possible methods of analysis which are inherently more interesting to behavioral scientists. One such approach was pointed out by Pike on the basis of an earlier suggestion by Fries:

... the analysis of the response to a question cannot usefully be treated without reference to the fact that it is correlated with the prior occurrence of the question which elicits that response, whether the response be verbal or nonverbal (1957: 136).

Pike suggested that language and interactional-communication behavior (which seem to be more intimately related than modern linguistics would admit) have a formal relationship in question-answer, interactional settings. That is, the answer or response to particular questions appears to be a formal (rule regulated), 'shared' system.

The focus of the present study will be, first, to inspect the relationship between verbal questions and responses — the Question-Response (Q-R) System — and, second, to inspect the classes of responses in terms of their membership, variations, and culturally relevant characteristics. Nonverbal responses (and questions) are considered to be discoverable after the fact of the investigation of the verbal material — in the context of the present essay.

The problem of relating language and culture, or of using the language as an entree into the inspection of nonlinguistic, cultural systems has various roots in both linguistics and anthropology. This theme was succinctly stated by Malinowski in the following form: "I submit that the linguistics of the future, especially as regards the science of meaning, will become the study of language in the context of culture" (1944: 5). The problems inherent in using the structure of language as an inroad to the study of culture are reflected in the works of Sapir, Whorf, and their students (Hoijer, 1954). Whorf considers the grammar as molding cultural systems: "... that the linguistic system (in other words, the grammar) of each language ... is itself the shaper of ideas, the program and guide for the individual's mental activity" (1952: 5). Sapir claimed that " 'The grass waves in the wind' is shown by its linguistic form to be a member of the same relational class of experiences as 'The man works in the house' " (Mandelbaum, 1949: 10).

In the actual attempts at such analysis, from the structure of the language as these scholars conceive of it, success has been felt to be far less than complete. Hoijer reflects this lack of success in spelling out his conception of the steps in doing "ethnolinguistic research" (Hoijer, 1954: 98-99).

Part of the problem of procedure seems to focus on the selection of units or parts of language to be taken as beginning points for the analysis of culture. Questions of the order of "What is a grammar or sentence?" — with reference to the culture — seem to be relevant. Are there other parts, levels, systems of language which are more useful for cultural analysis? Pike does title a section of one of his works, "On linguistic units larger than sentences ..." (1954: 73).

More recently, Frake stated: "A successful strategy for writing productive ethnographies must ... discover those features of objects and events which they (the anthropological subjects) regard as significant for defining concepts, formulating propositions and making decisions" (1962: 34).

To restate the problem, the linguist-anthropologist observer-interviewer attempts to allow the native speaker to categorize reality in his native world, preserving the contexts, while the observer manipulates some formally discoverable and describable part of language to show up those kinds of categories and concepts referred to by Frake. One basis for this mode of procedure can be found in Bloomfield (1933: Chapter 16, "Substitutions"):

A **substitute** is a linguistic form or grammatical feature which, under certain conventional circumstances, replaces any one of a class of linguistic forms ... the substitute replaces only forms of a certain class, we may call the **domain** of the substitute ... its domain is grammatically definable.

... One element in the meaning of every substitute is the **class-meaning** of the form-class which serves as the domain of the substitute.

... In addition to the class-meaning, every substitute has another element of meaning, the **substitution-type**, which consists of the conventional circumstances under which the substitution is made (pp. 247–248).

Bloomfield also discusses the fact that the various types of substitutions represent "elementary circumstances of the act of speech-utterance" (1933: 248), i.e., the culturally defined interaction.

According to Bloomfield, there is a part of language which does relate directly to the culture: the grammatically definable, linguistic substitute for classes of similar members. The domains or class meanings of such linguistic classes can be discussed in cultural terms; the class is linguistic, its domain refers to some set of similar cultural events. The fact that, for an informant, some form is a substitute for some limited class of forms would indicate that this class is culturally isolated by a native speaker on the basis of the cultural similarity of its members — to him, as a member of his culture.

If this line of thinking is pursued, one arrives at Frake's idea and perhaps, a methodology which would meet Malinowski's requirements for linguistics in the context of culture. A series of attempts which essentially follow Frake and Bloomfield were conducted by several scholars (Sturtevant, 1964) who do Ethnoscience. These studies concentrated on an 'area' of culture (e.g., firewood, sickness) and attempted to allow the informant to come up with names of categories: **head words** for substitution classes. This procedure is followed through to break up these categories in many and various directions until it is felt that the area is essentially broken into its significant component elements as the native sees them. The formulation of this is, then, a **cognitive map** (Frake, 1962) of some piece of culture. Descriptions which are yielded by these procedures appear to be excellent in mapping some elements of a cultural universe.

The presently proposed methodology attempts to stay within and preserve cultural contexts by entering the language from observed, situational behavior, systematically manipulating question forms to yield response classes, and testing hypotheses derived from the domains of response classes in the prediction of new forms, again within observed interactions. It will examine the formal properties of questions and responses as a **single entity** (the Q-R system) to attempt to see how aspects of linguistic and extralinguistic systems interrelate.

The basis for the use of the domains of classes is to be found in Bloomfield. A method for getting at such classes in some other language devolves upon the relationship, suggested by Fries, between questions and responses, which may be phrased in these terms:

> Question words produce classes of responses. At least some of these responses are appropriate responses to one question word, and not to others.
>
> Question words – expanded by other forms into question frames – introduce other variables or parameters. These further restrict and subdivide classes of appropriate responses into subsets or subclasses.
>
> Some of the 'other variables' or parameters are themselves appropriate responses to still other question words. When introduced in a given type of question, these show the intersections, the 'dimension' — time, space, etc. — through co-occurrence in the same responses.

This method allows the investigator to discover and manipulate a general logic in the language, to produce, as a limit, all classes of responses, thus to be able to investigate all possible culture domains, all areas of culture. This method strives to maintain the linguistic elements in their cultural context and is always returned to the context, the analyst doing no more than he does in, say, effecting phonemic analysis.

Theoretical Discussion

The relationship in language (and culture) between questions and responses is taken as a given.[63]

I. Definitions

    A. **Interaction** – the Q-R system inherently involves a relationship between two (or more) **persons**, who must implicitly share a sense of what the question **and** response 'mean' in any particular context.

> 1. **Contiguity** – the response 'follows' the question. In this study they are assumed to be of a single piece, the order properties being necessary, but insufficient.
> 2. **Answer** – the response **answers** the question. There

are right or acceptable, and wrong or 'silly' responses to any particular question. This is agreed/shared by the interactors.[64]

3. **Context** – particular questions occur in 'real' situations which are culturally relevant, and which partially define an answer as 'correct' or not.

B. **Question** – a question is a type of 'sentence' which 'demands' a response: i.e., it is somehow 'incomplete' by itself.

1. **Question word** – is that part of the question which relates directly to a **set** (class) of responses. It may consist of one or a number of morphemes or words, and cannot be *a priori* listed without reference to its co-occurring responses.

2. **Question frame** – the sentence in which the question word is embedded. It is made up of a number of ordered classes – one member of each occurring explicitly or **implicitly** in each question.

C. **Total response** – a sentence (or part of a sentence) which answers a given question or set of questions.

1. **Response** – a class of members, all of which relate to a particular question word. It may range from a single morpheme to several words in length. This part of the response frame must occur (other parts may not).

2. **Response frame** – made up, as the question, of a number of ordered sets. Most of these do not answer the question, but belong to other systems which may relate to context, interaction, etc. While all parts of the response frame (except the response itself) may not occur, they always exist in the context.

II. Units

A. The elements of the question frame are units on the present level of analysis. Each represents a substitution class which may range in size from one to several thousand.

A unit may consist of one or more ordered morphemes; e.g., *where* is a unit; similarly, a syntactically 'complex' form as *in the red schoolhouse* is equally a single unit. *How* and *how many* are both single units. Although *how many* is syntactically complex, it is conceived of not as *how* plus *many*, but as a single entity, equal to and different from the form *how* (since they relate to entirely different response classes).

Units are never smaller than morphemes; thus an initial separation into morphemes is useful. But it should not mislead us into thinking that morphemes are the question-response units merely because many of them overlap or are identical in form with units on the level of the Q-R system.

B. The Question – the 'left side'. Since the question word occurs with or delimits its response class, the other forms which may occur in the question frame are things which may differentially affect ('modify') the response classes. They never co-occur with a greater number of responses than the question word alone, but break up or divide the total response class into subclasses. They define the 'state' of the system. (All *places* are possible answers to *where*, but only a few such places are actual responses in any given situation. The remainder of the question frame – the nonquestion word parts – directly reflects those situational variables.)

It is thus impossible, *a priori*, to know what the units (or unit classes) are on the left side without considering the class of responses. The exact shape of the question word can only be determined in an interview/observational situation where an informant is asked a set of questions (which may well have an inherent order). The question word may well be 'divided' in order as in English *what*? vs. *what ... name*? which 'yield' entirely different response classes.

Question frames seem to be defined as a set by the question word they contain. They have different **properties** in these terms. Most question frames introduced by *where*? implicitly contain a set of 'temporal' terms – *Where is he going (now)*?; *who* questions do not. **The fact that the temporal set member does not occur in a given question cannot be taken to mean that it is not implicit in the question.**[65] Its presence, explicit or not, affects the subset of answers (although not the total set) which are likely to occur in any situation.

C. The Response – the 'right side'. The response is a member of a set of possible responses to a given question word – often a large set. The particular response which occurs is a function of the situation, not of the question word; the task is to separate the class from the particulars. The response may occur as an isolated form. So much of the question frame is repeated or repeatable in the response form that it is often redundant in context. *He's going ...* seems completely predictable as part of the response to *where is he going*? Its actual appearance in any response frame is a function of some-

thing external to the question-response system; e.g., style, polite-
ness, etc.

The isolation of the response from the response frame necessitates
an interview situation. Often, in conversation between friend and
family members, a question is not fully answered. In the Tzotzil
data between the informant and his wife, he asked:

k'u ca? ta wutun ca?i?	*k'u ca? ta sa? ?amul ca?i?*
'Why do you argue with me,	'Why do you look for your sin,
then?'	then?'

He then responded: *k'u hmul ca?i?* 'what sin?', answering part of
her question. This is not an unfamiliar gambit in the English-speaking
world. There is, however, a 'patterned response' to *why* questions
in Tzotzil introduced by the particles *porke* or *¢oh* 'because'.

The informant was fully aware of this, however, and was quick to
point out the 'gamesmanship' involved in conversational repartee.
Most questions are indeed answered, and the range and pattern of
responses is clear to an informant.

The problem of isolating the response from the response frame is
part of the procedure of isolating its question words and must be
done with 'same-different' interviewing techniques. The Analysis
section will outline one way of doing this.

III. Data

The data for this study were gathered mainly from a single,
major informant (Bartolome Sawanilla) Venustiano Carranza, Chiapas,
Mexico.

Data for the descriptive grammar on which this study is based
were gathered during an initial field session of some ten months
(1960-61). The major informant was taught to transcribe in Tzotzil,
and was also capable of rendering high quality translations and
writing in Spanish.

The grammatical data included a detailed descriptive analysis
(Sarles, 1966), a dictionary (about 3,500 words), and some forty
transcribed texts, twenty of which are currently in the files of
the University of Chicago Chiapas project.

The data were checked during a second field session (6 months):
(1) in the analysis of the recorded conversational data; (2) by this
observer's ability to learn to comprehend the spoken language
during his second field session, based on the grammatical model;
(3) by checking with other linguists working in the area; (4) by
checking with other informants.

Some amount of reworking of the grammar was done, since new data occurred during the second field session. The grammar appeared to be adequate for use as a tool in doing the second part of the present study.

The present study, dealing primarily with the question-response system and general, contextual statements, is based on data derived primarily from the single informant who also worked on the grammar, dictionary, and texts.

The data for this section of the study include the following:

(1) Recorded Conversational Data — 12 conversations of some 2-5 minutes duration between the major informant and several others. The others were selected in order to have at least a wide age range. Included are three conversations with females. These conversations were completely transcribed in Tzotzil, then translated into Spanish and analyzed linguistically. Several new or revised statements were made concerning the grammar. Lists were made of questions and responses which occurred.

(2) Elicited Data — based on the lists of questions and responses which occurred in the recorded conversations, a series of further procedures were used to isolate units of the question-response system, and to amplify each substitution-response class. The informant gave substitutes for each response form or class, arranging and delimiting the classes as he feels them to be.

By combining the morphologically isolable forms which have occurred in the lists of questions, the analyst placed these in all combinations and asked the informant which of these may occur, and in what orders. In this manner the syntactic limits of each question word were determined.

There are several possible checks on the quality of the data. First the data were checked in order to see if the informant was, himself, consistent. The amount of data was great and such checks made often, so that consistency seemed to be a significant check. Actually occurring inconsistencies in the course of the study most often indicated that the observer was doing something wrong.

A small number of questions were directed at other informants. These concerned the limits of response classes. Usually, two possible responses to a particular form were presented to an informant. Then a third, morphologically similar but nonpossible response — according to the major informant — was presented. These were almost always reacted to negatively.

IV. Analysis

The analytic procedures employed are quite standard substitution methods, but the difference here is that the conceptualization of the question-response system is simultaneously seen as both formal and cultural — rather than one or the other having *a priori* centrality.[66]

The questions and responses which occurred in the Tzotzil interview data were collected and examined. The attempt was made to see: (1) what **parts** or **elements** composed both the questions and responses; (2) how these related to one another; (3) how they related to the context. No assumption was made that the parts or phrases were *a priori* known (this was much simpler using Tzotzil data).

Two forms glossed 'where' had been noted in earlier field work; though the informant felt that they were different somehow, he had no way of expressing the difference which made any sense to me: *bu* or *buk'al* 'where ...?'

The solution lay in the response classes which occurred in answer to the two forms. The difficulty in separating them — and which may underlie most studies of meaning — is that there exists a domain in which they are, in fact, identical. They share some aspects of meaning, but not others.

Six questions introduced by the question particle *bu* occurred in the interview data:

Questions	*Responses*
(1) *bu na? ay naš?*	*ni?ay ta si?be.*
'Where did you go earlier today?'	'I went to gather firewood.'
(2) *buk'al ?akuc?*	*šokon keš.*
'Where do you gather it?'	*šokon keš.* (a 'place').
(3) *buk'al ?oy ?acob?*	*mu?yuk hcob.*
'Where is your milpa?'	'I don't have any milpa.'
(4) *bu nakal ca? ?ame? ?atote?*	*tah ta pinyantutike.*
'Where do your parents live?'	'Yonder, in Barrio Pimienta.'
(5) bu *ša?n nakalot?*	*te?oyun, tah tasnayol, hwiše.*
'Where do you live?'	'I'm there, yonder in the house of the daughter of my aunt (or older sister).'
(6) *bu hecukal ?oy ca? numtoe?*	*tah ta c'ul martile.*
'Where does he live, then?'	'Yonder in Barrio S. Pedro.'

At this point in the analysis it is difficult to know what is related to what. After the year of field work, I had a fairly firm idea of where most of the 'morpheme' boundaries lay. But close work with the major informant based on this set of sentences was necessary.

First, the 'necessary' parts of the responses were examined – the part that 'answers' the question. The **minimal response** was one which occurred in (2) *šokon keš*; i.e., a particular place. In (1), a minimal response would be *ta si?be* 'to gather firewood'. In other words, the response – the part related solely to the question – is a place or action done in a place.

It was easily determined that the *ni?ay* in (1) was formally related to *na?ay* in the question 'you go – 'I went'. As part of the 'syntactics' of the Q-R system, there are not just questions and responses, but other intersecting systems – here an interpersonal one which is reciprocal for *you* and *I*. But this system has essentially nothing to do with the class of questions and responses, except to 'modify' them situationally. In other words, any person can ask any other person potentially any possible question, and can expect potentially any answer which falls in the total response class to that question. But the number of actual possibilities, situationally tied, are remarkably restricted (i.e., responses are unlikely to be **novel!**).

This still yielded no idea of the difference between *bu* and *buk'al*, but increased the number of forms of *bu+particle* as in (4), (5), and (6), *bu nakal* 'where', *bu ša?n* 'where?' – all of these were glossed identically by the informant; **he felt**, but still could not express, the differences (to me).

I then began to elicit other possible responses to the original questions. The informant was asked to consider these merely as questions either out of context, or in all the possible contexts he could imagine. This yielded a large number of responses which were partially the same, but differences also began to show up, and some idea of the conditions which make the differences so subtle. (See table 1, p. 172.)

These are all place names as responses to the question, *bu* 'where?' But their distribution is quite peculiar. It is now possible to infer the differences in the meaning of the questions from the response subset distribution – but not the other way!

Note that questions (2) and (3) which began with *buk'al* have two subclasses, introduced by the particles *teno* and *k'al*. In presenting many more questions of this form to the informant, this is consistently true and all responses to questions of the form *buk'al* have two subclasses in the responses, which do not overlap. From geographic knowledge of the region it was possible to see that subset members introduced by *teno* are all closer than responses introduced by *k'al*. One may infer that the questioner had in mind two kinds of places – relatively near and relatively far from the place of the interaction – when he phrased the question in this way. (He could have asked the question *bu* without *k'al* if he did not have a two-part scheme in mind.)

By comparing the responses to (2) and (3), it was discovered that the responses are tied to the verb – i.e., to the 'activity'. Responses to (2) which are relatively **far** (introduced by *k'al*) are exactly those places which are relatively **near** (introduced by *teno*) in response to (3). It is inferred from this that far places to gather firewood (2) are, indeed, the nearer places in which farmland is located (3) – confirmed by the informant.

So the meaning differences between questions introduced by *bu* and *buk'al* are different in these fairly simple, but subtle ways – and in ways which are probably 'self evident' to the Tzotzil speaker, but unimaginable to the English speaker who ordinarily does not use a conceptual apparatus such as *buk'al*.

Sometimes the two classes occur even without the presence of *k'al* in the question frame. This happens with a class of transitive verbs and objects – e.g., *to gather firewood* – most activities which may occur only in well-known places, which have stable geographical locations irrespective of the place in which any interaction may happen to occur. In these cases the presence of *k'al* in the question appears to be redundant.

In the case of example (2), it was discovered that there exists a question which usually has no linguistic reflex. Most generally, this concerns repetitive activities, referable to a calendar or clock, about which everyone agrees, and to which verbal reference is rarely made. In example (2), the *k'al* would occur as part of the question only after about 11:00 A.M. Since people go to gather firewood between 5 and 7 A.M., they could have returned to the town from the 'nearer' places by about 8 or 9. They could not have returned with their firewood until about 11 A.M. if they had gone to a farther place. Therefore, anyone who asks the question before 9 A.M. would 'know' that the firewood had come from a nearer place and the *k'al* would not occur: After 11 A.M. the questioner would not know which place the gatherer had gone, and the *k'al* becomes necessary.

It is also clear that the knowledge of the questioner involves his seeing the person return with firewood, his having seen him leave to fetch it, etc. If the questioner saw a person leave the town late – at 9 or 10 – and saw him return with firewood at noon, the *k'al* would not occur.

In the absence of *k'al* in the question (4), (5), (6), some subsets of responses occur which are similar to those in response to *k'al*. Question (4) began with *bu nakal* 'Where do your parents live, then?'

The answers were of basically four forms:

(1) *li²e*
(2) *te ta c'ul kalwaryoe*
(3) *tah ta c'ul kalwaryoe*
(4) *ta kolonya*

Classes introduced by *te* and *tah* share **some** (but not all) members in response to their question frame.

There are several factors which appear to be significant in attempting to account for the differences among subsets of responses.

(1) unit size
(2) boundary
(3) contiguity

The response *li²e* can generally be translated into English as 'here'. In Tzotzil, as in English, this presents a problem concerning *which place?*, *how big a place?*, and so on. A word of 'relative' location such as this form is probably meaningful within some contexts, and to the interactors. It points to a series of methodological problems.

In response to this particular question, *Where do your parents live?*, the reply, *li²e*, would probably refer to some 'unit' contained within the town. This might be 'large', a *barrio* (a named section of the town), or 'small', a house or yard. By contrasting all subsets of responses to this question frame, some more definite statements can be made.

There is a subset of responses to this frame which is introduced by *ta*. All of the members of this set are places located **outside of the town**. Members of the other subsets include only members referring to places approximately within the town — actually including places on the 'edge of town'. By contrasting the set represented by *li²e* with the set introduced by *ta*, it may be concluded that 'here' can refer to a unit no larger than the town. This may be confirmed by combining *li²e* with some response ordinarily introduced by *ta* in response to this frame — e.g., *li²e, ta kolonyae* — in contrast with *li²e* and any response introduced by some other form (*ta, tah*) — e.g., *li²e, ta c'ul kalwaryoe* — and offering these to the informant as possible responses to the given frame. He agrees that these are all linguistically possible responses, fitting the 'rules', but consistently rejects the 'here, outside of town' responses. This confirms the previous statements.

The concepts of 'contiguity' and 'boundary' become important in discussing the differences between classes introduced by *te* and *tah*. At first glance, these sets appear to be analogous to those introduced by *teno* and *k'al*. Some of the members of the *tah* set are further away from the place of interaction than *any* in the *te* set. **They are never closer.** However, they do have some members in common. This suggests that there is a distance factor, but that there are also other differences which are not the same as those which contrast the classes introduced by *k'al* and by *teno*.

The distance factor can easily be shown to have to do with relative distance, by contrasting subsets of responses to one question frame with those of some others. In response to some other questions than (4), the distance of both *te* and *tah* may be far greater, referring to places distant from the town.

Other factors involve the idea of contiguity. Given a particular type or size of unit, the major difference between the *te* and *tah* responses has to do with the fact of something 'intervening' between the place of interaction and the place referred to. For example, two other Indian barrios touch, border on Barrio Convento. In response to (4), these two barrios must be referred to with *te ta* ..., the other barrios would then be *tah ta* ..., since they do not touch Barrio Convento. In referring to a unit the size of a barrio, the fact of another barrio intervening between 'here' and 'there' determines into which subset the response falls. In other words, the size of the unit and the notion of something intervening seem to be related ideas.

However, it has become apparent that what appear to be much different kinds or sizes of unit can have the same effect on responses, as things which have the same name or form. In the original recorded conversations, the form (4) occurred in *El Centro* 'the center', the *Ladino* or non-Indian part of town, which seems to act like a barrio. The response was *tah ta pinyantutike* 'yonder in Barrio Pimienta'. But we were near the edge of this barrio, less than a block away, and the Centro itself borders on all of the barrios.

This was pointed out to the major informant, who agreed that this was a proper response, *te ta pinyantutike* not being proper in that context. The explanation of this, which was subsequently tested, was that there was no contiguity (among the Indian population) because some Ladino-Mexican houses or property intervened between the place of the conversation and the place of reference.

The presence of a non-Indian house or yard has the same effect as the presence of a barrio in defining contiguity among these kinds of units. The **observer's** idea of size of a unit, and similarity among units, is not necessarily related to the reality of the Tzotzil world.

Another interesting case of contiguity or not, concerns the *sitios* 'yards'. In most cases, houseyards are bounded by low stone walls. In some cases, these walls are broken, so that there is a well defined walk between two adjoining‹yards, usually between close relatives. When there exists such a break, the yards seem to be considered as a single place — *li ʔe* — if this size unit is referred to. If there is no such break, the form is *te*, regardless of the fact that everyone can easily see over the wall.

The problem of 'boundary', which often includes problems of contiguity, is also important in the present discussion. **Outside of town**, as it is most often used, is related to the last houses in town, but also to the 'purpose', the context of the question frame. The 'smallest meaningful distance' out of town appears to be the distance away from the last house, where people cannot be seen; the most usual reason to go there is to defecate during the day. In this case, it is clear that the effective boundary is related to the context; in most other cases, the problem only becomes clear when walking through the town with various people, asking them to determine where, say, one barrio ends, and another begins. There appear to be no precise points except in reference to some contexts, some question frame.

The form, *li ʔe* 'here', can be seen to have a large number of possible meanings. Its definition depends on the examination of a large number of question frames, contexts, a more complete ethnography employing the methodology described in this study.

In answer to the original interview questions (5) and (6) introduced by *bu ša ʔn* and *bu hecukal*, neither the total response set nor the subset organization varied. From this it was inferred that the particles *ša ʔn* and *hecukal* have essentially no relationship in reference to question and response, but must belong to some **other** intersecting system, having to do with situational or contextual variables. In further eliciting it was discovered that the 'person' system was involved with *ša ʔn*; it would only be used between or to elderly people. A similar form in English questions is *might*, as in *Where might you be going*?, which would be asked of 'special' people.

Given only this much data and analysis and a good informant, a fair approximation can be made of the syntactic (order) form of the class of question introduced by *bu* and meanings related to 'where → places'.

(1)	(2)	(3)	(4)	(5)	(6)	(7)	(8)	(9)	(10)
bu	*ša²n*	*k'al*	*hecukal*	*ca²*	Verb	*ca²*	Object or *naš*	*naš* or Object	*numtoe*

It has been determined that slots (1) and (3) are related to the responses – (1) to the total class, (3) to the formation of two sub-classes. (2) is related to the ages of one or both of the interactors and might have some effect on the question asked.

This approach can be expanded by considering other question particles. These utterances also occurred in the recorded conversation:

(1) *k'u* **wan** *ba kaltik*?	'What might we say?'
(2) *k'u ta pas*, **tata²**?	'What are you doing, sir (mister)?'
(3) *bak'in ta pas ctal* **ca²i**?	'When is he coming, then?'
(4) *bak'in ta batik* **h²ipša**?	'When are you (pl.) going again?'

By trying each of these 'new' slots with *where* questions, it was found that they were all part of a question frame which could 'potentially' occur **verbally**. In other words this raises the problem of a 'complete' question: do all of these slots occur in any question situation regardless of whether they have a **linguistic**, verbal reflex? May some aspects of the question occur nonverbally as part of the knowledge a questioner has from observation of the scene or from some other source? For example, a person would have asked one question before about 11:00 A.M., another after.

V. 'Complex' Question Words

In Tzotzil there are a number of different questions beginning with the morpheme *k'u* 'what', 'how', etc. Treated by a morphological analysis, these would all appear to be similar. Instead, in many cases the form *k'u* plus some other forms combine to form **entirely distinct units** which themselves operate as question words. If the questions are analyzed without considering the accompanying responses, it would not be possible to see this kind of difference.

Here, several question forms which occurred in the conversational data will be contrasted as a function of the type or pattern of response which occurs with the different forms:

a1. *k'u yepal la kuctal*?   *ʔošib pešu*.
    'How much did you   'Three pesos (worth).'
    carry here?'

a2. *k'u yepal ca ʔ šcobe*?   *wakib almul*.
    'How much are your   'Six almudes' (a land measure)
    farmlands then?

b1. *k'u šaʔn wan ʔabi*?   *htukutan*
    'What is your name?'   Tukutan
    (What might you be
    called?)

b2. *k'u sbi ca ʔ ʔaniʔe*?   *htatik wan ni*?
    'What is his name   'Mister Juan Ni?'
    then, your father-in-
    law?'

c. *k'u caʔal*?   *porke   muk'lek,   k'ušʔelan*
                          kušulote.
    'Why'   'Because it's not good, how
                          you live'

d1. *k'u tba mantan*?   *bahman dulse, bahman hbalde,*
                          hrišton.
    'What will you buy?'   'I'll buy candy, I'll buy my
                          pail, my ribbon'

d2. *k'u tal ʔapasik liʔe*?   *tal hpastutik hulaʔ alnoʔo*.
    'What are you doing   'We came here just to visit.'
    here?'

This collection of question forms is most similar to the *What?* series in English — e.g., *What?*, What color ...?, *What time* ...?, etc.

The frames, a1-2, have a particular type of commonality with respect to their responses. If the form *k'u yepal* occurs, a number occurs in the response. This is true not only of this *k'u* form, but the same type of response occurs — a number/'enumerator' — with an entirely different question word, *hayib*, 'How much?'

The number of *what* in the response (*pesos, almudes*) appears to be independent of the question word. It is a function of a different kind of relationship — not in the question-response system — between the kind of verb or noun appearing in the question and the term used to express their measure. The form, *three pesos*, is translatable by all Tzotziles into dry measures (referring to some transportable produce as corn or beans) while the extent of one's farmlands is never expressed in these terms.

The (b) forms are much different from the point of view of the underlying morphology. In (a) the question words are composed of two particles (*k'u* and *yepal*). In (b) the question word is formed as a particle (*k'u*) plus a verbal (*bi*), prefixed by a person marker (*a-* or *s-*). They may be separated lineally, as in (b1) by some of the same honorific particles which are part of the *bu* questions frame (*ša?n, wan*). If this question word, *k'u ... bi* occurs, the response is always a personal or family name or a reference through a relationship to some known person (e.g., Bartolo's father). The responses to this question word also overlap with those of another, *muc'u* 'Who?'

k'uca? (al) is best translated as English 'Why?'. The pattern of the response is the presence of the form *porke* or *ɗoh*, usually introducing the response frame.

It is thus impossible to determine the form of the question (word) without considering the class of responses to it. If the total response class is different with, e.g., *how, how many, how much,* then these are different question words, regardless of their internal composition. And the question form which relates to a total class of response forms the class of questions in any language.

VI. Productivity Via the Question-Response System

Although it is often said that there are essentially an infinite number of possible grammatical sentences in any language, an examination of the question-response system leads one to wonder if this is completely true.

This study has thus far suggested that a relatively few question words are related to an equivalent number of total response classes, but each response class may be composed of many members, or differently arranged subsets. Thus a small number of question words are actually related to a very, very large number of potential responses.

The remainder of any question frame — the non-question parts — seems to constrict the actual subset of responses which may occur in any given situation. Thus, there are probably only a very **small number** of possible responses to any question! How might this operate?

If a syntactic question is considered to be made up of a number of ordered slots, each slot being occupied by a **set** — much like a total response class — it is easier to conceptualize how this might happen.

Consider a sentence like: *Where are you going*? From the Tzotzil, we learned that *where* questions have an implicit time dimension. That is, there is a slot in Tzotzil and in English which contains the class of responses to the question, *when*?:

Where are you going *when*?

        now

        later

        tomorrow

Where did you go when?

        yesterday

        just now

If not expressed verbally, this class is nonetheless **implicit** — usually being **right now** (itself not a simple concept).

There is also implicit in the Q-R system a slot at the end of the question in Tzotzil and in English which contains the response class to the question, *who?* This is rarely expressed in either language, but is inherent in the interaction: *Where are you going tomorrow, Bob?*

In any actual situation, much of this is never expressed, since it is clear in context and would be redundant, but it is **always** implicit, and points to the likelihood that a 'program' is pretty much in effect in any Q-R situation — there are probably a small number of possibilities which may occur situationally. This sets up the possibilities for many types of joking or teasing behavior — and when this is examined it may yield more insight into how 'situational boundaries' are defined. It is quite devastating to be asked, for example, *When are you leaving?*, when you had no idea you were expected to leave.

VII. Summary

In this study, twelve conversations were recorded in the town of San Bartolome. The recorded conversations were first transcribed, translated, and linguistically analyzed with the help of the major informant. The observer was present during each interaction, and recorded time, place, people present, and so forth. The major informant handled the portable tape recorder and microphone by himself.

Several lists were made, based on the informant's identification of questions in the transcription. Morphologically separable elements which introduce the questions form the basis for each list. Since the number of questions which actually occurred in these interactions was not extremely large, all of them were incorporated into the lists.

In addition to the question forms, the utterance (usually of a second person in a conversation) following each question was included after each corresponding question in the lists. These utterances were tentatively taken to be the responses or replies to the question — on the part of the second person.

The questions which seemed to be introduced by so-called **question words** (such as English; *when, where, who*) which occurred most frequently, are called **question frames** — which include the question words. The replies are **response frames**, containing the **response** itself, i.e., the response frame may contain elements which are not relevant to the question word. Both question words and responses can occur alone. The system being analyzed concerns the relationships between question words and responses.

The next step was the determination of the **total question frame** for each question word. (The total question frame is a syntactic statement about the lineal order of elements which can follow each question word.) This is done by combining, one at a time, the morphological elements which occur in any question to see if they are possible occurrences with any or all question words, and in what order.

Based on the frequency of occurrences, syntactic statements concerning the limits of morphological shapes of each response class can then be made; e.g., in English, the responses to *Where?* frequently are of the form, *in the ... (thing), to the ... (thing)*. These are often useful in predicting new responses to any class.

The question frames are then manipulated, via more elicitation, in order to see if parts of them, in various combinations, affect, or have no effect on, response classes. Those elements which have no effect are eliminated from consideration. Others set up subclasses of the class of responses to a given question word. Thus, a configuration: $Q'a\ b\ c$? represents a question frame. There is a class, R, whose members are possible responses to $Q'\ \&\ a$; one may discover that the response class, R, is not affected. Or it may be discovered that the responses occur as before, but they are arranged into, say, two limited subclasses of R.

By systematically dealing with each part of the question frame, as potential variables, lists of potentially all classes and of all subclasses can be made. Since the number of elements comprising the various question frames is large, this process is somewhat theoretical. But it could be done with the help of a patient informant and a computer which can be programmed to vary the forms in terms of all the discovered rules. Nonetheless, a series of significant statements can be made even from a small sample.

The observer then examined each class and subclass in order to derive some idea concerning the cultural domain of each. For example, *bu* 'where' defines or co-occurs with the class of responses which seem to have the cultural domain of 'place'. When *k'al* is added, (*buk'al*), two subgroups occur. All responses in these still refer to place, but some to relatively 'nearer' places, the others to 'farther' places – from the point of interaction. The form *buk'al hecukal ...?*, which is a possible question syntactically, gives the identical subclasses as *buk'al*. So the form *hecukal* can be eliminated from present consideration. It has no relationship to the response class.

By examining various classes and subclasses, their similarities and differences, one is led to postulate statements like *nearer* and *farther*, and thus to infer that the Tzotzil world – at least with respect to forms like *bu* and *k'al* – is divided, for some purposes, into two parts. That this distance, in the Tzotzil scheme, is relative to the kind of action, can be seen by varying the verbal parts of two otherwise identical question frames introduced by *buk'al*. Thus, *places to fetch firewood* are of two kinds: near and far. But 'far' places in which firewood is gathered are 'near' places with respect to farming.

One may also infer, for example, that there exist units, boundaries, etc., by which 'near' and 'far' are defined in the Tzotzil world. These inferences may be tested by dealing with new events, by being able to make predictive statements about linguistic response forms and their use in particular new situations.

The methodology presented here points toward a procedure which relates language and culture. By beginning with a culturally occurring situation, using grammar to isolate elements, and concentrating on a two-person scheme, the observer is enabled to make statements concerning some other cultural universe. He uses the question-response relationship system in the language.

Although various parts of the structure are manipulated, this method seems to preserve the essential context of the response. The analyst allows the informant to give him these elements, and to arrange them in classes according to the native model. The discovery of a systematic relationship between questions and responses allows the analyst to use the language to generate response classes. Furthermore, the observer poses no questions which are nonnative to the language being examined. He manipulates the form of the question frames, nothing more. The method would seem to provide, in the last analysis, a systematic mode of entering into the other culture's world of 'tacit agreement'.

TABLE 1

(a)	(b)	(c)	(d)
			ta kalwo
ta pinyantutik			*ta kolonya*
ta k'asaltik			*ta ti? ?uk'um*
ta konmento			
			te ta ?olone
ta sna yol,			*te ta ?akole*
hwiše			
ta hna ta	*teno ta ya?al ?oke*[67]		*te ta howe*
konmento	*teno ta hkec te?e*		*tah ta howe*
	teno ta koral ka?e		*te ta c'ul kalwaryoe*
	teno ta taki?uk'ume		*tah ta c'ul kalwaryoe*
li?e			
tee			
tahe	*k'al ta tontik*	*teno ta tontike*	*tah ta ti? nanatike*
	k'al ta cobtik	*teno ta cobtike*	
	k'al ta nab	*teno ta nabe*	
	k'al ta stenlehtik	*teno ta stenlehtike*	
		k'al ta suytik	
		k'al ta hec ho bel	
		k'al ta ti? ?u'kum	

(10) ON HUMAN GRAMMAR

One can analyze any event, event-string, or process into its 'component' parts, their relationships, and ways in which they might be combined to generate or synthesize the original event. This can be done for any such event that we recognize as occurring or existing in any moment, or over time. A person as event complex, for example, can be seen as composed of cell, organ system, or levels of consciousness. Each conception is in many senses adequate and 'correct', and we must ask more about the context in which the question occurred than about the description *per se*, in order to judge its descriptive and predictive adequacy.

This is not, however, the usual perception of those who work at the various levels of the body. Microbiologists rarely get to see any psychic phenomena through their perspective and tend to deny that behavior of organisms will ever be a meaningful area of investigation. To study the effects of poisons or traumatic injury, they may be essentially correct.

In interesting ways language has also been treated as a natural property of the individual organism. In what contexts have linguists asked questions about its components? What does one choose as the analogue to the body or organism? Biology has been 'fortunate' in that its subject matter appeared to be wrapped in its own boundaries – its skin. Language has been seen to be a property of that same organism, but one which developed later, rather than earlier, in its development.

Within the contexts of life, it has become clear that the individual organism, of whatever social species, is not the only meaningful unit. Many phenomena, previously considered to be biologically individual, are beginning to be examined as social; e.g., one's 'face-shaping'. I believe the development and use of language must also be considered, in the first instance, as social. (This is not to deny individual differences – they still remain ample. It's just that they do not seem to be the repository of language in any deep sense.)

Locating most behavioral and biological phenomena in the body has had the effect of guiding thinking about such phenomena as, say, pulse rate and language in certain directions, to the essential exclusion of others. The possibility of language development as a social phenomenon has never been discarded. It has simply not been pursued, apparently because most thinkers' ideas of social have been very limited.

Within the single-body context, it is completely understandable that the usual dualisms have arisen in our thinking. Children literally increase in their abilities to manage themselves and their worlds.

How do they increase? How can we account for the outstanding abilities they come to have?

What about the possibility of something like a 'social-grammar'?

Lest we accept — or reject — this as reasonable, let us ask what we might consider as the outstanding features of life and grammar to be accounted for:

First is the philosophical problem of knowledge — how does an individual know anything? The usual answers are to posit an associationist ability to the learner; or to assume that he had stronger, deeper abilities built in. Each of these theories imputes a different set of abilities to the organism; the associationist regards him as an essentially passive connector and retainer of relationships he experiences. The innate knowledge position presumes a more special being who is 'pre-wired' to do some things he has never personally experienced.

The human being has been presumed to have a special, unique kind of knowing — call it consciousness or rationality. This belief has influenced the features of language which linguists have been impressed by — namely those which seem to be uniquely human; e.g., creativity, intentionality, reflection.

Within this complex of thought, man and other species have been presumed to have bodies which are essentially alike (for reasons which continue to perplex me), but their minds are different. The causal leap trailed the thinking: because they have language.

None of these notions seems to be terribly convincing, because they haven't shown strong signs of being or becoming productive, and because they limit rather than broaden our perspective. Intuitively, on the other hand, they match the common logic in terms of which most of us were raised.

The idea of a social grammar? Where does meaning come in? How do children learn to learn, to speak, to understand?

Its units to be analyzed couldn't possibly be sentences. Sentences (appear to) come from each individual in some peculiarly spontaneous, 'creative' sense. It would also be very difficult to do any cross-species study of some entity like the sentence, since that would carry the imputation that other species deal with or have thoughts and ideas. Few scholars consider that nonhumans are very good 'thinkers'.

I'm more attracted to a kind of grammar which is interactional — e.g., questions and their answers. The semantic aspect of this grammar enters as we consider that questions do **have** or imply answers in some senses.

One could conceptualize the development of language as a kind of dialogue between mother and child in which mother phrases the humanly (culturally) appropriate questions, sets up and responds to the universe of proper (for her) answers.

In this sense, children's utterances of one or two word phrases are to be considered not merely as internal, individually motivated, productions, but (also as) responses to their mothers' queries. Language develops in individuals, but as a filling-in of a semantically meaningful universe presented by parents to each individual child. (Children who don't or won't play this game are, of course, considered to be extraordinary in the sense of being 'defective'.)

One of the questions in grammatical thought is concerned with how an infinite or indefinite system — the domain of all sentences — could exist within the finiteness, the skin, of any individual. The soul or mind, infinite in some sense, has been the postulated answer.

We must show either how that could be, or suggest alternatively that the system of all sentences is not so infinite as it appears. There must be, in other words, a way to account for a relatively simple system being extremely open-ended in some aspect or other.

It is, in this context, extremely interesting that responses to questions are both **open** and **closed**. That is, there is an acceptable **range** of answers to most questions and a clearly unacceptable set of answers. Response sets to questions are 'well-bounded'.

If a mother points to a dog and asks her one-and-a-half year old: *What is this*? The child may say, *dog, doggie, bow-wow, ruff, mine*, etc. All of these are either acceptable to the mother, or she will **correct** him by using one of them. There seems to be no single right answer to questions of this sort.

There seem to be several sorts of 'wrong' answers — *cat*, or *cow*, or *meow* gets **corrected** to *dog, doggie*, etc. He could have said *two, sun*, etc. But I don't think these ever occur in real life. 'Mistakes' are made within some **semantically delimited frameworks.**

That is, I believe that language development always occurs in semantic contexts. It is not just a process of vocalizing or saying 'de-semanticized' words, phrases, and sentences – it is a process of doing all of these **correctly** as the universe is presented to a child. Most mothers don't insist – at least at early ages – on a single correct response, so this process leaves open a vast range for individual differences and preferences, and some number of familio-syncracies which we all recognize.

Or the child can 'choose' not to respond – to not vocalize. This is acceptable up to age two or so with different expectations and demands from different families. The choice to not respond will be interpreted by most mothers as within normal ranges, or as a problematic child – depending, I believe, on many social factors such as age, social class, sibling position of the child, etc. The definitions of speech from the 'outside' and the ensuing pressures are, I believe, the **strongest** forces on any child to 'learn' language. He must 'exhibit' language behavior or get pushed fairly hard and constantly by the interactional and 'controlling' forces which he experiences.

Granted that most children have a fairly limited perspective and a small circle of actual interactants, in whose terms they learn language, how do they come to share enough with other speakers of their native language to be able to understand and be understood? How do they arrive ultimately at a sense of logic?

In the 'Question-Response System' there are a very few **relation-ships** which seem to be basic. The child has to somehow come to know about this. He has to **know** about the nature of the relationship between question and answers; he has to know, in some sense, that responses are part of the interactional system.

How does a child come to know this – or does he? It is very tempting to *a priorize* this knowledge. But I think it is much more a case of an organism which has always been in essential contact with an 'outside' and has responded to it successfully. Continued survival is predicated on this ability. Perhaps responding verbally is in some essential sense different from other types of organismic response, but I doubt it.

In what sense do questions elicit responses; or, conversely, how do responses complete or answer questions?

Consider two related kinds of questions: *where* and *when* questions and their responses.

We can discover quickly that they have a semantic-cultural component, because they 'elicit' different **sets** of responses. There are hardly any overlaps. Whatever the differences are between these set boundaries, they have to do with a 'semantic'.

A developing child could hardly **know** that *where* and *when* conjure up 'places' and 'times'. I question whether we know this in any but a derived sense, i.e., space and time are derived categories.

A developing child (I speculate) first gets to know about the question-response relationship (it has to do with subtle phonetic relationships, I think); that is *where* can be answered, *when* can be answered. His job, his strategy, is to 'fill-in' the response set. To *where?* he learns to say *here, up, bed*. His analytic job is to, first, know that they are in some sense the **same** — i.e., they share common features (to his mother in the 'real' world!). Then he has to know which responses **belong** to which question. Finally, one can begin in his worldly experience to gain a notion of what *where* or *when* might mean.

Most early speech of children is, in effect, circumscribed by mother. The child's single words are, in my experience, overwhelmingly related to what his mother says, her observations, and thoughts. Rarely do they seem to be completely independent of her and her definition of the scene; e.g., child sees airplane overhead and 'names' it. But even here, the naming is done in part, at least, to elicit something like approval or agreement from his mother.

In other words, there is no 'single-word' stage of speech development located in the developing child. There is a single-word interactional stage — acted out, displayed, occurring in the child's speech. But it's not only or merely in him. Words, in this view, have just as little independent existence as the developing person.

Children seem to be able to 'use' response sets to 'store' words they don't 'understand' as yet (much as my puppy puts all his important things in one place, and has only to note that place to find whatever he might want). In the *when*-Response relationship there are many words which most children seem to 'know', but some remain opaque or 'unpacked' for a couple of years. Three-year olds seem to know that complicated word-notions like *yesterday* and *tomorrow* belong to *when*-R. They are like *now, right now, morning, Sunday, 8:00*. But most children can't use them very fully for another year or two.

Response sets, in other words, can act like 'semantic repositories'. A child can know, initially, that something belongs to a particular response set. He can derive a useful but incomplete analysis of the common features of the set. (I hesitate to use the term *simple* for this; the child 'does what he does' at any point in his being — he seems to be an active strategist at all points. In this context, 'complexity' is no more than a hindsight notion of those who come to analyze their semantics in more ways than they did previously.)

As he experiences more, he will get to analyze the membership of each set in more ways. He'll use **subsets** of various kinds within the larger sets and come to 'understand' more fully notions like *tomorrow* or *truth*. These response sets are clearly useful for increasing. one's vocabulary (by 'small' and 'large' jumps) and having ways of 'increasing one's knowledge' by using this notion of response sets.

The dynamics of using response sets remains speculative, but it does seem that one can use the fact of question-response relationship to delimit the possible world of meaning to a very great extent, e.g., the notion of 'being as being-not'. By knowing a very simple relationship, e.g., <*who*-name>, a child knows a great amount about what's **not** being talked about. If a child hears a **name** of someone, he may not know who it is 'exactly', but he knows it's not a thing, a place, a color, a process, a time, etc. So any set-relationship which is **productive** — a relationship between a small number of items and a large number — **defines out** what's not at issue and implicitly carries with it a great deal of knowledge. Thus knowing, in the first instance, seems much more a process of delimiting than of positive identification or precision. But it's knowing a great deal of the potential universe of knowledge, from the perspective of the developing child.

Not-being most places, one is somewhere. How does one travel within a response set? On being asked how they 'were' at, say, age eight, most people I've asked get into being eight, perhaps in similar ways to being 'into' a particular response set. Everyone I've asked 'conjures up' an image of himself standing somewhere. In or near school, at the family home, seem to be favorite places. One then proceeds to 'move' imagistically from that perspective. One 'sees' one's third grade teacher and acts like he believes he might have with respect to that personage. This then expands through another set of imagistic metaphors to other happenings at 'age eight'.

I think we use response sets in similar ways. Once we're **into** a response set with, say, a new word, we can travel within the common features of the set and seek for subsets which are 'used' like this new word. We can get a good grasp of the meaning of new words in this way and can gradually come to explore its entire range of features.

Interestingly, we don't seem to have to carry around (remember?)

the entire range of meanings of all words or sentences in some random access sense — at least not in the same way, all of the time. At the most 'superficial' level, all we need is the first eight-year old image, or the most encompassing set to which a response word belongs. Once 'there', we seem to be able to imagine further activities or relationships that occur in that domain (Luria, 1968).

(My own experience in trying to play the violin is much like this — one gets more practiced and he can 'put away' techniques that he had to work at actively just a short while before. Once it's learned, one can simply *do* it. But I can, for a while at least, remember when I was still struggling. It's different now, because I can do it. So remembering has changed because my [bodily?] perspective has changed. As long as I want to continue to improve, I seem to have to 'carry around' an active set of problem techniques which I don't possess as yet.)

Later in language development, children are said to speak two-word and longer phrases and, ultimately, sentences. Can a Q-R framework begin to account for these abilities?

What may happen is that the child begins to 'attend' not only to the response-set and question relationship — which is linear, but not directly — but to the linear relationships in the question phrasing.

It's probably irrelevant to a child, for example, to use *your* or *you* in a question, early in his development. If he doesn't already know that he is being talked to from visual, tactile, and verbal cues of direction and loudness, then he's not really part of the interaction. But mothers and babies seem to work very hard to be within each other's *vis-à-vis*.

What do you want? Where's Bobby? Most of the question, at first, is in the question: *what ... want?* and *where*. Interestingly some questions consist of more than one word, using the criterion of an independent response set to determine what a question-word is: *What ... want? What time ...? What ... doing? What color ...?*

In the Q-R semantic, the child must come to differentiate not only single-word questions such as *where, when,* or *who,* he must also respond (correctly) to longer question words. The object or person involved still seems to be incorporated within the nonverbal and nonlinguistic verbal aspects of the scene. But the child must begin to distinguish between longer question words, or he gets corrected.

At the same time, there seems to be a kind of natural 'sequence' in interactional question-response, which must also be part of the languaging. This may contribute to the setting up of subsets within response sets along such dimensions as: general-particular; meta-phorical-literal; etc.

(1) *Where's Amy?* → *here*
(2) *Where?* → *bedroom*

(1) *When are you going?* → *tomorrow*
(2) *What time?* → *10:00 A.M. in the morning*

At the same time the child learns Q-R sets and subsets, he learns an order to the formation of the situation. Obviously much of this occurs in the face-to-face, nonverbally. It appears that the original knowledge about questions is located in the way parents and children interact. The mother in responding to a cry by giving milk, in effect, is posing a question to the infant about his (internal?) state. If he takes a fair amount of milk, that activity is presumed by the mother to be the infant's answer. Even though mothers appear to be uncanny in their 'knowledge' about their children, they must act as if they were diagnosticians of their infants' states. Children must also learn ways of eliciting responses – perhaps the 'smile' is really of the form of a question. It, in turn, usually evokes a strong response in his mother.

The appearance of logic, at least during early development, may well be 'located' in the order of the presentation of Q's and R's rather than in the verbal behavior. In the range of acceptable/possible responses to general questions, the child has a 'choice' in many questions. R's to *where* or *when* can usually be of the form of *here* and *now*. But in the logic of posing questions, this **causes**, in effect, the question to be asked again. (Obviously, this is situation sensitive – if *here* happens to be in a 'dangerous' place, the next question may be of the form: *What the hell are you doing there?*)

But the problem of what logic is – and how a child comes to share it – is not necessarily or only located in the formation of the sentence, but in the ways in which questions can be used in order to specify more 'closely'. To the extent that any response could be called 'funny', it appears that it is due to toying with the order, or giving more (or less) specific answers to questions than was 'expected'.

Ongoingness is also implicit in the logic of the Q-R situation. A child's use of a too general response will elicit the reasking of the question. This seems to be a mutually enjoyable game between young children and others.

A more full exposition of Q's and R's can, I believe, show that the infinite appearing set of sentences in any language is an illusion. Consider the child's language at any point in development as composed of a number of Q's and R-sets — plus the logic of the question formulation. Is this (knowledge of) language sufficient for him to do the kinds of things, think the kinds of thoughts which we have thought to characterize language? Is there, in other words, a syntax of the Q-R system? Where does the infinite part come in?

In most grammatical expositions, each sentence which differs by a single word is said to be different. Sentences which begin with: <The + noun> must amount to the order of 10^5 or so forms, multiplied by a similar number of verbs ... very, very large.

As suggested earlier, however, there seems to be a **set** of responses to questions which might reduce this number to something believable or reasonable. What might this have to do with sentences?

Consider a more full, complete question beginning with the word, *where*:

(1) *Where are you going now, Sam?*
(2) *Where ...?*

Note first that <R> is potentially the **same** in essentially all questions of the form <*where* → R>. There is an open, indefinite (infinite, by implication) number of places or things to do in response to <*where*> questions.

Thus responses to <*where*> in the form of declarative sentences: *I'm going home, I'm going downtown ... to eat. ...*

Not only are there an infinite number of sentences in any language, there appear to be several different infinities; there is a potentially infinite number of sentences in response to each of these: *when, who, how many*, etc. But they are different and we **know** that they are different kinds.

The infinitude has to do with the 'world', the culture; the idea that the universe of 'numbers', 'places', 'times' is open. But the particular infinity of sentences is closed with respect to which question it answers.

Each of the different infinities of sentences is restrictive of meaning to a very great extent. But obviously, a semantic which allows us to operate as well as we do (and I think we're extremely good at understanding one another — the idea of several infinities only increases my respect for how well we really do understand and comunicate) is much more specific or exact than the notion of

Q-R's would seem to point toward. There must be other principles at work which also restrict or define-out.

If the boundaries of response-sets are the locus of a semantic, as claimed earlier, then the encapsulation of its meaning is associated with the question word. The question *where* has its 'meaning' in the most general features shared by all members of its response set.

A likely place to look for more semantic delimitation is in subsets of responses. Are there meaningful subsets? Are these also associated with some part of the question – some *other* part of the question in addition to the question **word**? I'm convinced that there are, indeed; but first we need to take a closer look at the notion of (human) interaction ... because not all the 'parts' of any question need be said out loud. But they are implicit in the question whether stated or not. (A 'total' analysis of all 'occurring' questions would **not**, I believe, approach the perspective of the developing child. He must deal with the question-response situation in its fullest sense. I doubt whether any toddler can be committed to the notion that potential meaning is strictly verbal. He does deal, I believe, with a meaningful universe all the time – with no strong commitment as to the efficacy of explicit vs. implicit statements.)

In the interaction there are always people – two, at least – perhaps more, to an infant. When any question is asked there **always** exists an implicit term of address – to one's interactant. This is true whether it actually occurs or not – in most settings in American English, it is, indeed, fairly unusual to state it aloud.

What is the 'range' of this term – where does it occur in the question? Does it 'belong' there, whether or not it is said? Is it 'different' from the rest of the question?

It is, first of all, very different **sounding** from the rest of the question when it does occur.

Where are you, Sam? Sam is much, much lower in pitch, and probably in other ways, too, from the remainder of the question. (A Martian, hearing this?)

But note that any name (or title: *man, sir* ...) is much like *Sam* in this question. There seem to be a very real acoustic difference between all occupants of this slot vs. the remainder of the question. The difference is a feature of the **position** or **slot**, not of any particular name or title.

Without carrying this acoustic-semantic notion to an extreme, it may be pointed out that the question part of the question-response – minus the name or title – may also be seen as a linearly ordered set of sets. The 'term of address' is merely the last set in order. Its features as a set are 'stronger' (at least acoustically) than any of the differences of different names or titles. Are there other sets in the question? Or is each question a syntactically unique sentence?

Again, I must appeal to the context of the interaction. Implicit in any interaction is, among other things, a sense of time. Sometimes it's stated, often not. Unless otherwise signified, it is a fairly general 'now'; i.e., *Where are you going?* and *Where ... going, now?* are essentially the same question.

(As with terms of address, the actual stating of a word which is usually silent can itself be a message, but usually this seems to be a message 'about' the situation in some sense different from that in which using one or another word affects the message!)

By substituting various words for *now* in this *where* question, it appears that essentially any 'time-word' can be used. Syntactically, they all appear to want to go in the same location. (**Now** *where are you going?* is also possible, but it's quite a different sort of message!) *Where are you going – at 10:00, tomorrow, tonight?* The completive forms require a couple of other changes: *Where **did** you **go** yesterday?* But the time slot stays where it is.

Now, one interesting thing about the so-called time slot is that it may be occupied by all members of the potential response class to a <*when*-R> question. So a <*where*-R> question is, indeed, composed of slots, positions, or sets – not just words. The sets are ordered. A Q-R syntax is a syntax of ordered slots, not a syntax of words. Each slot is also, in some senses, semantic.

What about 'phrases'? Is there a Q-R phrase level?

One of the parts of the sentence-grammar beliefs in indefinite structures is that sentences are indefinitely 'long'. This idea would seem to oppose the view that sentences are made up of a finite number of ordered slots; a fairly small number, at that.

Consider the response set to <*when*>. It is made up not only of single words like: *now, tomorrow* – but also: *at 10:00 in the morning on Friday*; three-phrases, probably (and with their own small/large semantic!). Each of these is but a single response.

In other words, the indefiniteness of the length of a sentence does not lie within the domain of sentence-syntax, but within the already restricted membership of the response class.

One could say in the exotic kinship terms of the languages that seem to intrigue social anthropologists the most, things like: *I'm going home, mother-in-law's father's granddaughter of the fabricatin' clan.* The entire phrase is a **single** term of address. Acoustically, it

is all like the **Sam** of our earlier example. But it can be 'stretched' —
one could have said **Sarah** in place of the entire phrase or left it out.
There is still a **single slot** for names or titles. One response fills the
slot — regardless of its (internal) length. (There are interesting
apparent exceptions; in color terms, for example, one can combine
two — say, *red-green* — to specify whatever *red-green* is. But, again,
it's said differently, acoustically, from: *red, green*.)

So, question sentences are, in part at least, made up of ordered
slots. Since some slots can be indefinitely long and have an indefinite
membership, this notion can easily account for there appearing to
be an infinitely large set of sentences in any human language. (It
also makes the possible learning of language appear to be the explicable and reasonable process that it seems to be!)

What about other questions? A closer look at <*when*> reveals
that it is 'reciprocal' with <*where*> questions. That is, <*where*>
questions contain a <*when* → R> slot; and <*when*> questions
contain a <*where* → R> slot: *When are you going ... downtown,
home*? (Maybe it will turn out that our space-time-event percipient
structure is really a function of the reciprocal nature of *where* and
when-questions.)

Questions are not merely the question-word, but are defined or
gain 'structure' by their relationship to a distinct response set. There
are a fair number of <what + ...> questions: *what time? -color
-thing -name*? Obviously the question word is *what* plus another
word — the minimal unit which relates to a response class.

This is also true of <*how*> questions: *how many? -much, how ...do it*?

Some questions themselves relate to subsets of other questions.
That is, they are more specific in the very asking. *What time ...*?
relates to a subset of <*when*> responses. All responses to <*what
time*> are also responses to <*when*>; but the reverse is not true.

There seems to be a hierarchy, of sorts, among questions; perhaps
there are several; both logically and developmentally. Some of it is
located in the question-words (e.g., *when, what time*). Some is
located in the logic of question asking: e.g., <*which*> and <*how
many*> already presume that the object(s) of discussion are known
and shared. <*Where*> and <*when*> usually presume a fair knowledge of the activities of the interactional participants. <*Why*>
questions seem very different from most other questions and are a
favorite source of gaming and confusion to toddlers, who only seem to
know about the first part of the response: *'cause*. But they don't
seem to have a good idea for another year or so about the semantic
of the rest of the response.

How is a fairly specific 'meaning' reached in the context of the Q-R system? My guess is that one begins to attend not only to his first 'image' — the whole potential set of responses to a question word — but to the subsets as well. But most of the subset relationships occur with respect only to particular question words. Where are the other relationships found?

My guess is that the rest of the question **frame** — the sentence in which the question word is embedded — begins to be attended to.

Where are you going **now**? — *now* is a very peculiar notion and certainly must be from a child's perspective. In the 'defining-out' framework, it must be obvious pretty soon to a child that he can't do anything 'now', which has already been 'finished'. One can't get up from bed, when one is already up. At the interactional level, one must already have developed a sense of eventness: inclusion, boundaries, before one can even deal with a sense of 'present time'. I think the notion of time is not a purely intuitive human notion; one has also to buy-in on how others event the world. Surely a good part of development is to take one's child 'out' of his own time and into the world of others. One must learn to turn off math and turn on spelling in the early schooling situation. Earlier there occurs the gradual shift of operating in baby's time, to the baby's operating in family time. New parents look forward to the first time the baby 'sleeps through' the night — as if that were somehow a natural human function.

In any case, much 'sensitization' of the child has already been done before the great verbal thrust is cast upon him. This sensitization is heavily in the direction of an adult's view of the world. We tend to respond to a family who operates more heavily in the child's realm as raising a 'spoiled' child. In terms of later social development this is persuasive. But note that a child is essentially made to take on the situational definitions of the adult world in order even to be able to speak sensibly. Sense — thus rationality — seems to be a shared, social definition of being.

Where are you going **now**? — only a few places or activities actually exist in anyone's world at any moment. At night, a usual answer is: *to the toilet*. One could try a number of responses such as: *to the moon, downtown* — both are about equally likely from a three-year old perspective. I think one tends to fill in responses from one's experience — tending to form subsets of likely responses from unlikely ones. Thus a three-year old view of places feels much like a few plausible responses as opposed to the entire remainder of the set of places: *downtown* and *the moon* are, in this view, about equally unlikely. The problems involved in getting to one or the other have not yet affected the subset relationships.

Similarly, many children seem to use <*when*> responses in a kind of dual fashion. There is *now*, and there are all those other times gathered together in a single subset. *Tomorrow* and *next year* and *never* may well be collapsed together. If this be true, no wonder we regard children as 'impulsive'. (This leaves open for future study how we and other cultural groups organize our subsets of time responses. Moving into someone else's implicit time organization is resisted, even in one's own culture, and occasionally in one's own family.)

It must also be clear to a child that only some people in his world ask certain types of questions.

(11) TOWARD AN ANTHROPOLOGY OF DEVELOPMENT

The study of meaning is a central concern of all behavioral scientists: the meaning of life, nature, being, language, communication ... the meaning of meaning. In fact, one good way to appreciate the history of the sciences of behavior is, as approaches to meaning. But they are all overlain or interwoven with a virtual latticework of paradoxes, illustrated by the nature of dictionaries: dictionaries are fine for people (or beings) who already know a great deal of language; definitions depend on other definitions for their substance — they are **circular**. But where do we gather and become that knowledge by which we begin to use a dictionary? When do we buy in on that circularity of definitions which some have called Culture?

Those engaged in the study of meaning have used a number of devices to 'approach' this problem area, since it seems to resist any direct attack. A favorite is to look for structures or systems which seem to exist in some independent sense, to examine and analyze them. Whether such systems really exist — in what sense are they independent — remains unasked. A promise — a putative or speculative promise — is made that knowledge of these structures will be related to other behavior, to the brain, or to 'things' once the structures are 'well known'. As far as I can tell, none of these promises has ever been kept. Fashions in academic gamesmanship thrive on their existence in a future which see new promises develop before old ones are kept.

Rather than making promises, or approaching the study of meaning in any 'formal' sense, let us sneak up to its edges — jabbing and feinting at our own feelings — using as vehicle a parable on development. This one is addressed to physicians concerning the fragility of growing up normally. Its audience understands this only too well, but is already committed to curing the (already) sick. Physicians operate professionally from an implicit model of **health** — presumed, defined normality. They have no model for studying this normality;

only a method of diagnosis and intercession to 'help' or 'cure' people who have somehow deviated from 'it'.

Human ethologists must be witnesses **to** and **for** the story; they sympathize with the role of the physician. But they should understand that pathology **and** health are dynamic, social issues – not merely matters of individual problems. ('Death', we should recall, is a matter of legal definition, not merely a physical 'fact'.)

As an anthropologist, I suppose that it's my job to ask about all children in all times, in all places: to ask who they are, who they become, and how they become. For the concept of pathology rests in large measure on these questions, and the notion of curing turns about their proposed solutions.

My intellectual father in this enterprise is the pathologist Rudolph Virchow (1849), who introduced the theory of cellular pathology into Medicine and is accounted by modern physicians as one of the founders of scientific medicine. He wrote the following passage in 1849:

If medicine is the science of the healthy as well as of the ill human being (which is what it ought to be), what other science is better suited to propose laws as the basis of the social structure, in order to make effective those which are inherent in man himself? Once medicine is established as anthropology, and once the interests of the privileged no longer determine the course of public events, the physiologist and the practitioner will be counted among the elder statemen who support the social structure. Medicine is a social science in its very bone and marrow. ...

The anthropologist deals with peoples' stories about the world, with their myths, how they believe reality to be, and how they treat their myths as truth. All of us have our own stories and truths, but we rarely talk aloud about the more basic ones. Contrast, if you will, two prevailing stories about human nature: first, that people (children, infants) are basically sinful; as opposed to the second, that children are neither inherently good, not are they bad. These are indeed old stories. But both are true to the extent that people believe in them, acting in everyday life as if their children **are** actually one way or the other. For who gives life – who sustains and directs it on a daily as well as lifelong basis – who nourishes it, who can threaten it?

Most of our popular children's stories clearly state that continued existence is not guaranteed, is always open to threat; and further, that the moral forces of 'good' and 'bad' may constantly be called into question. The stories I'm thinking of involve one or more children (with debatable sibling ties — and which ties aren't debatable??) with one or a pair of older people in the guise of parents or parent-type characters. Keep in mind that the relationships are usually ambiguous; more importantly, something in the children's lives is at a point of change, or at least of quite unusual activity.

Now, in the ordinary course of just growing up, the developing child who merely unfolds true to his nature — innately — is hardly likely to be a victim of the whims of bad parents or bad luck. But this story — of individual developments — is merely one more of the fairy tales, not even a very enlightening one, and quite probably not one which is partial to those actually doing the developing.

The idea that development is a fairly even, day-to-day kind of thing underlies our usual notion of **models.** Early in life a few basic things like gender (Stoller, 1967), which are sometimes said to be most importantly in the parents' minds, must be 'worked out', the child adapting the parental belief as his own truth. If models are present — say, a good, strong male model for boys, a typical female for girls — with good thoughts and good actions, their children will turn out O.K. But why should our scientific statements account for a simpler view of the world than our myths? Have we merely exchanged an elegant set of stories-to-grow-up-by for a more simple-minded group merely to work at setting straight those children whose models are somehow deficient or aberrant?

If we retain the implicit idea that life's stages are preincorporated in each child at birth, it's not hard to understand why a several-staged child, why a fairly simple construct of development has prevailed. But it's my role to take a questioning position, and to ask if a five-year old is **only** going to become a man; for isn't he also going to become, among other things, a six-year old, a first grader — a wholly different (or almost wholly different) character from what he is now?

Recall that when Snow White reached her magical seventh birthday, her stepmother became angry quite without provocation — except that of Snow White's being perceived as no longer the same:

And so the little girl really did grow up. Her skin was as white as snow, her cheeks as rosy as blood, and her hair as black as ebony; and she was called Snow-White. ...

But this queen died; and the king soon married another wife, who was very beautiful, but so vain that she could not bear to think that anyone could be handsomer than she was. She had a magical mirror, to which she used to go and gaze upon herself in it, and say,

'Mirror, Mirror on the wall
Who is the fairest of us all?'
And the glass had always answered,
'Thou, Queen art the fairest in all the land.'
But Snow-White grew more and more beautiful; and when she was seven years old, she was as bright as the day, and fairer than the queen herself. Then the glass one day answered the queen, when she went to look in as usual,
'Thou, Queen art fair and beauteous to see,
But Snow-White is fairer far than thee.'
When the queen heard this she turned pale with rage and envy and called to one of her servants and said, 'Take Snow-White away into the wide wood, that I may never see her any more!' (Grimm, 1956)

Since anthropologists deal with the whole world, we can ask the following question in cross-cultural perspective: What does the child become? Very simply, he should become a good American, a good Ashanti, a good Aztec — if his parents are that and believe it to be good. That is, a child will adapt, within pretty narrow limits, the same way of being — of looking at the world — as his parents. Anything short of this, or perhaps different from it, might be perceived as pathological. But the perception presupposes a picture of what a good Samoan or Spaniard is. **Where** is that picture? How does the child get to partake of it, to share it?

Consider a situation I have seen: a two-month old infant with an almost two-year old toddler. Grandpa of the toddler says: "Don't scratch the baby's eyes!" — toddler proceeds almost immediately to go for the baby's eyes, and eventually the toddler is banished from the presence of the infant as he persists in this activity. What is the message from the toddler's point-of-view, besides the fact that grandfather's view of toddler's intrinsically sinful nature is confirmed — after all, his son, the toddler's father, was a no-good little ... but then we all know that story.

Our toddler is typical only of some households — those which don't **trust** two-year olds in a series of situations like this. He is repeatedly advised of a possible number of things; for example, he is told **not** to do something which he hadn't even done — he does it — he is punished. If the child wants attention, he has learned a most useful technique. If, instead, he had merely wanted to stay in the room, he learned that some verbal messages from often trustworthy sources aren't worth a damn sometimes; that there are messages and there are **messages**, and selection is fraught with interpersonal and situational ambiguity. Perhaps he learned to not only listen to what grandpa says, but to watch him more carefully!

Let's return to a make-believe girl, Cinderella! (Perrault, 1956). Let us suppose, for fun, that Cinderella **has** a father, that she is really not a stepdaughter to that 'Lady', her father's wife, but merely that she is the youngest, and feels discriminated against just because she's young. We are all reminded, fairly often, by our own younger children that the eldest does, in fact, get special privileges. The dialogue changes with the age of the children; the message is more constant.

If Cinderella is merely the youngest, she might well perceive her plight in dreadful terms; see herself as filthy, underprivileged ... and plot constantly for change, yea, for deliverance! We might suppose a sociologist casually suggesting that she wants a change of status. But how can that be achieved in the context of a given family structure? The particulars of Cinderella's case seem peculiar, most probably, to her age; but the idea of change, the foreshadowing of a 'new' being, with new rights and privileges, is repeated.

In a way, the idea of rights, privileges, a good or bad life, suffering, a positive approach, are all kind of relative. One man's optimism is another's form of fright. Yet we talk of normality, of productivity. How does our story, of how things ought to be, jibe with the way things are?

Consider a rather basic human operation – naming an object. Now, it might be supposed, looking at ordinary objects in an ordinary language – our own language, whatever it may be – that this is quite straightforward; words have meanings, meanings have words, and all that.

But looking at what is apparently the same object in the contexts of different languages, we gain a degree of insight into a more indistinct, a more complicated world. It turns out that a two-year old doesn't learn names of 'objects' as much. He really learns names for a set of properties which stay constant in a variety of contexts, usually social contexts.

So then, what's a **table**? and how does a child come to know it? In fact no one is ever 'taught' what a table is. He must abstract from ordinary contexts what a table **must be** to the older persons around who use those sounds to mean a particular table, in a particular place, time, and circumstance. The developing namer must, in turn, try out his knowledge, this apparent abstraction, in other situations. Usually, in all cultures I have heard about, he gets corrected if slightly wrong – say, he calls *a cow, a horse*; but his naming is merely accepted as correct if he was somehow correct. I don't know what happens if a child is 'very wrong' at naming something – say, a horse for a table – or that it ever happens in real life.

The impact of this is that even a simple, rather basic human operation — prelanguage in many senses — can be clearly seen as an attempt on the part of a child to get in tune with how the others in his life seem to organize and to split up the world. We know, cross-linguistically, that all objects (rather, their properties) can kind of shift in many different contexts. The important thing is that the child develop the **correct** — in this case, the **same** implicit — model of the world as his models have.

Perhaps we are raising the question of how is it that individuals grow up. The idea that we are, indeed, all individuals and only individuals, pervades many of our intellectual approaches to the understanding of development. One approach, which has had currency in the study of language acquisition, suggests that meaning of words in real languages is acquired by association and repetition. This makes the same assumption about words that we often make about people — that is, that they are single entities; that they have only one meaning, one role, one age. This idea oversimplifies the processes of growing up, and practically mechanizes the child. It is as if we really believed that a single, monolithic set of facts represent the entire developmental processes of the child. It is as if we merely had to correct deviance in some constant manner — bad behaviors, bad pronunciations — in order to get a normal product. On the contrary this story of development does not seem to be at all accurate. It appears much more to be the case that it is the constant, yet varying with age, implicit interpretations of correctness, of cultural rightness to **not** react when a child's speech seems to match his parents'.

It has been noted that some foster parents do well or do best with children of particular ages (Von Mering, 1965). When the children get too big or too old, they tend to be traded in for fresher stock. However, most of us don't have the opportunity to trade our children in, and merely have to live with the changes. But **we** also have some pictures of what children are or ought to be at different ages; our own, and I suppose, other children. We have pictures of what parents ought to be, that may or may not vary with children's ages.

It's a curious fact that the Anglo-Saxon fairy tales we read most to our own children usually mask children's interaction with one another by making them different in one way or another. In the Three Bears, Goldilocks only talks to bears, and then only after she spilled the beans; the Three Billy Goats Gruff only talk to a troll; Snow-White only talks with dwarves. The few times that children do talk with each other is when the children talk as one with respect to an outsider such as the witch in Hansel and Gretel.

But doesn't this fairly accurately reflect the world of the family from which most of these stories gain their depth? With respect to common family problems, the children are a kind of unit; their identity and loyalty unquestioned, not meaningful as individuals. Inside the family, however, sameness is truly a fiction. Then how do children get raised from day-to-day, year-to-year; how do they get 'grown-up'?

At perhaps the simplest level, how does an infant's mother 'know' what cries mean? Because **she** has provided the infant a model by reacting to past cries as if they had constant meaning? But what if she reacts inconstantly — or has no such model in mind? This being an oral metaphorical tradition, it's really quite hard for Dr. Spock to put it in writing.

Similarly, a three-year old who called *a table, a horse* might get laughed at; a five-year old who did the same might get 'laughed down' — unless he did it 'for real' — in which case the parents might wonder.

The 'for real' aspects of growing up are played out most strongly for most of us within the family. Yet familial definition and perception of **correctness** is redefined from age to age. What has been alluded to as 'age-grades' are not merely the different calendrical ages of children, but, more importantly, age-grades are the shared perceptions of what normal or pathological acts are for a four-year old, a six-year old, a 15-year old. While we all recognize the simple fact that eight and ten-year olds are quite different, we hesitate to really believe that the difference is not somehow inherent — doesn't just belong to the child — but in large measure rests in our adults' definitions, shared beliefs about what each age-grade **ought** to mean; and in general does mean.

Granted the existence of such 'actual-perceptual' mechanisms at play in the raising of children, we can ask several questions about **transitions** from one phase to another. While we are accustomed to thinking that growth is a rather even and continuous phenomenon natural to each particular child, there is a fair degree of evidence which suggests that growth occurs in 'spurts'. Rapid transition and 'aha' perceptions of these changes by parents is a more common parental expression once the question is raised than I would have supposed. Such comments by parents to one another as: "Look at how long he is!" or "Those clothes are too babyish for her!" are usually expressed as sudden observations; they seem to transform other parental perceptions as soon as they're made.

Now, if age-grade transitions are even relatively rapid, we might suppose that the child at each particular stage must have a fairly good idea of 'where he's going', of what he is moving toward. Or is that necessary more than in outline?

Recalling our favorite fairy tales, it was pointed out that the children were all in some unhappy state (usually not of their own making). Perhaps that means merely a kind of 'precognition'; a vague 'feeling' of malaise, of dissatisfaction with whomever they are or feel themselves to be. Since children know that they are several things with respect to different people, it might only affect a small part of their being, at first. But we also recognize by now that their definitions of themselves are in fact mirrors of their parents' (and perhaps of societies') models of them as 'correct' kinds of children. So we might surmise that the transition about to occur, happens first in the parental 'fancy', the children's unhappiness or threatened feeling relating to their apparent incompetence or incompleteness as the parents begin to observe that their children have 'changed'.

We have in our literary traditions many ways of signaling change. Usually it's handled by a trip away, crossing a bridge; often it's associated with water; one can go to sleep and dream. But we return from the journey − none of us really becomes anyone different in entirety. We might really think that the parents had changed, and not the children.

Two areas of potential pathological reaction occur immediately in the context of this way of thinking: first, that the parents might have a 'peculiar' clock of age-grade change; and second, the parents might not want change because they feel, like some foster parents, that each transition in the child 'causes' a change in them. Particularly in the cases where he is sensitive to changes in his close friends, or where neighbors or other adults perceive an imminent age-grade jump − the child may be caught in a kind of 'squeeze'. On one hand, he knows he is in transit; on the other, he is told not to be. He might react to such a bind by showing up with a variety of symptoms, but then where is the 'locus' of pathology???

In speaking of models my first tendency is to believe that, like objects, they're singular things. We already know, however, that objects are constant properties of things rather than the actual things. So we have good reason to guess that no model is an entity, and no one ever knows exactly what he is to become except with fairly constant reference to the people around him. If he behaves correctly in their terms, he is merely accepted; if his actions are perceived as incorrect or peculiar in others' minds, then he is corrected, punished, maybe shunned. For the parents who believe in original sin the return to correct being is always possible and likely; for another child, the first show of peculiar behavior may be defined by his parents as his natural and enduring state. There may be no return.

Think of how Snow White's model of womanliness is presented to her; her first (most real) mother dies, presumably at about the time the child becomes 'oedipal'. The older she becomes the more vain the queen becomes — and when Snow White is seven, and beginning latency (the first obvious signs of femaleness to the old lady), there's hell to pay; and she's merely banished. Now, being banished, no one (that is, mother) has to endure the pain of watching her become a demi-female. As one of my favorite professors often noted, it's quite likely that we call the post-oedipal child latent and act as if it's somehow inert, because the **blatency** of the behavior of this age-group is simply too painful to watch. We can empathize with the idea of exile. While Snow White is picking up the skills she's supposed to get — she learns less about females than of males who are in about her own state; about halfway beings.

Then poor Snow-White wandered along through the wood in great fear; and the wild beasts roared about her, but none did her any harm. In the evening she came to a little cottage, and went in there to rest herself, for her little feet would carry her no farther. Everything was spruce and neat in the cottage. On the table was spread a white cloth and there were seven little plates with seven little loaves, and seven little glasses, with wine in them; and knives and forks lain in order; and by the wall stood seven little beds. As she was very hungry, she picked a little piece off each loaf, and drank a very little wine from each glass; and after that she thought she would lie down and rest. So she tried all the little beds; but one was too long, and another was too short, till at last the seventh suited her; and there she laid herself down, and went to sleep. (Grimm, 1956)

Life is even rougher when the adult female model makes her final appearance. This time she even looks like the witch we've always known her to be, and in merely doing her motherly job of feeding, Snow White throws a real fit; the energy necessary, we would guess, to make it through the transition from maidenhood to womanhood.

Those of you who recall the Bergmann movie, *The Virgin Spring,* will agree that transitions are neither simple nor gentle in Anglo-Saxon and Scandinavian folklore. Pity the poor father who can't figure out his role at all, or even if he has one; one minute a dwarf; the next prince charming; the next an outsider, an old man who's treated as a group of beings he never even thought he was. ...

We are faced with this curious fact; namely, that models are likely to be presented negatively. The child at whatever point in his development doesn't learn what to be, anything like as solidly as he is taught what **not** to be. I suppose that might leave him quite vulnerable if he doesn't have other supports or supporters who help him learn what he's supposed to be, or abandon him by perceiving the 'worst' aspects of his character and defining that for him as the 'real him'.

One of the peculiarities of the so-called civilized world is that the models we believe to be shared by all parents do vary. They vary in some ways which seem to be quite destructive to the developing child; but they may also vary with geography, with the 'kind' of family in ways in which 'outsiders' might 'see' as pathological.

Consider an extreme case, that of a real princess like Queen Elizabeth when she was a little girl. While she was like any female, she was always 'special'; nonnormal in various ways. But, in her case, that was all right because she behaved properly for who she was and was to become. If, however, we didn't share with her family the belief that she really would become a queen, we might judge much of her childhood as outside of normal development; many of us would, doubting the idea of the divinity of the royal family, be tempted to believe that her models of growing up were indeed mostly fantasy.

The problems of diagnosis and curing are tied, perhaps strangely, not only to well-being *per se*, but to well-being within particular social contexts. A psychiatrist friend suggested the following as problematic and to this point:[68]

An 18-year old girl consulted him. She was, in his terms, a 'poor Pitiful Pearl', very passive. She began to 'move' in therapy and showed up one day with an engagement ring — usually a pleasant happening from the therapist's point-of-view. In this case, however, she had been presented with the ring essentially in public and with no previous knowledge that she would get it. This took place in front of a very tightly knit group which operated much like an extended family, say, of Italian descent; in this case it was a square dance group to which the patient, her fiance, and both of their families belonged. She arrived about a week later for her therapeutic hour; she had not yet seen the boy alone since the presentation of the ring. As far as she knows, the boy is 'flighty'; the girl is unsure of his work. Is her solution a good solution? It may be very appropriate in its context — the dance group. To continue therapy may be an attempt to impose the therapist's value system, even if primarily medical and well motivated, for another value system; the one in which she will have to continue living, and which contains the lateral supports of family and friends which may well make for a successful or at least enduring marriage and family life. Further therapy may make life within the group very difficult; yet, that is where she may well have to live or essentially abandon her family and friends.

Different groups and subgroups, economic, ethnic, social are different in many respects. While groups rarely conform to their external stereotypes, there is good reason to believe that children are brought up by parents who tend to see the world like their own families and neighbors; but different from people who came from different parts of the world, even a long time ago.

Consider the plight of the unlucky physician called upon by a concerned mother or neighbor to do something in the context of the following tale:

The country was lovely just then; it was summer. The wheat was golden and the oats still green; the hay was stacked in the rich, low-lying meadows, where the stork was marching about on his long red legs, chattering Egyptian, the language his mother had taught him.

... In amongst the leaves it was as secluded as in the depths of a forest; and there a duck was sitting on her nest. Her little ducklings were just about to be hatched, but she was tired of sitting, for it had lasted such a long time.

... At last one egg after another began to crack. 'Cheep, cheep!' they said. All the chicks had come to life and were poking their heads out.

... 'Quack! quack!' said the duck; and then they all quacked their hardest and looked about them on all sides among the green leaves; their mother allowed them to look as much as they liked, for green is good for the eyes.

... 'Well, how are you getting on?' said an old duck who had come to pay her a visit.

... 'This one egg is taking such a long time,' answered the sitting duck.

... 'Let me look at the egg which won't crack,' said the old duck. 'You may be sure that it is a turkey's egg! I have been cheated like that once, and I had no end of trouble and worry with the creatures for I may tell you that they are afraid of the water. I could not get them into it, I quacked and snapped at them, but it was no good. Let me see the egg! Yes, it is a turkey's egg! You just leave it alone and teach the other children to swim.'

... 'I will sit on it a little longer. I have sat so long already, that I may as well go on till the Midsummer Fair comes round.'

... At last the big egg cracked. 'Cheep, cheep,' said the young one and tumbled out; how big and ugly he was! The duck looked at him.

... 'That is a monstrous big duckling,' she said; 'none of the others looked like that; can he be a turkey chick? Well, we shall soon find that out; into the water he shall go, if I have to kick him in myself.'

Next day was gloriously fine. ... The mother duck with her whole family went down to the moat.

Splash, into the water she sprang. 'Quack, quack!' she said, and one duckling plumped in after the other. The water dashed over their heads, but they came up again and floated beautifully; their legs went of themselves, and they were all there. Even the big ugly gray one swam about with them.

'No, that is no turkey,' she said; 'see how beautifully he uses his legs and how erect he holds himself; he is my own chick! After all he is not so bad when you come to look at him properly. Quack, quack! Now come with me and I will take you into the world and introduce you to the duckyard; but keep close to me all the time, so that no one may tread upon you, and beware of the cat.' (Anderson, 1956)

The ducklings' mother provides a definition of good, moral duck behavior – at least for ducklings. She tells them how to quack, how to swim, whom to address and how, whom to shy away from. She has the good grace to observe her brood and to decide, from their observed behavior, whether or not they are 'normal'. She is, in our terms, quite a good mother.

But if she lacked confidence, didn't trust her own observations or ability to observe, and believed the ugly duckling to be imperfect in some 'important' way, the story might be different. In this actual story – our case study – the duckling was, in fact, attacked for being different; the duckling assumed that he deserved it merely for being so 'ugly'. Presumably his mother's support wasn't strong enough to counteract it. He left the nest on his own, and in attempting to escape, came upon some hens, and after a while:

... An uncontrollable longing seized him to float on the water and at last he could not help telling the hen about it.

... 'What on earth possesses you?' she asked; 'you have nothing to do, that is why you get these freaks into your head. Lay some eggs or take to purring, and you will get over it.'

'But it is so delicious to float on the water,' said the duckling; 'so delicious to feel it rushing over your head when you dive to the bottom.'

'That would be fine amusement,' said the hen. 'I think you have gone mad. Ask the cat about it, he is the wisest creature I know. ...'

'You do not understand me,' said the duckling.

'Well, if we don't understand you, who should?' the hen asked.

Indeed, who should? If a consulting physician, asked to come in at some point in this case, believed deep down that he 'knew' the society (that is, duck or swan society) and tried to get the Ugly

Duckling to adjust 'successfully', he might well be doing a disservice on two counts: first, the 'patient' is, at best, marginal as a group member — merely for being the age he is. While the ducks and he have some claim on each other, it is hardly a strong one from either point-of-view! Second, any therapeutic gambit, which makes sense with reference to living in swan society, might be nonuseful, even contra-indicated for life among the ducks and for making the transition to swan society. So it seems quite important to judge the nature of any illness with reference to the real world in which a child lives and is becoming, without prejudging the facts of some other sub-culture's world, by carefully finding out how one transits from stage to stage in growing up to live among the swans.

(12) FACIAL EXPRESSION AND BODY MOVEMENT

Facial expression and body movement are communicative, just as language. Given this similarity of function, they may be compared as static or dynamic processes. Although language can be seen as being 'related' to expression, this essay opts for a view of language, gesture, and movements as different actualizations of essentially the same processes. This view as it is developing within the context of Human Ethology seems to require a reconceptualization of language structure as well as language function.

Facial expression and body movement are inseparable from linguistic activity in the communication process. Being wed to a tradition which accepts as given the 'independence' of language, however, linguists have been willing to jump to explanations of language as reflecting deep-seated, well-buffered neurological mechanisms (Chomsky, 1968). There has been little attention paid to other aspects of behavior which **occur** together with language, and are also part of the growth and development processes. Linguists have tended instead to consider gestural and other body movement phenomena either as commentary on language, *per se*, or as some kind of uninteresting independent communicational system.[69]

The field of **expression** as it relates to language is a neglected area of study. This essay will show how it may be seen as an integral part of a study of language, as opposed to a language-expression dichotomous **interface**. Among the interested disciplines in the area of expression are anthropology, cognitive or developmental psychology, psychiatry and ethology-behavioral biology. It appears likely that the emergent cross-disciplinary field of Human Ethology will consider this problem area.

The rallying issues are many. One is the realization that natural behavior is understudied. Psychology has been content to study a limited variety of responses to stimuli in controlled experimental situations. Its picture of man as a perceptual mechanism is presently being challenged (Gibson, 1966) in a movement which will have repercussions involving all of the observational disciplines which have accepted an implicitly passive, analytic picture of man as a bundle of essentially independent sensual systems.

A second issue is the increasing realization that the view of man as an individual is not complete. Man – and other animals – are **social** animals, and one's developing adult models are **socially** successful; not simply as surviving organisms, but as people who can mate, communicate, and raise their young to live in the same cognitive sphere as they do.

In the context of man as a bio-social animal, it is simplistic to proceed from the assumption that language is an independent system. Linguistic phenomena are central to the maintenance of bio-social groups. Language is not merely a collection of rules for sentences or sounds, but a part of our ongoing behavior. It is thus necessary to consider verbal and other expressive behavior in many contexts to gain an understanding of how people become and maintain an **apparently** rational (i.e., social) existence.[70]

Traditional linguists must suspend their picture of language as purely verbal. A comprehensive approach to language includes recognition of larger patterns of behavior. Yet, there is no explicit recognition of some simple facts of lip and mouth movement as seen on faces; for example, on faces of parents as they recite popular children's poems. 'Baa, baa, black sheep' has a contrastive lip and mouth change on every syllable – as seen in the face-to-face (vis-à-vis) setting.[71] Every bilabial and all palatal sounds (at least in American English) are characterizable not only as sound, but also as gross changes in the facies of the speaker. A child spoken to in the face-to-face sees as well as hears. And in this context, it is noteworthy that most children seem to be unable to transfer these 'language' skills to the telephone until they are in control of quite extensive grammatical and contextual 'machinery'. Seeing and hearing are part of development,[72] and the face-to-face setting may be so much a part of one's interaction that only older speakers are able to speak and understand 'telephonese'.

In the vis-à-vis we interact with others on a number of levels, all of which may be operating simultaneously.[73] We watch skin and clothes, and see whether the mouth or eyes are open or closed. We attend to fairly gross changes in the dynamics of mouths or eyes in motion. We feel and sense the underlying muscular changes of others. We smell body odors distributed differently by skin, clothes, and hair.

The problem of what expression is also must reflect a long dual definitional history. Typically, two types of sense are given to the word; one which is essentially **social** (how do other people react to certain facial appearances or changes; do they reflect 'emotional' states?) and the second, a more bio-structural account (which muscles are involved in expressing 'happiness' or 'disdain'?).[74] The so-called 'muscles of expression' are also referred to as the 'mimetic muscles', suggesting that anatomists believe that children mimic the movements they see, translating from parents' faces the reflections of underlying muscles. Part of the cooing, handling, and TLC which infants need to socially and physically develop is an increasing muscular or proprioceptive sense of their own bodies. Apparently, they learn much of this sense from felt contact with other people (Frank, 1957). From this point of view language can be seen as muscular as well as auditory.

Phonological tradition has made use of a few facial observations in constructing descriptive systems – 'open' means simply that the mouth is open further than in producing 'closed' vowels (it also means that the listener-watcher can usually see teeth and tongue movements); rounded means lip rounding (yet the English affricative consonants seem never to be described this way).[75]

On the other hand, much has remained unnoted by linguists; the vertical striae on lips are perfectly clear within the distance range of the usual *vis-à-vis* showing extremely slight changes in underlying circum-oral musculature. These striae indicate impending change, such as mouth opening prior to speaking (and there is a perceptible delay between these two events!).[76] People's eyes are also changing contrastively at frequent intervals; it has been demonstrated (Spitz and Wolf, 1946) that the smile response in infants, which is claimed to be so characteristically human, is intimately tied into reacting to **human** eyes. People breathe, and it is very unusual for people to speak as they inspire. We can rest assured that children are aware of this. Traditional linguistics has been willing to deal with deep, out-of-awareness phenomena of various kinds to the extent that they fit into certain linguistic structures. In this case, the phenomena of expression are comparable to linguistic phenomena, yet have not been considered to function in its structures.

Expression: Tonus and Set

The study of expression must deal with the physical presence of bodies as seen or otherwise sensed in face-to-face interaction.[77] If this is restricted to surface phenomena, skin, clothes, and hair, changes in them represent or reflect underlying muscular and vascular changes. Any serious consideration of expression will consider both the anatomical structures which are the foundation of expression and the 'surface' of the face.[78] The skin or surface of the face is organized into several areas. If we note change and contrast, the areas immediately apparent are the eyes and mouth. Color or pigmentation of the eyes and skin enhance such contrasts in different persons and populations; 'steely' eyes are usually green or light blue and quite low contrast, and changes (winks, blinks, eye shifts) may be less obvious than in darker-eyed people; mouth (and eyes) are enhanced in relation to darker skin.[79]

The remainder of the facial skin seems to be differentially organized by 'folds' or muscular groups which seem to vary much like linguistic dialects. It appears that one tends to 'use' his face much like the people in his family, community, etc.[80]

Relationships between the skin and the deeper structures are not well known. Perhaps this is because anatomists and surgeons have been interested in structure, not relationship, or because skin lesions are amazingly self-repairing.[81] An important aspect of this relationship is the highly flexible and plastic nature of the skin, as opposed to the muscles and bones beneath it. The skin is not strongly attached to bones or muscles, except at relatively few points, so it is free to move almost independently. This enhances or exaggerates muscle movements.

The bony parts of the face may be seen as a kind of foundation for the muscles. These muscles are called 'voluntary', but this term implies no necessary sense of awareness, rather suggesting that most of us can move them when we want to.[82]

The expression of a face reflects the underlying structure of muscle and bone, the superficial structure of the skin and the relationship between the skin and the other structures. The areas of the face in which expression occurs may be divided, for expository purposes, into an eye component and a mouth component. The set of the muscles in these areas and the movement of the skin around them defines expression. What seems to be meant by looking like oneself is some relationship between the muscle tone (**tonus**) in which muscles are ordinarily held, over the bony structure underlying. Our ordinary facial expression is not passive in the sense of expression being a change from flaccid (**at rest**) states of muscle **tension** but changes in tension or tonus from already 'tensioned' muscles. This is often referred to as **facial set**.

Enlow (1968) in his elegant monograph on the growth of the

face clearly shows that the development of the bony structure of the face is related to the use of the overlying muscles. Facial set is a reflection of the family in which we grow up and, equally, the group to which the family belongs. It is consistent that this facial set will be translated by the muscles to a bony set, or dynamic shaping of the skeletal face beneath the muscles.[83]

There are a number of aspects of **body** set which can be thought of in much the same way as facial set.[84] That is, we have a range of possibilities of how to 'arrange' our shoulders (high or low — giving us the 'appearance' of having short or long necks); pelvis thrust slightly forward (adult female) or backward (adult male — both 'middle majority American'); to hold our legs such that our feet come down 'straight' as we walk, slightly in or slightly out. Women's posture make center of gravity adjustments to breasts. Again, these 'adjustments' seem to be cultural-dialectal to a great extent: one walks like his group, holds his shoulders similarly, etc. The amount of individual variation which this allows still remains great, however, and we can identify most people at least of our 'own group' by face, and often by manner of walking at fairly great distances.

Expression and Language

A linguistically sensitive rationale for the study of expression must proceed from the assumption that language relates somehow to other behavioral phenomena. This might take place within the individual at, say, the neurological level; or may involve more than one person. Whereas language seems to have lent itself to individual-oriented models of language function, expression is usually seen as reflecting social-interactional behavioral variables.

Many linguists have, indeed, considered a 'functional' model of language 'use'. The most popular phrasing is of the sort: 'Language is (used) to communicate.[85] In this context, expression can also be seen as related to communication in a similar functional manner. It is thus possible to consider several formulations of expression, facial and body, and relate them to language in terms of their similar functions.

The possibility of comparing functions must relate to the kinds of 'structures' in which they are seen to operate. This requires a fairly full examination of what interaction and communication might be — yet these are neglected fields compared, for example, to the efforts of language scholars.

This has resulted in a very few formulations of the nature of communication structures, and the form of expression studies thus far can be seen as reflecting one of the following: (1) communication as message or information transfer; (2) communication as a constant social process.

Most models of language which have developed in the twentieth century (proceeding from Saussure) has utilized to a greater or lesser extent the first model; i.e., language as the exchange of ideas/words or thoughts/sentences. The speaker gives 'new' information to the listener. Developmentally, language acquisition has primarily meant learning words, sentences or the rules for 'understanding' or 'creating' them.

The second model of communication is that which will characterize the emergent field of Human Ethology, and towards which models of language are just beginning to develop. This implies, among other things, no necessary distinction between verbal and non-verbal processes as they function in communication, and truly seems to open up a potential area of comparative study.

Information Exchange Models

In the context of the informational model of communication, the study of expression has taken a number of interesting directions — with the possibilities not yet showing signs of completeness or exhaustion. Most of these have considered units of expression to be much like words or sentences, to be examined as if they represent essentially independent structures. In the absence of any full explanation of communication, a variety of *ad hoc* operational definitions of structure have had to suffice. These have been rooted in the analytic traditions which consider behavior to be constituted of a number of separable (if not independent) acts or events which characterize our different modalities of operation: auditory, visual ... smell.

The study of 'gesture' has also capitalized on the option of a traditional dualism between **expression** vs. **emotion** to establish legitimation. It has associated a movement (or set of movements isolated into a discrete segment somehow) with some emotion or 'meaning'. Heirs of the traditional dualism seem to equate the terms, 'expression, rational and language structure' as opposed to 'emotional, irrational and non-verbal or verbal, non-language' which had hitherto been considered to be essentially unstructured (essentially Saussure's *parole*).

The emotions have been considered in the mind-body dualism as more 'primitive' than language; the usual equation seems to be irrational, primitive, animal-like. Biologists thus regard them as prior to man and the origin of 'true' (non-emotional) language; psychiatrically-oriented workers regard the primitive as prerational in each person's development; thus we see a similar set of studies emerging from these two disciplines.

Excellent examples of this approach are the work of Eibl-Eibesfeldt (biology) and Ekman (psychology) which have interesting correspondences. Each selects out of the world of movement a set of operationally defined gestures, which they presume to be 'universal'. Both are engaged in testing across cultures to see if or how the 'smile' or other 'meaningful' facial expressions are handled by different cultures. The quest for universality would seem to follow from the presumption that emotions are primitive and pre-linguistic — thus they must (from the biological and psychoanalytic points of view) occur in all humans. In this formulation (a 'progressive' or additive notion of evolution) we humans have all of the general attributes animals have — plus we have language.[86]

The works of both of the authors (e.g., Eibl-Eibesfeldt, 1968; Ekman *et al.*, 1969) are well worth pondering in the context of the possible relationships between language and expression. The first point of contact or interface is located in a **semantic** realm. Eibl-Eibesfeldt considers the 'smile' to have essentially the 'same meaning' to all people, almost regardless of experiential differences among them. He does this apparently on the grounds that it is part of what distinguishes men from animals (just as language is presumed to do) and so all people 'must' have it. Similar or homologous movements in animals are interpreted to be non-similar in the same way as animal verbalizations are assumed to be non-language (Smith, 1969:145).

Ekman *et al.* tested the same set of 'emotion-showing' facial photographs across cultures, to see whether a variety of different peoples label them 'identically'. A number of facial expressions are indeed universally 'recognized'. Unfortunately Ekman does not tell us how the inter-language equivalence of terms or labels was determined; so we can only be certain that different populations are consistent in applying the same labels to particular pictures.

On another level the relationships between expression (gesture) and language must lie somewhere between putative structure and experiential behavior. Language is considered to be a structure with a grammar; gesture, in order to be comparable, must also be considered in this light. Thus, it should follow that students of expression-as-acts or gestures should attempt to find a grammar of gestures. Differences between language and gesture are immediately clear in terms of linear order, and immediacy of contiguity. Nonetheless, the postulation of the notion of a **gestural grammar** would lead to the search for similarities, probably at the level of sentences composed of gestures as units – and sequences of gestures as analogous, say, to phrase structures.

Another relationship between gesture and language – in the context of static studies – has to do with the understanding of individual behavior. If gesture (or any other unit of bodily position) is considered to take place on the face or on the body of the individual, then the observer can match what he says with that gesture or its immediate context. This kind of study would have relevance for the learning of behavior (gestures) possibly associated with certain forms of language. In addition, it might lend insight into both correlational and causal behavior at deeper organismic levels, such as neurological, in the context of the emerging field of Brain and Behavior (Pribram, 1969).

Dynamic Studies of Communication

In its essential opposition to more atomistically cast studies, a dynamic approach might begin from the assumption that 'new' information is a fairly rare commodity in the real world, and as such might well constitute the basis for a study of 'residual', but not 'central', phenomena. A study which concentrates on the exchange of a really new or even a fresh bit of information is thus seen as an unlikely way of proceeding to find out about communication. This is one reason why linguistic approaches which consider grammatical structure as a central human function seem (to me) to have decreasing relevance.

Another consideration of the dynamic study of communication concerns the fact that the notion of the truly individual-existential self seems about as rare a part of one's being as the notion of new information. Most of our actual behavior takes place in 'well-known' contexts such as the family, neighborhood, business establishment, classroom or bureaucracy. New information is thus truly important, if only by contrast. To better understand this effect, see Kuhn (1962). Again there is no question that messages which embody new information do occur – hopefully even in teaching contexts – but it seems less useful to concentrate on essentially 'unusual' processes as the very foundation of our approach to the study of communication.

It is in this context that ideal language structure may be seen as only one of a number of such structures, some remaining not well known, which enter into communication. A sample question of possible interest to linguists, which arises in the present context, is of the following form: assume, for the moment, that children do not 'have' to learn language — it is neither innate nor an incumbent process. Grant further that young children communicate very effectively with those around them (and if they did not, they simply would not survive; Blauvelt, 1954) through tactile processes, 'grunts', contextually relevant eye movements — i.e., the behavior of a healthy 6 month old. Why, then, do they 'learn' language?

Immediately we are forced, on the basis of these assumptions, to search within the organism. But we are also forced to search without — among the other people in the infant's home who begin to 'demand' speech by about 1½ years at the latest. Models for speaking may be less in the individual infant than in his mother's 'working image' of him.[87] Remember that many infants do not speak — we label them retarded or autistic or pathological in some way. But they may simply have made life adjustments which are different from the rest of ours (Virchow, 1962). Here we may begin to see language development as part and parcel of social development. And we might even begin to ask why aphasic children are that way, rather than jumping to indeterminate diagnoses such as 'brain damage' or other such imponderables which admit of no understanding and of no possible change.

The consideration of dynamic views of communication also imposes the necessary consideration of time variables, even real-time variables. Whereas the ideal structures of language, physiology, individual, or society can be seen as existing essentially out-of-time, people communicate in fairly continuous fashions. In one sense, discrete units such as sentences, phonemes, or percepts exist all by themselves; yet it might be argued that such 'essences' only emerge from the reality of interactions in which they occur. One doesn't just work out his rules for creating sentences; he talks to someone about something; and understands what's happening to a fairly remarkable degree. People are social beings in addition to being generators of disembodied sentences.

Another question which might be phrased is how do people understand one another; in what sense is language intelligible in real time? It seems to me that this question might be interpreted in two ways, first as a non-question; e.g., the real question is how does communication 'fail' or why don't people communicate better? Secondly, by noting what a remarkable thing it is that there are so few communicational confusions in an otherwise messy world. The latter is clearly the appealing one to students of communication dynamics.

Examples of approaches to studies which have used time include those by Miller, Galanter, and Pribram (1960) and by Birdwhistell (1968a, 1968b), Scheflen (1964) *et al.* Most of them have tried to work with the notion that peoples' ideas about the future often (if not always) influence their present or ongoing behavior. On the level of the sentence this might mean that, say, the first words of otherwise similar sentences contrast as they are embedded in differentially long sentences. Or that a phrase final word might reflect in its occurrence some features of the kind of phrase in which it occurred, and something about what's coming next. (This, as opposed to 'explaining away' such actual dynamic variation by attributing it to such inexplicables as 'allophonic' or 'free' variation).

Another idea pursued by Scheflen, Birdwhistell *et al.* is that many such plans operate much like structures in time. Although these might be better conceptualized as being 'generative' ultimately, they have been considered to operate much like a symphony, a baseball game, or a wedding in which the outline of the form is to be 'played out'. Scheflen and Birdwhistell have approached 'The Interview' in this way, searching for patterned repetition of movement on the part of patient and therapist.

But such culturally defined ritual scenes might also be unusual in the same senses discussed earlier. Communicational processes go on many hours on many days when only a more highly leveled notion of 'plan' would seem appropriate. Indeed 'chronobiologists' are only now demonstrating that we vary in many physiological traits across the day (circadian rhythms) as well as through the week, month, and year. From the present point of view of dynamic approaches, the emergent field of 'socio-chronobiology' will have to consider the variation in behavior as related to bio-social cycles such as the symphony, or the classroom hour. (How is it, for example, that people in varying stages of their daily cycle, can come together for an hour to listen and attend the same lecture without disruption? Or can they?)

Finally a dynamic approach might see itself in essential opposition to the universal (language or gesture) approaches which rely on the assumption of cross-cultural or pan human similarities to be raised to the level of causation 'because' they define human uniqueness. It seems to me that this rests on such an increasingly tangled mat of assumptions of the nature of human nature that they can lend little understanding to gaining new insight about it.

Summary

The study of facial expression and body movement is still in its infancy, especially in regard to possible linguistic relationships. Reasons for this general neglect of such obvious aspects of man's behavior are various, but the most important are traditions of thought and conceptualization of problems to which linguists are heir. Careful description, while necessary, will not itself solve the mysteries of expression and communication.

Part of the difficulty is that our philosophical traditions of thinking about man are very individual-oriented, with a primary emphasis on adult, rational, male. It is no accident that these terms are equivalent in so many senses, but this focus surely does not tell us all there is to know about behavior, linguistic or other.

The face, or 'parts' of it, are in constant motion while speaking. The listener's face(s) and body is quieter, but not 'at rest'; and his feedback is an important part of the face-to-face interaction where most of our ordinary conversation and communication take place. Traditions of observation have, however, called attention only to the speaker as the transmitter of 'new' information, and not to the listener.

Linguists and others have acted as if such information takes place without regard to audience and context, but also as if it occurs without regard to bodies. The sentence and the word indeed appear to be independent of one's body. And a grammatical approach to facial expression through 'emotions' can also treat expression as independent of bodies – though this requires a more creative imagination.

The 'factual' basis of what humans are about – is not really very strong; the traditions are, on the other hand, perhaps overly seductive. We might all agree minimally that children turn out to be essentially like their parents – except that there is variety and change upon the basic model. One way of phrasing the outline of the enterprise is, 'How does this happen?' Instead of concentrating on pathology or operationalism to define normality, we might reopen the consideration of cross-species studies where children also turn out to be pretty much like their parents. Instead of assigning varying percentages to an intrinsically dualist position of nature vs. nurture, we are presently able to begin to phrase testable questions which might transcend this peculiar traditional division.

Further, observation of language should include what happens on the faces and in the bodies of the interactors. It is intriguing to note that bodily relationships also shift when conversational topics shift from, say, the 'here and now' to a narrative. There is good reason to believe that all such behavior is structured and patterned, if only because ordinary communication is so effective. There are very few 'confusions' in the every day world within the relatively constant cultural contexts of family and work.

(13) THE DYNAMICS OF FACIAL EXPRESSION

The **human face** is as distinctly **human** as any aspect of our being — yet it remains virtually unstudied. It is a most active center of inter- action: A completely facile, mobile area, its relationship to the underlying tissues is one which is enhanced rather than restricted by loosely-fitting outer surfaces. It is a set of highly contrastive surfaces, these contrasts heightened by interlaced muscle fibers whose movement abilities are quite marvelous. It is the area of one's body which other persons relate to as the center of one's being.

The human face is as stable and continuous as it is dynamic and variable. All of the present peoples of the world have clearly human faces, and have had for eons. An individual retains a few features, at least, as he grows, develops and ages, so that one's photographic history retains a sense of uniqueness. We look like our families, the families of our parents, and those around us; we look like ourselves. And it is tempting to emphasize those facial features which are stable and continuous in accounting for how faces are, and how they are formed and shaped.

Because our faces seem so characteristically human, it is easy to believe that they are as stable as our species — and that facial move- ment is a dynamic, played out on the surface of a static skeletal form. How difficult it is to remember that the skeleton, itself, is a dynamically derived form dependent for its shape on the interplay of constancy and dynamism of the forces acting upon it (Enlow, 1968; Moss and Salentijn, 1969).

What is a face — how do we come to look like we do? Should we attempt to explain the variability we observe, or is it more interesting to account for the constancy?

In what senses do populations look alike, and continue to look alike? What features do we count as those individual differences by which we distinguish one another and ourselves?

The sensibility of these questions has entered a new phase with the knowledge and insights of dynamically oriented-anatomists.

Enlow's monograph, in particular, provides a solid foundation for considering these questions which could have been only roughly speculative even a few years ago. Do bony structures completely determine what faces look like or do faces in some sense determine the forces shaping the underlying structures?

Associated with these puzzlements are questions about the location of the face-shaping mechanisms, as well as about the nature of those mechanisms. Since the continuity of facial features appears so strong to us, it has been tempting to attribute them to internal-genetic processes. On the other hand, anatomists have been so impressed by the facile imitative abilities of the external facial muscles, that they have called them the 'mimetic' muscles. Anatomists have felt that the face is a place where one can transfigure the expressions of someone else's face into one's own. Less frequently have they asked how this might be done.

The history of the study of the face and associated structures may account, in part, for its virtual neglect. In a way very similar to the study of Language, the face and head have been considered to be almost extra-natural. Darwin himself came closest to a productive study of the face in "The Expression of the Emotions in Man and Animals", but this was neglected and discounted until the recent rebirth of interest in animal behavior. Broadly speaking, the face has been considered an area which simultaneously reveals and masks something **about** us — a glance into the depths of our personalities. Little is known about its workings as any kind of physical-biological arena — as a thing in and of itself.

A number of common facial observations remain well-known, but anecdotal. The face changes throughout all of life — for most people in fairly characteristic ways. All of us are extremely sensitive to the face as a major clue to our age; we constantly label one another in terms of these inexplicit, folk-taxonomic features. We are quite **accurate**, if changing, observers as our interests change in different phases of our lives. Yet even Enlow (p. 251) portrays the 'life-history' of facial development as a series of photographs which covers the period from eight months to 20 years. Perhaps structural changes from age 20 to age 70-plus are presumed to be either very minor, or somehow normalized.

It is also well-known that the micro-time dimensions in which faces are observed confounds the problem of facial dynamics. **Still photos** are highly stylized if posed, yet often represent some inexplicable abstraction from reality if taken from the ongoing dynamic. The habit of interpreting, of reading into such transitory moments, some total — usually emotional expression — must be tempered by experiences in working with dynamic video or movie techniques. It would not be inaccurate to suspect anatomists of attempting to 'cadaverize' the more external structures of our bodies, as they have so long resisted looking at the functional-dynamic aspects of deeper skeletal structures. But by doing only this, one is likely to be especially impressed by the continuity of form, by the apparent complexity of expression, and to remain wary of the possibility of its study.

Speaking as a linguist, I consider that the face is no more unstudiable than language; no more-or-less dynamic, human, yet continuous in so many features. The face is an active part of the processes of communication, of speaking, listening, encoding and decoding. It is not merely a commentator about the so-called messages of interaction; it is, like speech, both message and commentator. It is, in my view, as much the essence of our being as the ability to think and conceptualize.

It is useful to push the analogy between language and facial expression if only because they are so peculiarly intertwined. From a dynamic point of view, language is a set of muscular movements, whose complexity and beauty matches that of the fine dancers and athletes. Like a study of the hand movements of a skilled dentist or musician, the more one studies these processes, the more one is impressed by the capabilities of the human form. Not only is speech so impressively complex, it is virtually error-free. Imagine the constantly changing dynamic of the tongue moving through fairly great distances, knowing so much, so well.

Consider further that these muscular habit abilities are also situation appropriate. They are congruent with our eyes, sizes, and vary remarkably well with the nature of the room, the audience, and the ambient noise levels. Further, they are remarkably like the muscular habits of the people around us; i.e., we all speak dialects, familiolects, 'profession-olects'.

The concept of 'dialect' means that we sound essentially the same as others; muscularly, it means that we share their articulatory habits, to a large degree — especially when contrasted with speakers of another dialect or language. A so-called 'accent' is the projection of one set of muscular habits carried over into a setting in which most people share another set. And they are, in my view, 'felt' as well as 'heard'.

One other facially relevant characteristic of dialects is that they have a reasonably short time dimension, for many people at least. They can be remarkably plastic and changeable. If a person is thrust into a situation where all the others around him have different speech habits, he is likely to change, to speak as he perceives them to speak. In some cases one is virtually compelled to change in order to be understood. But some people are highly resistant to such change and one can think of their muscular speech habits as being extremely stable, operating within a rather long time span.

Besides the dynamic aspects of speech, there are some dialect-language habits which are likely to be very stable: for example, where we usually hold our tongues when we are not speaking, the amount of tonus and tension in the various parts of our tongues, and to what extent this tension is translated into actual pressures against the teeth, lips, palate and pharynx. And consider the kinds of tensions with which we hold our cheeks, lips and teeth. Speech is a release of air from a finely tensioned mouth.

I think it is extremely useful in conceptualizing the shaping abilities of the tongue to think of the mouth as a rich cognitive center in which the tongue is the prime mover, tracker of information, processor and manager of food, and particularly of saliva. The very ability to speak seems to be very much intertwined with how we manage saliva.

The tongue is so 'concerned' with its domain that any change in it provokes an almost incessant tongue movement to that area – a new filling, an ulcerated surface seems almost to yearn for the tongue to come and inspect it, and to 'understand' it.

The tongue can reach so many places. Even to swallow can be interpreted as the need of the tongue to contact the pharynx every so often – and it does even this with a degree of pressure.

The interior of the mouth — a large part of the interior of the face — is thus extremely well-known and understood by our tongues, if not exactly by 'ourselves'. In the case of a newly discovered, sharp dental carie, it takes a rather strong 'willing of the mind' to keep the tongue away from its self-appointed rounds, and to keep it from 'self inflicted' damage.

Now, does the exterior surface of the face share any of these features of speech, with the interior of the mouth? Is the face as well-known to us as our tongues and mouth? Can there be said to be facial dialects, muscular habits, a tensioned dynamic? What is facial time?

Looking around, one is impressed by the diversity of faces – they all look different; so different, in fact, that it seems surprising that we can somehow remember what a lot of individual people look like.

Yet, as we travel across Europe, or any part of the world which has remained less of a melting pot, we become impressed by the facial types we meet, the changes from the last place we were, and how alike the people look in any one place. We may also discover that we are obviously 'American-looking' to most other people, essentially irrespective of how long our families have been here. In some senses our faces are indeed much like those around us — there are facial dialects. Boas noted long ago with reference to head and nose shapes, that there seems to be a kind of Americanization process of at least some facial features (Boas, 1940).

Is this process a muscular process — much like the muscular habits which comprise speech dialects? Or is it an internal-genetic process of some sort? My belief is that the face is, indeed, a most active place, and that it is also very dialectal — our faces do share many features with the faces of those around us. Further, I wish to affirm that the underlying skeleton is determined, to a very great extent, by the shaping processes of the external face. What are the **mechanisms** of the external face which apparently cause this to happen?

First of all, it is necessary to consider what the term **mimetic** means, and how it is that we can be said to mimic anyone's face.

Mimetic seems to mean to copy, most basically. Yet what is copied? What does an infant respond to whose mother opens her mouth in order to stimulate him to open his mouth? (Essentially all mothers, everywhere in the world that I've been and asked about, seem to do this). What it seems to mean is that the infant can make some muscular **translations**. He translates what he sees as his mother's external **surface** into some sense of his own facial muscles. He may also translate his facial muscle feelings into how it appears on his own face; and he may even have a translatory sense of what the facial muscles of his mother are doing. In any case, his own muscles 'respond' to her movement.

Although this is a common observation, it has many interesting implications. Our bodies can, to some possibly great extent, translate how other people's bodies are. Not only is this true of faces, but we have an apparently uncanny knowledge of how other people maintain their own balance, at any moment. In other words, we seem to be uncommonly good at translating from other people's bodily surfaces into our own muscular-proprioceptive feelings.

What I'm suggesting is that our own knowledge of our muscles — here, our facial muscles — is related to what we see on other peoples faces. (Presumably we can get to this through tactile, auditory, and other senses as well as through visual means.) The fact that we continue to look relatively alike, and to look like our own phenotypes is largely due to holding and using our facial muscles in about the same ways as the people around us. Facial dialects are like speech dialects: muscular habits, tonus, tensions.

This is, to me, the outstanding factor in facial shaping and facial expression. Unless, as Enlow and others have implied, the mandibular muscles keep the mandible in tow in very complex ways, we would not continue to look like we did a few years earlier in development. The facial muscles are the major shapers of the face; we use them like the others around us.

But there's more to this story — as there is to speech. The face is in almost constant movement. The mouth and eyes, circum-oral and circum-orbital muscles, are ever-changing. Why are they always moving? What do they move for? Are there any people who don't move their faces much?

If one looks at a movie of a new-born — preferably in slow-motion — one is impressed by the rapidity, distance, flexibility of the head, ears, nose, mouth, tongue, eyes and associated parts. It is useful to have a movie if only to check one's observations and note that it really is all happening.

Down's Syndrome children, especially those who are clearly diagnosable at birth, seem to lack most of these movement abilities. Whereas their eyes and tongues are highly mobile, they seem to move against an essentially immobile background. The rest of their faces move very little, if at all. Probably this is the essence of their appearing diagnosable at birth.

Noting the Down's children will appear to be retarded intellectually in thought and in speech, as the years pass, we may ask how their lack of facial movement might contribute to their dilemma. Is facial movement itself so important in development; does lack of movement necessarily imply a damaged brain; or do our faces play other parts in development behavior?

Granted that people have a fair muscular sense of what others' faces are doing, how can one relate to a face which does not move? What do mothers 'use' their children's faces for — in addition to their essential food-dispensing service? What is a face?

Faces are external information centers. Mothers use the movement in their children's faces to determine a great deal about their infant's internal state. Children — it's more obvious in toddlers — attend to other people's **faces** primarily. The relationships between people are, to a very large extent, relationships between faces.

What sorts of information show up on faces? From my linguistic bias, the first is information about speech. While we adults seem to believe that speech comes 'out' of mouths, it is probably more apparent to children in the face-to-face situation that our lips are **moving** with the noise.

Interestingly, linguists have shared the fiction that speech comes out of mouths, because they've never done a 'visual phonetics'. But think of what an adult does in talking to a one-year old: in the face-to-face, one articulates clearly or carefully. What this means **visually**, is that one moves his mouth, lips, and circumoral areas a great deal further than usual, with more lip tension, and maybe a bit slower than usual. It seems to be mainly a visual happening, much less an auditory one.

It turns out that many of the poems which are early childhood favorites are also highly visual. "Baa, baa, black sheep" has a major visible change on every syllable. In terms of facial muscular development, the visual aspects of speech appear to help the child discover and exercise particularly those muscular aspects of his face which his parents use in speaking.

Conversely, a child tends to not exercise, and in many senses to **lose** effective muscular abilities which he already had as a newly born infant; not just the inability of most of us to wriggle our ears, but also the kinds of tensions, movements and muscular awareness which are enhanced or disenhanced by being spoken to by speakers of different languages. French, for example, not only sounds different to us, but the lip tension of speakers of French is much greater than ours, and their lips much more rounded; essentially all French speakers compared to essentially all native speakers of English. The southern British **hold** their upper lips with a great deal more lateral pull than we, much like many other northern Europeans. The upper lip tends to 'disappear' with increasing age — at least, less lip **appears** on the surface of the face. But the constant, high degree of lip tension, with its potential for facial shaping is very constant. Surely the faces of different national groups — and their language seen as a set of muscular tensions and habits — are highly related.

By several months of age, some of the limits of future development of the face seem to be set for most people. The enhancing of some features, the non-use of others, seems to be enough to account for many of the gross differences; e.g., the tremendous symmetry of most Russian faces, and the non-symmetry of most English ones. Just as the 'curling' of one's tongue seems to be difficult to do unless one practices during development, it is difficult — but not impossible — to regain or relearn how to use the other facial areas (at least to use them easily and 'on purpose').

The relearning of facial movements seems to be almost impossible for most of us. Learning to move both eyebrows independently as an adult is very difficult. Yet the experience of musicians, for example, is that techniques which appeared impossible at one point, are part of one's bodily repertoire a few months later. The body — and face — really appear to be quite plastic — if one's experience really changes. The apparent fact that most adults continue to look very much 'like themselves', I take to mean that their world of experience and contact remains extremely limited once they have reached adulthood. Those people who move to new places, across some socio-cultural line, or otherwise move out of their former groups are quite open to major facial changes.

To return to the facial development issue, not only do mothers see dynamic visual changes on their infants' faces, they **interpret** these changes. The information that they believe to occur on their infants' faces is some blend of the child's actual states and the mother's belief system about what's happening. Each of these systems is in flux as the mother confirms her own observations by having her infant respond as she thought he would. The infant comes to sense that his mother **reads** him correctly — as his 'needs' continue to be met. Bear in mind that the information might 'mean' quite different things to mother and infant; the fact that they can discover and work in terms of a shared interface of interpretation seems to be the most critical issue.

The mother's view is that the infant is variously: hungry, wet, messy, or hurts. But the infant's notion may well be of this sort: that it will feel good, pleasureful to expel air rapidly from his lungs; the sound is nice, the sucking may look good, smell good, and feel good to all the surfaces of his mouth and tongue which come into play.

The important point in development, most probably in evolution, is that each child comes to interpret his own muscularly derived feelings in about the same way as his parents interpret them. If he does not, he runs that very real risk of being unable to interpret the rest of the world in about the same way his mother does, and he will be called by some such labels as 'retarded' or 'autistic'.

Down's Syndrome children are an interesting case in point. No one really knows whether they are truly intellectually 'defective'. By a kind of retrospective prediction, we assure ourselves that the third body on the 21st chromosome has done something bad to the brain. Loss of normal function, especially in behavioral terms, will result. We **know** their bodies are peculiar – the most anomalous of all the congenital syndromes according to Shapiro (1970). But the designation, **retarded**, is, above all, a behavioral statement.

In the context of the history of progressive evolutionary thought, the Down's are thought to be not just different, but **biologically** deficient; unchangeable except within some relatively narrow limits. I wish to suggest that all the data is not yet in, and that there are alternative ways to think about the problem, especially if we take the area of facial dynamics seriously.

As noted earlier, Down's children have a very passive, non-moving face. Their external facial muscles – the mimetic muscles – do not move much. Whether their nervous innervation is anomalous, or the muscles are lacking, is not yet known. Some of their deeper muscles seem to function normally; they can suck, move their tongues, move their eyes. Both the 'informative' surfaces display little hint of subsurface movement.

This peculiar muscular anomaly syndrome can easily lead to behavioral anomalies – of the sort which Down's persons display as a population. They have unusual speech, they are 'moody', often hyperactive, and they continue to use their faces and bodies peculiarly. Not only do they look different, they act differently as well. Why?

A possible explanation has been hinted at: namely, that their faces are used by mothers as information centers, as windows into their bodily functions, needs and wants. A great deal of facial movement and development involves the sharing of expression; in my terms, the ability to translate what appears on the mother's face, into the child's own external facial musculature. Muscularly, behaviorally, this seems to be the major problem. The mother has difficulty in reading; the child in translating 'properly'.

Most Down's children seem to try to move their faces as their parents do. This can be seen most clearly in some older children who have fairly massive brow ridges. These children seem to try to substitute deeper facial muscle abilities. Some of them do remarkably well, most do not. (In fact, an ongoing study at the University of Minnesota is trying to see whether more constant mother-child interaction, with a lot of external support for the mother, will help their children to look and function more normally). Perhaps the ones who do best have in some sense 'discovered' their facial muscles.

The other, most characteristic Down's expression, seen in older children, is the typical 'tongue-hanging-out' (mimicked so well by most people who work with Down's). Why do their tongues hang out?

Earlier, I suggested that the mouth is a kind of cognitive center, and that the tongue operates as a most knowledgeable and interested member. It acts, for most of us, within a well-known, essentially closed sphere. But for the Down's persons, the tongue is different, and different in a way that most of us picture as 'stupid'.

I wish to argue that the Down's tongues are not necessarily stupid, but they surely are different. These differences create and/or reflect differences in speech, and in mentation.

Perhaps there is something 'wrong' with the Down's tongues, but to rethink the issue, let us imagine how they could be different, and what a tongue difference of this sort might imply. It appears that 'normal' tongues must use the external facial muscles to help them determine the extent of their boundaries. A face is a statement about the relative tensions of the interior and exterior portions of the oral area. With less operative facial muscles, Down's seem to lack a great deal of the external information about where their mouth is, or ought to be — using their parents as models of what a tongue 'should' do.

I speculate that the Down's tongue-out is an accurate representation of how he perceives his parents' faces to operate. He simply has no way of interpreting the external facial muscle part into his own picture of his face. I think that he believes that he is operating about like his parents, much as any other child does. The dissonance comes in the normals having a different image of the Down's person's abilities, not necessarily from the Down's person himself.

This can help account for some of the usual speech difficulties which are characteristic of this syndrome. Most of what we call speech is a direct function of tongue movements, articulations, and shapings. Simply stated, a different mouth-tongue orientation virtually must affect speech production. The fact that many experienced Down's Syndrome observers have noted that there is a characteristic speech associated with Down's only seems to imply that Down's persons' muscular orientations are very similar. Even if a part of the syndrome were a rather specific neurological effect, I suspect that we would note more variation in Down's speech than seems to be present. Ultimately, the tongue and associated structures directly determine the quality of speech. In other cases, these are highly compensatory mechanisms; in Down's they are not because, I suspect, of a muscular orientation, of which they have no way of becoming aware.

But we have not yet asked about how the face might contribute to mental abilities in any direct sense. Here, again, there is virtually no data, but theories have existed for millenia. It is these theories which seem to have called attention away from the face — usually directly toward the brain or to some function associated with the brain. It is enticing to believe that the true person, the down-deep reality resides in that disembodied interpreter.

The mental functions of humans have always been thought to be very special, human, and extra-natural; call it the mind, the soul, language, it has had the same effect. The effect has been to block or to restrict comparative, cross-species questions and research, and either to concentrate on those features of man which are thought to be unique, or to focus on the shared areas which are directly the body — physiology, anatomy. Here, too, the belief that we share a kind of primitive 'emotionalism' with other species, has become a part of the evolutionary emergence story of man. Only rarely has the human form, itself, been considered as part of the mental abilities of man. Study has centered instead on a few features — bipedalism, opposable thumbs — which can contribute to different life styles from other species.

The last serious work on comparative facial muscular development was completed by Huber (1931), prior to 1930. There have been a series of ethologically oriented and motivated studies on the facial sur- face in the 1960's and a few still continue. As far as I have been able to determine, few scholars have tried to relate the appearance of the surface to the morphology, to the underlying muscular dynamics.

The theories, which claim that man's mind is so special, have not only determined the research interests and strategies to a remarkable degree, but they have allowed us to believe that we could account for our observations of faces as simply **reflecting** (or 'masking') the workings of the mind or the emotions, not directly contributing to those workings. And so the face has been neglected.

But I believe that human faces are at least as important in life and in evolution as our brain or any other feature of our being. Somehow we have been duped into believing, like linguists, that the surface of the face mirrors and plays out mental and emotional states. Until now we have not seriously considered that the face itself may itself affect or determine the brain, and that one's reading of one's own facial expression is a statement to himself about his own state, and about his state as related to other persons' faces.

One's knowledge of his own face, particularly as it is able to empathize with or translate from others' faces, is a critical feature of our being. There is some evidence to suggest that faces of infants do not translate directly from parents'; that is, the analogues from parents' faces are not all 'muscle-for-muscle'. Instead, infants' smiles are mainly circum-oral movements which are not tied into parents' mouths, but more especially to their eyes — when the heads are in a direct face-to-face within certain distances (Spitz and Wolf, 1946).

Again the parents' and infants' interpretations of the 'same' activity are likely to be quite different. For the child, it may simply be a pleasant set of movements; for the parent, a rewarding interaction which bespeaks of future deep rapport. As observers, our anthropomorphic leanings are not applied only to non-humans, but to developing humans as well.

Infants use their parents' faces as information centers, not just of their emotional states but also of the state of the situational world in which the infant lives. Any unusual noise, any call, and the infant snaps up to look at his mother's **face**. Infants are probably extremely astute students of their parents' faces   and any interruption or loss of practice may result in a difficulty, be it of knowledge, reliability, or trust.

Human eyes seem the more remarkable, the more they are studied. Not only do they help tie-in our infants to us, but in the highly contrastive light differences, they are extremely obvious, as are their movements. And they have what appears to be an almost infinite number of states of focus and direction. One can read where another person is looking with remarkable accuracy. The whole world of meaning, of objects and activities, is reflected in one's eyes, probably more clearly than in any other part of his body.

For most of us the contrasts are enhanced by other facial areas, and particularly by the facial hair — eyebrows, lashes, hair, beards, moustaches. It is important to note that we have exquisite muscular control over all of these areas. It is not terribly far-fetched to suggest that these facial muscles are in some ways tied-in to our cognitive processes. The face is never really inactive, even when we are alone and 'thinking' to ourselves, or day-dreaming. Remember also that the mouth interior is as active, tensioned, managing saliva during the reading of this paper, as when the body is engaging in interaction. The tongue is busy, constantly. (For most of us native speakers of English, it is currently pushing up against the upper alveolar ridge or the upper teeth — its tip is playing with a small bolus of saliva which we become extremely interested in swallowing as we become aware of it!)

What about the children who have no eyes, or no facial muscles? Do they smile; how are their cognitive processes affected by their different perspectives? Blind children smile — Down's children seem to be awfully sober; they have difficulty in moving those muscles which we parents will interpret as smiling. There is little question that we consider blind children as much more intellectually competent than Down's.

It may well be that Down's children cannot read where their parents are looking, nearly as well as normal children; but they try to do it visually. Blind children have no vision and must organize their bodies and faces through quite different mechanisms than Down's children. (I suggest trying to read braille as a test to gain some insight into the remarkable tactile sensitivities of blind persons.)

The eyes embody the kind of dual status which has characterized theories about faces: they are sensate moving parts of our bodies; simultaneously, they are an arena through which to look at the real person. Most observers regard vision as our principal sense, **the** way in which we come to know the world, the major reality-testing mechanism of our being. But an infant sees highly mobile, contrastive, ever-changing surfaces; we have no idea of whether an infant knows about his own eyes as analogues to his mother's eyes. Mothers interpret and impute to their infants the notion that their eyes are the same kinds of things, and the infant must gradually come to interpret them in about the same way.

The child's 'ability to see' is not the proper biological question in asking about his potential development. The question must be of the form of whether he can come to see and interpret the world and his own body in much the same way as the others about him. I suggest that much of this is done through the muscular mechanisms by which we analogize our bodily processes to those of others — as self-knowledge, knowledge about others' bodies, and how others interpret the world. These seem to be as much bodily processes as any other function of our existence and center on the human face.

To conclude, the face has a kind of dual existence in that it has at least two aspects, a surface and the external facial muscles. This is not particularly interesting or even apparent until the face is considered as an interactional center. If the focus of study remains only at the level of the individual, faces will inevitably appear to be primarily genetic and self-caused: heritability of looks, continuity of populations would seem to be self-evident; retarded persons to be biologically deficient and inherently unchangeable; cognition, a function of the mind; and curing will be offered in the form of management and good nursing. Facial movement could only reflect our mental and emotional states — weak faces, weak minds.

However, once the face is considered as an intricate set of moving and movable structures which are tensioned, constantly changing through life, we are forced to explain what the face does, how it does it, and when. We note that we, and infants particularly, use others' faces for information about them, about us, about the world, and how to interpret all of these.

The people around us have favorite tonus and movement habits. They see these habits developing in their children as the children come to adopt similar ways of holding their own muscles. Face-shaping seems to be as much a social as an individual process. I consider them inseparable.

The variation which this process permits is still remarkable. It is a statement about the unbelievable ability to use and control our faces, but also about the equally remarkable ability to distinguish and to remember faces, at least in populations with which we are most familiar.

The face has an **interior** which is also a highly mobile, tensioned area, in constant interplay with its external surface. The muscles of the face and the inside of the mouth are in some dynamic balance all of the time — talking, listening, dreaming. These tensioned muscles would seem to be the major long-term facial shapers. We sound like we sound because we hold and use our tongues inside the kind of resonant cavity that we shape for ourselves — very similar to those of the people nearest us.

The face can now, I believe, be reexamined. I have tried to stimulate a sense of the dynamic, the variation, the richness of the human face: surface, muscles, as well as the underlying bony tissues. And I have tried to point toward some of the mechanisms, individual and social, which are involved in the shaping processes. I hope that the functional anatomists will continue their fine works to include the forces that **shape** the bones, and that they will expand their view toward the socialization processes as they affect the individual face.

(14) AROUND THE
CARTESIAN IMPASSE

> "One must either acknowledge that it is beyond one's powers to understand how body and mind are united, how they interact, or, if one claims to have any understanding, attribute it, not to philosophical insight, but having learnt the lessons of 'ordinary life and conversation'. This is the Cartesian Impasse ..." (Vesey, 1965: 11).

A Human Ethological Approach to Communication

I

Having spent an appreciable apprenticeship in traditional linguistics, paralinguistics, and kinesics,[88] it has seemed to me that deeper understandings of human interaction and human beingness were not available within these conceptual frameworks. No matter how carefully done, much more of the same approaches seemed incapable of producing the sorts of ideas and insights which many of us have felt to be lacking in the behavioral sciences. They seemed to yield excellent descriptions, but lacked explanatory power.

The aim of transcending one's (apparent) human experience was not obtainable in these traditions. We needed new vision to become finely-tuned critics of our beliefs; to grasp any sense of when and how a circular theory nears its cyclical consummation; to be able to look outside to be able to look back at man with new rigor and new reality filters. How else can one begin to observe the obvious: the dynamics of human communication?

It seemed a natural extension of my training (i.e., to think of language as all human languages) to think of how other species might perceive us. A search of the literature on animal communication seemed in order. But the animal behaviorists have looked at animal verbal behavior primarily as deficient human behavior (Busnel, 1963). Knowing how one tends to hear even other human languages in terms of his native language, the biologists' listing of other species' 'calls' in terms of what the human hears, appeared anthropomorphic in the extreme and uneducated at best. It seemed that the field of animal verbal communication had not yet gained ingress into its own subject matter. The inventive conclusions about animal verbalization only served to confirm the beliefs of those who imagine that human language is extra-natural and intrinsically non-comparable to the so-called 'speech' of other species who occasionally modify and vibrate the air expelled from their lungs (Lancaster, 1965). For one who was already secure in his beliefs that humans were indeed as unique as any other species, this seemed defensive beyond proportion. If other features of our being were similar to other species, what made language so super-special? I saw no reason to invoke a new 'creationism' merely to maintain man's dignity (an element of being which ought to be striven for in any case!) (Bronowski, 1965).[89]

But the deeper motive for looking beyond was to relook at assumptions and definitions of why we believe language to 'be', and to be what we say it is. Not that the beliefs are 'wrong' in some transient existential sense, but that they were either too simple or too complicated (one can't easily distinguish between simplicity and complexity from the 'inside'). Besides, the ideas seemed to be very old; deserving an occasional airing, but not necessarily true fidelity. And they pointed directly to the **individual** as the locus of being and believing, rather than as a hub in a social network. Interaction, in this theoretical orientation, was inconsequential to being, developing or even to reproducing. The mind of man appeared disembodied, a behavioral science developed, which is far removed from the personified bodies which most of us seem to occupy, if not to be.[90]

In Cartesian tradition, belief in the individual as the locus of knowledge, consciousness, and thought sanctioned the essential neglect of questions of interaction. Interaction remained as problem, not as fact; designated the 'Problem of other minds' (Ryle, 1949). One 'knew' that he existed because he thinks (has consciousness, language); but it remained unclear that he could or did relate to others' minds. In other words, an intellectual, philosophical basis for the very study of interaction appeared to be lacking.

Whatever their 'intellective capacities', however, different species do have different sorts of bodies which move differently in velocity and rhythm. Yet all socially reproducing species 'know' others of their own species: what, how do they know? If one considers the possibility that the ability and propensity of 'bodies' to interact is interesting, perhaps observation and conceptualization may begin again.

But there is more intellectual baggage borne on the wings of traditional thought. Theories of mind and language became interwoven with a theory of society (Cassirer, 1946). Man was presumed to be unique as he acquired language; this acquisition was followed in some historical sense by stable social interaction, the achieving of 'culture'. Individual man became social man via the vehicle of language. And this story, simplex to complex, pervades our views not only of human development, but also the ontogenesis of each human developing. Interaction is not considered to be a fact of life, but principally a problem in living.

But if one actually observes other species, he notes that they also live socially, in relative calm and peace. By all modern accounts, society must have pre-dated the emergence of man (Darling, 1952). While each animal appears to be no more or less individual than are humans, the actuality of the solitary, non-social feral being who evolved to wander in the Edens of the past, is a non-occurrence in the natural world. Evolution did not occur in non-social individuals; development does not occur in non-social individuals; language does not develop in non-social individuals. Why do our language **theories** not ask about the input of others into the so-called 'minds' of individuals? Who or what is language a property of? Is language disembodied, or just our theories about language?

Not only has ethology confirmed that society is as natural a condition in man as individuality, it has nudged the evolutionary biologists to grudgingly admit that behavior, like bodies, has continuity and species-specificity. Evolution, claims Mayr (1963), has taken place as much or more in terms of behavior as of the 'solid' more tangible tissues, soft and hard. In fact, even anatomy has shown recent signs of reconceptualizing the dynamics of bone shaping in terms of social interaction (Enlow, 1968). Behavior appears to be 'harder' and bones 'softer' than the 'objective' scientist had thought them to be. The cliche is that 'behavior is heritable' (Lorenz 1965: xiii); its serious consideration has raised to collective consciousness the old questions of nature vs. nurture which many had wishfully hoped were permanently interred.

In some mysterious *Zeitgeist* dynamic, similar questions appeared simultaneously in the behavioral sciences, but with a bio-morphological twist. Language was said to be heritable because of our natural properties as (normal, individual) human beings (Chomsky,

1968). Linguists, whose anti-body orientation made them essentially immune to observing the observable, fought to attribute this ability to the 'mind'; but a few of us suspected that this attribution was some sort of cover either for a new creationism or for a new biologism in which variation and continuity were to be eliminated from purview. But this era did educate us, intellectually, into the mysteries of idea shifts, and into the baser reasons thereof. Everyman's law of ideation: people prefer to have intellectual dressing on their beliefs!

But a more engrossing facet of the issue also appeared — if behavior was to be considered heritable, thus 'genetic' — would this affect the notion of genetic in any sense (Stebbins, 1965)? If 'normal' humans have language and reproduce, how do they get to be, or to remain 'normal'? Were they born with some fixed propensities for which interaction and experience could only provide nutrients, or was the concept of normality an emergent interactional dynamic of any sort? Can the study of face-to-face interaction be considered to be **biological**, in terms of its contribution to variety, continuity and evolution? Is there a conceptual pathway along which the biological and behavioral aspects of man can be seen to be integrated or coterminous?

Consider the human face: that aspect of our being which seems as rich a source of 'information' as our very languages. How is it to be considered? — as a surface projection of internal affective states; as a contrastive set of surfaces which highlight the myriad movements of eyes and mouth; as a partial representation of the internal dynamic of linguistic formation; as a place to yawn, smile, grimace, blink, wink, and smirk; as a place to imagine that the real 'I' is located; as a map of 'betraying' entree into our being; as a reactive covering through which other beings are personified and confirmed; as a net and network by which one can feel, image, mimic, project others' feelings, imagings, mimes, and projections of themselves; as a place which tells us not only about itself, and ourselves in reflection, but about the object-event-time of our discourse; as an array of territories which we love to study, to remember, and can recall in multiple dynamic contexts even after years have transpired between interactions; as the seat, the locus of our continuing moral feelings about ourselves as played out often in our imagined, so subtle re-creations of family; as the interplay of human surfaces which receive and direct the sounds of interactional speech towards our ears; as the obverse of its internal surfaces, the place which feels tongue movements, but refuses to show them to the world; as the prime locus of so many, so-called senses; as our largest unclothed surface;

as the most notably dynamic surface of one's body because its hair is so light reflective; as the region of our being by which we tell others about the state of our health, and beseech or refuse help; as our sex and age; as the site of one's external projection as a whole, successful person, or not; the determinant of whether one 'belongs' in a situation, or is a 'visitor'; as a class marker; a place to cream and color, to call attention to or away from itself; beauty, stupidity. ...

No notation system yet contrived can begin to describe the human face. What has been developed so far is a series of approaches to faces, mostly non-dynamic, which tend to obscure problems as much as they can illuminate (Eibl-Eibesfeldt, 1970; Ekman, 1972). We are susceptible to being led into appealing shortcuts as if they offer potentially complete insight – if the recent history of linguistics can be taken as any measure.

In the context of 'behavioral-biology-so-far', there has been a movement to look at faces and language as if their genetic-innate components were fixed in each individual sometime prior to his emergence into the social-experiential world (Eibl-Eibesfeldt, 1970). Instead of using a genetic-interactional scheme in which genetic refers to a potentially continuous aspect of living, the assumption which has gained popularity is that **nature** means 'built-in' forever, and **nurture** means modifiable. Some behavior(s) are caused in essence by in-built features of being; in this theory facial expression in the external mapping, the performance of a fixed humanoid set of affective states (Ekman, 1972). This represents a literal interpretation of the Darwinian exhortation that the face is the site for the **expression** of the emotions (Darwin, 1872). And it is a direct equation of the notions of biology with inflexibility (as if adaptability is a notion which applies only in the long run).

What happens to the 'normal' human notion in this view? Is it also an inbuilt feature of one's being? – once abnormal, always abnormal? G. G. Simpson admonished me: "Only normal human beings have language!" [p. 85]. Yet I was taught in human anatomy that each of us has some anomalies; that viability, growth, reproduction were the major issues; that there were either fairly wide parameters of being, or a variety of pathways.

Who decides on the issues of which 'anomalies' are to be considered within normal limits, and which outside the boundaries of acceptable normality? We might respond that 'nature' decides; but all of us need social 'tender loving care' (TLC) to survive. No human is fit to survive at birth. By this definition of normality we scarcely can be said to exist at all. Biological normality for social species cannot be said to exist solely within the individual. If the individual organism can be said to 'decide' anything which is precisely non-social, it may be able to decide to abort itself. Otherwise, it does not seem to have any sense of being which can be construed purely as extra-interactional. Continued viability of any individual must be some complex set of *quid pro quos* between its imaginings of itself and its other-bodied *Umwelt*. If organisms are **bodies**, then we must begin to account for their social-intellectual abilities without presuming a 'mind', a *Deus ex machina*, as an explanatory mechanism.

II

By construing the problem of human knowledge within a framework of dualist thought, in which one must impale himself on one horn or the other or try precariously to ride both, the issues have been obscured. Knowledge is either in-built and learning is chimerical; or experience is the be-all of existence. The notion of life-as-interaction contains the seeds, I believe, of alternative conceptualizations and paths of study of human behavior.

I think that this will be the basic conceptual contribution of an ethological approach to communication, at least for the foreseeable future; that it will be a most useful exercise to take seriously the empty half of the mind-body antagonism, place it directly into interactional perspective, and see where it takes us.

It will take great perspicacity to avoid the pitfalls of already assuming that which we desire to discover, a mark of essentially all theories which set out to explain man's presumed uniqueness. Most theorists, including behavioral biologists who examine man, tend to invoke 'psychical' explanations to account for behavior **before** they move to simpler, 'mechanical' explanations. Questions of the form of: 'how is man unique', must be addressed anew, or simply passed-by.

Let me submit a number of observations about man, which might be considered as 'case studies'. All are incomplete, but (I hope) suggestive of how we might begin to rethink, particularly in terms of how our bodies might 'understand' others' bodies.[91]

(1) An old anatomical cliche: certain parts of our bodies are highly **mimetic** (Goss, 1954).

While the notion of mimesis seems quite straightforward, it is essentially the only concession anatomy has ever made to the possibility that bodies are in some sense social. (Actually, anatomy has only recently begun to concede that bodies might be alive.)

Mimesis literally means copying. One's body can make itself to 'look like' another's (at least to express emotions, because it's precisely those muscles which anatomists call mimetic). That is, we have the ability to copy others' expressions.

It is the facial **surface** of another body which one sees – it has or is 'given' depth, shadow, color, contrast, many 'parts'. But one sees external surfaces. In order to mimic, to produce on one's face the same movements he sees on other faces (does an infant know that faces are faces?), one must produce an expression by moving his own **muscles**. One's face must see and analyze another's expression and **translate** a visual dynamic (or static) into his own facial muscles. I suggest that we have no understanding of the mechanisms for mimesis, but that they are critical for the deeper understanding of interaction and of the individual. Expression seems to be interactional as well as internal or innate.

(2) At an early age – three months or so – one can 'elicit' a smile on a baby's face. Upon testing, it was learned that a humanoid figure, principally our type of high-contrast **eyes**, would also elicit apparently the same smile (Spitz and Wolf, 1946).

Not only can an infant organism mime by, for example, opening its mouth when its mama opens hers, but the infant apparently can transduce interactional eyes into its own mouth dynamic. While there seems to be a lack of explanation for this almost universally observed phenomenon, it adds weight to the notion that our bodies can (and want to) respond to and with others' bodies in complex ways. Although some smiles may be due to a release of an internal affective state, others may indeed be related to other bodies.

A neglected question is why a smile should have 'positive affect'. What 'feels good' about a facial surface moving superior and laterally to the point where we judge it to be a smile? It might be due primarily to the fact that its occurrence in their infants has such a high positive load for parents who interpret it as a confirming sign of normal development and increasing love.

There are children whose attempts at smiling are not completely 'successful' – i.e., although there is oral movement, it seems not to be sufficient to be seen as a smile. Among the children who 'do not smile' are the bulk of Down's Syndrome (Mongoloid 21-trisomy) children who are diagnosable at birth by facial inspection. These children do not (cannot?) move their mimetic muscles very well.

Deeper muscles, eyes, tongue, sucking seem to work pretty well, but not the external ones, including those which do our smiling.

Is their inability to smile well, a function of a muscular weakness or due to a defective brain? Most of them will turn out to appear 'retarded', more-or-less severely. Will this have to do with their inability to properly demonstrate affective expression, not be able to 'tune-in' on others completely, and have a facial map which most of us will·label as 'stupid'? Or do they have an in-built intellectual defect which remains neurologically undemonstrable (or both)? 'Mind' theories posit defect, as mind theories seem particularly wont to do in 'exceptional' cases.

(3) Some aspects of our being which have dynamic facial components, seem to be 'catching' (mimetic behavior?). These include yawning, coughing and dryness of the throat, whispering (I find this really intriguing!), shortness of breath. Many essentially internal aspects of our bodies 'find themselves' interacting with other interactants' bodies. Mimesis is thus not only facial and external, but also internal in barely understood senses. What kind of pact is communication that it produces 'symptoms' in an observer-interactor's body in an essentially **uncontrollable** way?

(4) While there is no question that humans are rhythmic creatures, how are these rhythms shared and controlled?

Musicians are highly rhythmic creatures, trading on rhythm to make a living. Many musical instruments are held; supported by one or more body parts. Good musicians can and must 'suppress' the feeling of rhythm in those supportive areas, or their musical output will suffer (ask any amateur musician!). That is, humans can apparently 'control' the organization of rhythm distribution in their bodies.

In ensemble music, one must not only 'know' about his own internal rhythms, but must be able to tune-in on others' with remarkable precision and speed. Human bodies seem to have little or no difficulty tuning-in to the rhythms of others' bodies. One can organize his own body, and simultaneously track on and share an interactant's time.

There are certain situations and/or states or relational being in which people (bodies?) seem incapable of interaction. One of these is the 'jogging' state. Joggers have little or no problem in conversing with co-joggers, apparently regardless of how fare they've run. But there seems to be no way for a jogger to talk with or relate to (e.g., one cannot maintain eye contact) with a person who is in a normal state. On checking common pulse rates, it appeared that the pulse of the jogger was literally 'pulled down' during eye contact, a very precarious, and certainly a very uncomfortable, state.[92]

This suggests that interaction involves shared rhythms, that the heart or pulse rate is also susceptible of being 'shared', and that eye contact is sufficient to set up shared rhythmicity. On checking common pulses of people at rest, their pulses jumped together into a kind of momentary synchrony when they came into mutual eye contact, or related mutually to the same voice. Quite probably speech is also a rhythmic, synchronizing activity.[93]

(5) A way of thinking about speech is as a function of a continuously varying **muscular** dynamic whose rhythmic features have been considered outstanding. From this perspective, speech can be considered as muscular vibration altering a column of air.[94]

The aspects of language which are rhythmic may be 'felt' as well as heard. That the listener in any interaction is subvocalizing, has long been noted. It may well be that some of this activity is rhythmically related to what is being spoken in such a way that the listener then analyzes his own sub-vocal activity as representing part of the message. What this might imply is that at least some of (linguistic) interaction is primarily a bodily interaction.[95]

Perhaps, then, human bodies as perception devices are the sorts of things which resonate (in an almost literal sense) to sounds. In mind theories, the ability to 'understand and create' is attributed *a priori* to mind.

When the deaf men of Gallaudet College used to play football, play was started and stopped by whacking the biggest bass drum imaginable. Evidently this set the earth in motion in ways directly and rapidly perceptible by the deaf players. All of us 'feel' bass sounds of trucks and distant stereos. Yet the usual metaphor of speaking-hearing has only to do with the impingement of sound vibrations on internal ear mechanisms. Why, then, do small children find it interesting and necessary to do a lot of interaction in the face-to-face, instead of putting their ear to their parents' mouths? I suggest that the human body, particularly the face, is a major shaper (absorber, censor, amplifier?) of our sound perceptions (and all this may imply for the study of non-human speech!).

(6) On observing slow motion movies, it can be noted easily that there is a time lag between mouth opening and vocalization. Con-

sider the possibility that the infant, though he may both hear and see the face, has no way initially of knowing that his mother's (or his) face and voice are related in any direct sense.

Consider the mouth as a purely **visual** dynamic phenomenon, for the moment. Whatever the precise total relationship between speech and movement, there is no question that the mouth moves with, actually just preceding, speech. On examining the 'visual phonetics' of speech (akin to lip reading), it appears that the mouth is simpler, in the sense of having fewer easily differentiable positions or movement dynamics. For example, the mouth of most English speakers is pursed, the upper lips especially everted with essentially the entire class of palatal sounds. Phoneticians have indeed noted that high vowels are preceded or accompanied by relatively closed mouths and low vowels by more open mouths. Bilabial sounds involve mouth closings and openings; back vowels are **seen** as more rounded lips in English.

These movements are all 'exaggerated' in so-called baby talk – a special dialect used occasionally in many, if not most, languages for directly interacting with infants. Like mimesis, the notion of visual exaggeration is usually internalized but left undescribed. It consists principally of more-than-usually-tense lips, moving further; it may be slower than ordinary speech, but is certainly more *marcato*, the movements rapidly occupying the first part of the duration, leaving gaps or spaces in the dynamic. (Here, I can only analogize to the musical idiom.) It also appears that speech is more closely tied in to visible movements – i.e., it lags behind the lips by less of an interval than usual. It seems to be more evenly rhythmic, the 'line' being divided into more even event-moments than in ordinary speech. (To test this, imagine saying: "Baa, baa black sheep," to a young child.)

(7) The visual aspects of speech must be very **exciting** to an infant, especially as seen as occupying so much spatial figuration on the Brobdingnagian ground of the parental mask. It may very well be that this relatively limited silhouette of speech is the one which infants use as their first approximation to language. Recall that the first 'words' infants are universally said to 'speak' are bilabials; ba-ba, ma-ma, pa-pa; highly visual, vertical mouth movements accompanied by a relaxed tongue and vocalization. We parents interpret this composite as words and speech, and we presume that our infant does, also. It is just as likely, however, that the infant makes no such presumption (so it must be, except in 'mind' theories). At this point

in his development, all we can reasonably believe is that he is aware that his external and internal vocalization apparatus are to be considered as part of the same process. (Stated another way, the question might be: How and when does the infant come to know that his face moves while he vocalizes?)

Why do faces seem to be exciting, not merely interesting, to humans? Granted that faces are potentially rich sources of information about another person, and about ourself in the G. H. Meadian sense, why should bodies 'care' (Mead, 1943)?

A course of thought might be to ask about other visual aspects of being that seem also to be exciting, and to seek out which features we respond to. Although I hesitate to infer universality as my individual projection, it seems to me that fireworks, rockets, fire engines come close to being a humanoid 'turn-on'; practically any event which occupies a lot of visual ground rapidly with increased visual intensity — plus a lot of noise. These tend to be episodic events; bounded in space and time.

In the interactional *vis-à-vis,* the adult face seems to have many exciting features, especially viewed up close. Lips moving from a quiescent state to full open, to pursed; teeth flashing, tongue darting. A carefully watching infant, drawn to the vast change in observed lips, feeling his own lip muscles vibrating sympathetically, hears and feels a rapidly rising, seething noise, pulsing vaguely in time with the mouth changes. It stops. ... and begins again.

From this point of view, there is no strong reason to assume that the human infant knows about language in any direct pre-wired, innate sense. But it is necessary that he is strongly attracted to the perceived dynamic, and that he 'cares' about making it his own. He does this presumably by the muscular processes of mimesis, gradually coming to match what he sees, feels, and hears with what he does himself. Whatever the exact details, language learning appears to be a dynamic muscular interactional process.

If this is a useful perspective, a number of issues arise: how do 'normal' children become and stay normal? How do blind and deaf children learn 'language'? How much 'micro'-information is available in the face and speech dynamic; how much of this information do children and/or adults use — regardless of their awareness? How does a perceived dynamic become episodic or evented, and in what senses? Why has this perspective not arisen in a general approach to human behavior?

Within this context the most exciting event to humans is other humans. Through one's knowledge and interaction with other bodies, one gains a sense of himself and the external world. Does this approach allow us to observe language dynamics as an exciting event?

The amplitude of the voice is probably the most clearly body variable in speech. Beginning from silence, the voice can rise slowly or rapidly to great or lesser amplitude. If either the velocity of rise or the actual amplitude increases beyond some point (empirically discoverable?), most of us experience a severe bodily reaction, which we might be said to then interpret as "scaring the hell out of us!" The so-called 'angry' voice proceeds from a great deal of glottal tension and explodes to full amplitude. It is well-recognized across species as an 'alarm' call.

In 'ordinary' speech, the amplitude also is in constant variation. While adults tend to not be aware of the finely tuned control of amplitude (and tone), it is continuous and, in my opinion, both extremely subtle and studiable.[96] Although it has been given a highly restricted role in linguistic theory, or banished to paralinguistics, amplitude variation may be a major variable in interaction and in language learning. What we call 'clarity' may, for example, be a direct statement about amplitude control; the same may be true for frequency.

It is possible that the infant has some sort of inbuilt phoneme or distinctive feature recognition-analyzing device. But this is surely an adultocentric view. How do we know that a sound is that sound? Or is this even an important question in the context of studying interaction? It was pointed out a decade ago that whole words could be excised, even from out-of-context sentences, with little or no loss in intelligibility (Pollack and Pickett, 1964). Are sounds, or some sounds, inconsequential to understanding? What are the senses in which organisms try to understand one another?

How does a child come to know that a particular word is that word, when essentially every 'repetition' of it varies from all others in at least some respects? Presumably the 'formants' remain relatively constant, although the data base for this assertion remains out-of-context for the most part (Flanagan, 1965).

Each and every word spoken by humans is not merely or solely that word. It literally sounds different if spoken in various parts of sentences than it does 'in isolation'. It always occurs in a particular space and all spaces shape the wave form — the difference between males and females saying the 'same' word are acoustically great. The amplitude — which is likely to be the most apparent feature to infants — is related very directly to distance between interactants.

But what about the subtleties, the nuances of speech? Mood, person, audience, age, sex, 'type of person' (priest, professor, president ...), telephone, continuity – we hear them all, and must therefore have and use much better acoustical theories than acousticians do.

Sound is the disembodied vehicle for language! Sound keeps words apart – sound doesn't convey any information directly (in linguistic theory) which has to do with language. But these statements cannot illuminate since they're part of the explanatory device which assumes that language is a passive link whereby minds attempt to understand one another. And, I feel certain, these theories lend themselves to by-passing the necessity of life, as easily as the necessity to observe bodies as part of the human condition.

In ethological perspective, the question of how a child comes to 'know' that certain constant features of a (shaped) wave form are to be interpreted as a particular word remains an intriguing problem. It forces us, I believe, to a position of much greater respect for the entire human organism than is inherent in a view which sees the body as a circumstantial abode for its mind.

The fact is that we have only the barest glimmerings of how one person understands another – in terms of sound alone – and this fact should not remain obscured by traditional claims of what ears are, or sound is and is not.

(8) While appearing somewhat different, there appears to be no good explanation of how and why our bodies can relate to such **exciting** happenings as occur in sporting events ... to the extent that some people find themselves standing and cheering at home, watching sports events on television. And there seems to be little question that the 'porny' movies 'turn-on' a number of observers (or set a scene which people can 'use' to turn themselves on).

These observations suggest that our bodies are highly attuned to others' bodies – perhaps particularly to their rapid movements, and especially to deviations from 'normal' (our own?) states. But perhaps this is the sense in which we know what 'abnormal' is; i.e., that our own bodies find themselves forced to change or alter their images in ways that we label 'uncomfortable'. (But how does one's body come to its own ongoing homeostasis? – does the hoarse-voiced person 'know' about himself, or do we tell him as we respond to him?)

To extend this further into the realm of speculation, how is it that our bodies react to 'deviant' bodies in such interesting ways, often causing us to laugh or cry? Do we (involuntarily) try to create their infirmities in our own bodies and respond to our own failures as if loaded with affect.

Perhaps some extra-special extrapolation of this bodily propensity might shed some light on why we feel 'afraid' of some species; e.g., snakes. That is, do our bodies find it difficult and troubling to redo themselves into certain shapes? Possibly, the human ability to manage fires is related to our bodies; maybe we can begin to account for our 'humanism' by contrasting and comparing 'fears' in different species as related to their bodily organization.

(9) Eyes! Not only do they focus, but they are the 'windows into the soul'. Mutual eye gaze has received a good deal of attention with respect, at least, to the total effort of interactional study.

In body perspective, this curious fact may be stated in a slightly different way: eyes 'don't like' (?) to spend much time relating to one another! This seems to be true for lots of species, and those of us who try, feel that it is no more difficult to 'make' a dog, cat, or ape blink, than another conspecific.

Why is it that eyes find other bodies' eyes so sensitive to mutual eye contact? It's even true of nursing infants: If one moves his head in front of a (bottle) nursing infant and 'catches' the baby's eyes, the baby will either look away, or stop nursing and usually smile. (It's about as difficult to maintain even momentary eye contact with a hungry baby as with a jogger!?)

I suggest that the eyes are in constant motion in the sense of readjusting focus, and that mutual eye contact forces the inter-actants' eyes into a constant search for the very subtle dynamically varying focal plane(s) of the others' eyes. If they declare the 'staring game', children can stare at one another's eyes for a relatively long while – until it 'hurts' from dryness or from trying to balance a focus dynamic. And 'lovers' can stare – perhaps they are busy transfiguring each other's bodies, and the eyes diminish in interactional importance. It may also be that the dilation of female eyes during courting has to do with a 'willingness' to relax some of the eye focus movements.

I have noted that the ability to stare does increase with distance. After about 15 feet, it is a much less uncomfortable thing to do. In the context of teaching, especially, students in the back of the room can stare at the teacher for quite long periods – and it seems to be quite congruent with the situation.

Also, in the teaching context, I have noted that even a rapid 'fixation' – a momentary meeting of the eyes of teacher and each individual student – seems to **personify** the lecture. That is, the student seems 'forced', in some sense, to be more responsible for or to the course 'because' the lecture has been a one-to-one interaction. One or two such moments per class hour per person seems to have a notable effect. In my teaching experience, the rapidity which I can fixate on an entire 'array' of students has increased gradually to the point where it's very easy to do in classes of up to about 30, and can be done – with effort – in quite larger groups. Why this should have a strong apparent effect on the teaching/learning process might lead us to rethink at least some aspects of (human) vision.

(10) An uncanny ability of humans is memory of others' faces; taxonomizing them in dynamic completeness, for long periods. Many people seem to 'visualize' others principally as faces. But we do less well in distinguishing those faces with which we have less familiarity, apparently in some population senses: "**They** all look alike to me – and to mine!"

Perhaps we can infer that we attend carefully to the facial features of those who compose our surround; but how carefully, with what depth? Is this learned? Do different populations attend to very different aspects of faces?

To my knowledge, we don't yet know. Although most of us can and do distinguish male from female faces, there seems to be no careful accounting for what it is that we attend to. For this most usual and ordinary human ability, there is no adequate description. Why? My guess is that we are extremely bad (on-purpose) observers of these aspects of bodies which we use for our ordinary life-taxonomies. (My dentist complained that working on men's back molars was more difficult than on women's, apparently because most women 'hold' their lateral circum-oral muscles more loosely than do most men. Thus they can open their mouths wider – this is what we mean when we say, 'prettiness'?)

Is the ability to 'visualize' other faces and remember them of any deep importance to the problem of memory? Perhaps memory (and consciousness?) begins, at least, in one's ability to translate how others' faces represent their worlds into one's own body ... and brain.[97]

(11) Imaging? Obviously an individual/mind process? Upon reading Luria's "The Mind of a Mnemonist" (1968), one is struck with the visual imagery, layer upon layer of how the professional mnemonist

concentrated in remembering to remember to remember. Asking students in classes over the past year about: "What things were like?" — when they were, say, 8 or 9 years old — one is struck with the very common imagistic accounts of how they 'get into' such memories. The most usual picture was associated with either home or school, and they could proceed to 'remember' from there.

While I have no understanding of what this might mean, one striking factor in imagistic memory is that most people do not remember childhood in random access terms — rather they seem to have a way into the scene; once 'in', they seem to be able to visualize-imagine in apparently different ways or pictures. Similarly many colleagues report that they visually imagine (potential) audiences as they write, prepare, or review lectures.

In some cases, friends have reported difficulty in transferring images from one mode or locale to another. A co-student in a linguistics course many years ago, who spoke German natively only at home, had no 'accessible' German in the classroom. Some musicians I have asked find it difficult to talk 'about' their instrument unless they have it in hand. The carry-over of images from one context to another is clearly not a simple matter.

Yet, as pointed out earlier, we are extremely good at remembering faces, dynamic expressions of those we know well. I occasionally feel that I am still learning, at least comprehending more deeply, what some of my teachers said fifteen or more years ago. How is this possible?

It suggests to me that a lot of what is called memory is not exactly in one's 'head' or 'mind'. Perhaps it can be said to be located in interactional contexts; that in some, possibly deep sense, an individual really doesn't know or remember; what he 'carries' (words seem to be less than adequate here) is 'access' to the interactional scene. Possibly this is followed (in imagistic time?) by a 'personification' of 'how he would act' in that context. An example: I have asked a number of people how they (literally) place money in a salesclerk's hand when paying for a purchase. All have claimed not to know! But I have observed very few confusions or ambiguities occurring in such scenes. So they must **know**; but where, then, can that knowledge be said to be located? — in the two minds? in the interactions? Actually, most of my informants could easily 'visualize' themselves in such a scene and could (kinesthetically) **feel** the proper hand-arm position. In the 'memory' in their bodies, then?

A number of people who regularly do very concentrated work —

e.g., musicians, teachers who dialogue without notes, the mnemonist — report that such work is physically (as well as mentally) exhausting. Why? Does it take lots of (bodily) energy to utilize the brain? Or is the ability to do such work consistently (also) a bodily exercise? Perhaps all the necessary images are not stored (only) in the brain.

(12) Close your eyes — it is often much easier to 'visualize' images this way. Is this somehow paradoxical, or is it easier simply because so much ('real') visual input is eliminated?

Perhaps there is more to it, because imaging with eyes closed appears to be much more active than one might suppose. What seems to happen is that the closed eyelid actually presses **inward** upon the eye (stimulating it!), helping to create one's sense of visual image.

This — if true — suggests to me that our ability to create our own images in this active physical sense may be much more complete and subtle than we have thought possible.

It also suggests that blinking is more than an eye-moistening device. I have observed, for example, that shifting eye focus is almost always accompanied by a blink — if not, there is a sense of eye 'strain'. It is very difficult to maintain focus without blinking. Why? I know of no satisfactory answer to these questions.

Within a 'body' framework, one might postulate that eyelids act somehow as a locus of access information. One keeps or stores a lot of information-images of the sort, say, which enables him to 'remember to remember'. Perhaps we keep our attention-tenders in particular bodily locations. Rather than having to postulate a brain or mind which is operating and tracking on multiple levels simultaneously, it seems reasonable to propose that the brain operates primarily as an information switching center; not as the self-caused, self-knowing being which has to somehow constantly interpret its own interpretation, multiply regressed. No wonder it's powerfully tempting to posit a *homunculus.*

(13) What sorts of information or knowledge is possessed by one's 'dominant' hand, different from or 'more than' one 'keeps' in his other hand. (One begins to feel the existential thrust of free-willing minds saying: "Cut this out!") Having asked this question of a number of people, and not having found one who could analyze this most important (and apparently humanoid) difference, I felt forced to conclude that this sort of body-image information was so basic to one's being, that it was 'not available' for analysis (if one doesn't already know ...); perhaps it is simply a lack of vocabulary.

This problem leads one to an 'end around' approach. Lots of musicians, for example, have fairly direct access to what they do – much violin pedagogy (there is a large written literature extending back several centuries) is the teacher's analysis of what he himself does, demonstrating how to do it, and how to image it usefully (perhaps metaphorically). At any rate, violinists have two quite knowledgeable hands, but each operates successfully in extremely different domains.

A series of problems show up immediately in this context. One is coordination – the right (bowing) hand must just follow (in time) the left finger placement. In asking (here only a couple of) people about coordination problems, one of the 'perceptual' difficulties is that the musicians 'locate' the problem in the 'wrong hand'. One tends, say, to think of it as a left-hand problem, when the difficulty might lie in the right. This is also true of the dynamics (relative loudness and softness) – it's very difficult to keep one's left hand from pressing more firmly when the eyes see *forte*. But to play well, the left hand must become freed of this belief.

One has to 'assign' different techniques to various body parts. There are seven string and double-string combinations for violin bowing. One has to know where they are without looking, and with the right hand up to three feet away from the point where the bow actually contacts the string. In order to play well, one must 'feel' in his arm 'where' the movement primarily takes place and assign the various string bowings to arm locations. Most bowing assignations are, believe it or not, 'located' at various positions on the right upper arm and shoulder. It seems to me, that a lot of practice-makes-perfect is in reminding oneself about his own (metaphorical) bodily organization.[98]

This all suggests that in attempting to achieve any very deep understanding of human movement, in or out of interactional settings, we will be forced to learn much more about how we organize and know our own and others' bodies.

(14) Can there be said to be image centers in the body? A case was made for the eyelid being such a center or device. I suggest that all body surfaces which 'stick out' are possible loci for imaging.

Contemplate the tongue; Ask any dentist, and he will affirm that tongues clearly have a 'mind' of their own. Whatever else 'orality' may be, it is certainly a cognitive investigation of the universe by the tongue. The ability to articulate speech is the smallest function of tongue-dom. In addition the tongue distributes (the proper kind of) saliva and must manage it properly to even be able to speak. Management of saliva and speech are in some senses coterminous.

The tongue is no more a passive member in face-to-face inter-action than are the muscles of articulation. The English speaking tongue is in virtually continuous contact with the upper teeth or alveolar ridge; more important, it is delicately **tensioned**, pushing. In fact, this observation first arose in an oral biology seminar when the orthodontists pointed out that most malocclusion is effectively caused by 'tongue thrusting'.

One might suggest that the tongue is actively 'tracking' during interaction and might contribute to or be part of the mentation processes. In (13), I suggested that the interactional miming dis-cussed earlier is modeled 'incorrectly' by faces which are unable to copy another's face; e.g., Down's Syndrome.

The Down's/Mongoloid child who appears to have non-operant external facial muscles, and who will predictably be 'retarded', may be merely unable to use his tongue as others do. Professionals who work with such persons report that almost all of them speak similarly to one another. If the tongue has something to do with mentation, it is not surprising that they turn out to appear to be mentally 'defective'. But this form of so-called defect may not, in the first instance, be mental in the sense of an abnormal brain. Rather the apparent mental-mind defect may be seen as a problem in bodily interaction.

(15) This conceptualization of (some) mental 'defectiveness' as a problem in interaction leads to a reconsideration of the informative function of the face. Again the Down's Syndrome children who are visually diagnosable at birth provide a provocative example.

Apparently a great deal of information which parents seem to seek for and use is 'missing' on Down's faces. Since there is so little facial movement or accompanying color and tissue changes, the affective information which parents interpret as representing the actual state of the infant, is absent or severely reduced.

In interactional perspective, the effects of this are to make the infant's face appear to be less reliable and probably much less interesting than in the normal infant. This seems to reduce the level of parentally induced interaction and lead parents to assume that the child is less (internally) responsive to them.[99]

By spending less time, and quite probably from attempting to mimic adult faces without the full use of all the external facial muscles, the Down's child will not be able to become 'normal'. In fact, these children form the case paradigm caricature of facial **stupidity** which most of us seem to use as rough mental evaluators: mouth open, tongue down and exposed. This means directly that **we** interpret and judge the mental attributes as indicated on faces — as if faces directly represent mental powers. But the actual mental states of such people might be quite different in a variety of senses.

It seems useful to consider the following possibility: that Down's and many others, who we label as 'retarded', look like they do because in some senses they 'believe' that they look 'normal'. They attempt to 'get in tune' with their parents as much as any child — the aberrant result caused by their muscular/bodily inability to mimic properly; this, in turn, reducing and/or altering their parental inter-actions in such a way which effectively 'confirms' their beliefs and causes their faces to become (or remain) abnormal in the judgment of the community. Operating from 'false' assumptions, such children tend to misread, but in ways which they adjust to and find 'comfortable'.

Actually, a number of sub-adult and adult Down's persons do appear to look more like the general population. Many seem to have quite large brow ridges. I interpret this as their attempt to use or substitute 'head' muscles (parietal, occipital, etc.) for their missing facial muscles. Some of them seem to be able to do this pretty successfully. In the more successful cases, one feels that the sustained familial interactional effort with these persons must have been enormous (Hunt, 1966).

(16) About comfort: my Southern Mexican Tzotzil informant and close friend, Bal, having spent a great deal of time studying *Gringos* speaking English, commented several times that we must hold our tongues at the "top of our heads. How fatiguing that must be!" He tried holding his bilingual Tzotzil-Spanish tongue up to the alveolar ridge and reported vague distress feelings after about ten seconds. His usual interactional, listening tongue placement was on his mouth bottom, with the tongue tip tensioned against the soft tissue protrud-ing 'forward' below the bottom teeth.

But this vague feeling of discomfort arises in many other contexts as well. There are a variety of bodily positions whose shift or changes will provoke a sense of fatigue in a few seconds. This is clear to would-be musicians in small muscle movements — holding the violin is, for example, a ridiculous arm position. To maintain it for two or three hours is amazing. But it can be 'worked-up to' gradually.

There are also male-female body-holding or body-set differences which have been arrived at very gradually during development. The typical adult female pelvis thrust feels – on imitation – very 'peculiar'. Holding a cigarette 'like a woman', with the wrist held backward beyond about 30°, is also strange.

Trying to 'feel' Slavic or French or Indian requires one to reconstitute his mouth-holding muscles, and to literally alter one's appearance. And it causes discomfort!

The point of this is, I believe, that it demonstrates that we have organized our bodies in ways that become increasingly 'comfortable' and 'natural' to us. How did we come to that particular body organization which – upon change – causes us to feel uncomfortable? How do we (or did we as we grew up) maintain this essentially (body) **esthetic** view and what is its distribution by feature and population?

If, in a G. H. Mead view of interaction, we relate our faces (and bodies) to one another – are there mechanisms and limits to how we do this, which tie in the notion of discomfort suggested above? Does the sense or direction of mutual facial adjustment, say, place more constraints on the depth or quality of message interchange, or is there some 'intermediate' or 'neutral' mutual adjustment area which shapes the interaction?

If the old anecdote of married couples growing to look more alike contains any germ of truth, what are its structural dynamics?

Students report that some (usually 'effective') professors appear different in different settings. Assuming this is at least partially true, what might it mean? Does the person one appears to be, represent the teacher's adjustment to that particular scene, or are we dealing with some sort of illusion?

(17) In a body theory of interaction and being, there must be included an esthetic sense. The notion of body alteration being somehow uncomfortable must imply a sense of our being able and willing to judge alterations of our body (parts) as being relatively pleasureful or not (Cabanac, 1971).

Mind theories simply build-in a postulated pleasure-pain differentiation center, as well as a primary set of emotions. The body – in mind theories – is hardly more than a locus for the end organs which are sensately responsive to stimuli, which are thence passed to the CNS-mind loci for interpretation.

While I know of no well worked-out counter theories to that innatist-mind presumption, it is probably worth suggesting how some alternative theories might be conceptualized. Two sorts of ideas may be considered: 1. That, say, the 'body' tends to regard as 'pleasureful' those stimuli which are transmitted or move primarily 'along' (the fewest number of) surfaces — stimuli which may be said to 'cause' pain are those which move 'across' effective surface boundaries. Also important here must be the effective amplitude of the stimulus and its temporal dimension. Tickling, for example, is an **interactional** event which is usually interpreted as pleasureful until it begins to involve 'deeper tissues', and begins to be perceived as 'hurting'. 2. That the external body surfaces (such as the face and eyes) being (we assume) in a continuous tensioned dynamic somehow are sensitive to external stimuli in such a way that they form some sorts of representation of the external world — what we call perception would then be our (second order?) reading and interpretation of our bodies' representational configurations.

One could imagine, for example, that the human eye is itself effectively a many-layered organ. The eye, say, forms a 3-dimensional representation of the 'external' world by 'choosing' certain of these 'layers' for primary focus. Very likely one 'chooses' these foci analogously to how he chooses to speak like he does (which might help account for why myopia has its peculiar distributions!). 'Seeing' would then be a second-order reading not of the external world, *per se*, but of our eyes' representation of it. This notion might also help to account for why one-eyed people can operate as if they 'see depth'; why staring is so difficult; and it might enhance the reasonableness of reopening questions about why we blink.[100]

(18) If the 'emotions' are capable of being conceptualized in a body theory, they must be susceptible of shaping and structuring in the context of interaction.

How can we be said to read (correctly) 'tension' or 'fear' in another's body? We could be responding to his facial expression; somehow matching some mosaic in our mind with what we believe we are seeing. Or, in body theory, our bodies could be said to be attempting — in the interaction — 'to get in tune' with one's interactant. One then interprets one's own body's attempted representation of another's mood or emotional state. This theory begins to account for how it might be that some people become especially 'sensitive' (I don't think one can account for this in a mind theory!) and others not so sensitive; why we seem often to read badly or misinterpret across all kinds of human boundaries (age, language, sex ...). And it may even be able to begin to account for why it might be that we do seem to change through 'experience' – hopefully it may also lend understanding to why we are resistant to experiential change in many circumstances.[101]

To extrapolate even further, a body theory of being might even be used to understand some of the dynamics of speciation; it may be, for example, that our bodies find it difficult to respond to bodies which are in whatever senses, quite different from ours. It seems very easy for most of us to empathize, e.g., sexually and parentally with other species; but it seems to be extremely difficult to 'feel' like any four-legged creature in terms, say, of maintaining balance or running.

(19) What 'feels good'? Vanity, power, success ... Olympic gold medalists all report that winning 'feels' great. In what senses do these feel good so that people will devote all their energies to their enhancement? Are these any different from any other 'addiction'?

What feels bad? Depression, fear, horror ...! But some people find horror movies and stories titillating. Why do most kids like ghost stories?

Of those states of being which feel good, many have a high degree of interactional input – they involve others, bringing 'positive attention' to one. 'Famous' people 'walk famous'. Spencer Tracy is reported to have been able to demonstrate this.

Sickness feels bad; hurts 'hurt'; pain **is** pain. But these are all said to be individual, private.

Assuming all of these human feelings to be bodily in some sense, how might we formulate some ways of thinking about them which might lend some insight into their nature. In mind theories, it appears, these states of being are not deeply explicable except possibly in a descriptive sense.

Most long-term, committed joggers report that jogging also makes them feel good. Here, at least, some observations can be offered. Sheer movement becomes a joy to joggers; their energy level (if they don't overdo jogging) rises; their bodies become and remain 'tight'. I think they feel their total bodies much more completely, and mainly they feel good. So the feelings have something to do with maintaining certain degrees of **tension** in various body parts, of having 'command'. My guess is that this also somehow enhances one's ability to control whatever it is that feels good. And, I suspect, a lot of it has to do with being able to avoid a lot of what feels 'bad'.

Talking about these 'feelings' is obviously difficult. But that should not stop us from continuing to study and describe the (apparent) bodily changes with the variety of reported feelings. Much of this is in the arena of 'body image' and good and bad feelings must be, in some sense, a derivation of or deviation from an expected-desired set of feelings. It might be, for example, that obese people have difficulty in lower weight maintenance because they retain the essential feelings of themselves as fat people – instead of retraining themselves to 'think thin' which includes a necessary self-feeling of 'discomfort' upon eating 'too much'.

'Tension' seems to mean truly that the body is tenser than usual – who can tell if 'minds' direct or cause bodies to become tense; or if a tenser body is interpreted by one's 'mind' as, say, a 'headache', or an arthritic pain. How do people constitute their bodies to enhance good feelings, to avoid 'damaging' it?

(20) Congruence and Context – a major difficulty in describing bodily or vocal variation with situation or context – as **insiders** – is that we apparently are 'contextually appropriate' observers. What we tend to note is unexpected, incongruent, or unusual facial expressions. This places us in an observational position in which we seem likely to confirm our own normalcy, rather than to note variation. 'Natural history' recording of movements, no matter how carefully done, can do little more than to make us better micro observers; it can yield little new insight or lead us to observe the range of possibilities which do **not** occur (but might have) in any situation.

A first attempt to become better observers is to 'break context' – e.g., take a tape of a half-hour interview; cut, splice in a variety of orders, and listen to the same voice as it ranges over a variety of topics, mood shifts, and interactional changes. There is much more variation, and of more different kinds, than one ever 'hears' just listening straight through. So we must be contextually-tied observers.

Other correctives – in trying to become better observers – is to keep in mind how other species might hear us, non-native speakers of our language hearing it for the first time, how it sounds 'through' a closed door. If it seems rhythmic, say, in any sense analogous to music, it is useful to study the mechanics of musical production.[102]

At any rate, I believe that there is much more in the voice stream – especially in interaction – than linguistic theory has begun to suggest. It appears to be studiable if we can learn to become much better observers of the 'knowing body'.

In contrast to current linguistic theory, I believe that the sound stream can and does convey **meaning**: about the situation, the relationship, about continuity, context, and a multitude of social and temporal variables. The obstruction to reconceptualization has been in linguistic's claims that a phonemic description of language has been **exhaustive**. A critical reading of modern linguistic theory will reveal, I believe, that sound is as incidental to language as bodies are to minds!

NOTES

[1] The use of parentheses surrounding (*other*) ... *animals*, is maintained throughout to remind us that the status of man-as-animal is what must remain open to questions and to debate.

[2] [Yet] "It is a curious paradox that the greatest gifts of man, the unique faculties of conceptual thought and verbal speech... . All the great dangers threatening humanity with extinction are direct consequences of conceptual thought and verbal speech. They drove man out of the paradise in which he could follow his instincts with impunity and do or not do whatever he pleased" (Lorenz, 1966: 230).

[3] This statement is taken from several years of personal experience in defending my position concerning the possible comparisons between human and nonhuman verbal utterances. The response, particularly from academic philosophers and linguists, is that they are *a priori* noncomparable, as different as one can imagine. I merely asked — perhaps too insistently — how they knew that; how could they possibly know that?

Having done a fair amount of homework, having been a field linguist, having listened to animal behaviorists discussing their work on animals, I have been suspicious that the certitude about human languages being especially unique rests on grounds which are not merely intellectual, but are part of many peoples' views about the human condition.

Who is so uncertain about humans being unique that he must rule out such comparative efforts as being doomed to failure?

Who must defend the sanctity of human language by **accusing** its questioners of being nonserious or simply irrational?

[4] From a modern biologist's point-of-view, all species are unique — by definition. But who can say that man is more unique or extra-natural than any other species — why, by 'language'? Attempts to specify degrees of uniqueness are rapidly beset with all sorts of definitional and perspectival arguments.

What I am attempting to do is to remind us that humans are unique, but that we cannot discover the areas of uniqueness by **defending** a particular historical view about humans. The methods for becoming more objective about our behavior must remain broadly comparative and open. The 'origin of language' problem is neither open, nor is it comparative, as will be shown in the rest of this essay.

[5] Ernst Cassirer spells out the history of this issue with great care, pointing out that a great number of issues reflect themselves in the context of being human and having language (1955). In general, it has been assumed that man was both nonlanguaging and nonsocial prior to his 'possessing' language. It was

language which he obtained first: This, in turn, enabled him to communicate
with and to understand others of his own kind. In this sense, the history of the
'origin of language' problem is the attempt to account for how nonlanguaging,
nonsocial creatures might have 'discovered' language.

The view that humans were likely to have evolved as (already) social
creatures suggests that 'language' is quite possibly a very different 'thing' than
we have believed it to be. Much of my own work has been an attempt to point
out some of the aspects of human languaging which have been overlooked within
the current construction of the nature of language.

[6] Beginning most clearly with Spinoza, and the gradual development of
existential — as opposed to essentialist — thought, the human body has indeed
'reappeared' as an aspect of human nature, after Plato attempted quite successfully to 'hide' and suppress it.

My position is that social beings are in constant contact with the forms,
particularly the faces, of other humans. The very formulation of one's being
(e.g., how one 'looks') is dependent on how significant others imagine one
looks and treat him within that particular dynamic vision. I have attempted to
extend G. H. Mead's (1934) ideas to include the presence of what Mead took to
be an arena of symbolic interaction.

[7] Again, it was Plato who set the issues in the form that they presently appear
common-sensically to us. The 'mental' uniqueness of man is clearly constructed
in the dialogue Phaedo.

"In this present life, I reckon that we make the nearest approach to knowledge when we have the least possible intercourse or communion with the
body, and are not surfeited with the bodily nature, but keep ourselves pure until
the hour when God himself is pleased to release us" (112).

The underlying politics are portrayed in the "Republic" where the famous
'philosopher-kings' idea is drawn out (431). The argument is developed by an
extensive definition of what the ideal philospher is, or ought to be, and sub-
stantiates the claims of the philosopher-kings-to-be of possessing an ideal/absolute
form of political wisdom. A number of persons currently seem to be in the
running for this mythical office:

"Until philosophers are kings, or the kings and princes of this world have the
spirit and power of philosophy, and political greatness and wisdom meet in
one, and those commoner natives who pursue either to the exclusion of the
other are compelled to stand aside, cities will never have rest from their evils —
no, nor the human race, as I believe — and then only will this our State have a
possibility of life and behold the light of day" (431).

The reason language plays a prominent part in politics is that language is what
has been assumed to make man 'rational'. In Plato's view, the 'philosopher' is
man at his most rational. And man must be rational to know, understand, and
follow 'rules'; a *sine qua non* for the governance of a 'proper' Republic. One's
body and feelings can only muck up a clear, cool mind.

Perhaps what we are really discussing is: whose views of human nature should
we believe? on what grounds?

[8] The history of ideas, given these assumptions, is a development of what
happened. As particular problems arose, certain 'solutions' were considered to
be inadequate, others were proposed, became common-sensical, and so on. The
sociology of knowledge in this arena has to do with the tension and dialectic
between prevailing opinion, new solutions to old problems, who agreed or

disagreed with whom, and why particular solutions no longer (in any era) 'sold' in the intellectual or public opinion marketplace. In fact, this polemic arises presently because there is now a great deal of flux in the ideas of those (all of us) concerned with human nature; quite possibly there is more uneasiness at present about the human condition than in any other period.

[9] "And when real philosophers consider all these things, will they not be led to make a reflection which they will express in words something like the following? 'Have we not found', they will say, 'a path of thought which seems to bring us and our argument to the conclusion, that which we are in the body, and while the soul is infected with the evils of the body, our desire will not be satisfied, and our desire is of the truth? For the body is a source of endless trouble to us by reason of the mere requirement of food; and is liable also to diseases which overtake and impede us in the search after true being: it fills us full of loves, and lusts, and fears, and fancies of all kinds, and endless foolery, and, in fact, as men say, takes away from us the power of thinking at all. Whence come wars, and fightings, and factions? Whence but from the body and the lusts of the body? [...] The body is always breaking in upon us, causing turmoil and confusion in our enquiries, and so amazing us that we are prevented from seeing the truth' " (Phaedo: 120-1).

In the Cartesian form of this argument: "Thought is an attribute that belongs to me, it *alone* is inseparable from my nature" (Descartes: Meditations, p. 26). He attempted also to banish the body from being through his 'method of doubt', and claimed that our bodies are like the bodies of (other) animals. He set up the possibility, reified currently by Chomsky (1966), of language being the locus or entry into the essential, unique aspect of human nature, the human mind.

[10] Whitehead has attempted to make time on ongoing process rather than a mere attribute of being (1929). I agree with his position on the nature of being-as-process. However, he does not deal with the sociality of man, and its implications, as his is "A Philosophy of the Organism".

[11] "Phonetic animal expressions convey, almost without exception, subjective situations and aspirations. They are affective sounds which seldom tend to become objective designations or denominations. They express the idea of immediate time only, of a present situation or one which will occur in the immediate future. They cannot express abstract ideas which are unconnected with organic behaviour" (Busnel, 1963: 69).

These statements do not necessarily have anything to do with (other) animals. They merely follow from the uniqueness assumptions about humans; (other) animals and (human) bodies are assigned the 'leftovers'; a mere embellishment of Aristotle:

"The animals other than man live by appearances and memories, and have but little of connected experience; but the human race lives also by art and reasonings" (Metaphysics 980b, 25).

[12] If human reason-language 'raises' us to a point where we are extra-natural in some sense, then an area of enquiry appears, in which the 'fundamental' or 'real' nature of man seems open to dispute. As I point out later, Lorenz *et al.* have entered this apparent arena of study, with strong claims of knowing the true and underlying nature of man. The argument is forceful, but is accompanied and/or motivated by an ideology which, one suspects, is theo-political, and not purely scientific (Lorenz, 1966).

[13] "For the body which is moved from without is soulless, but that which is

moved from within has a soul, for such is the nature of the soul. But if this be true, must not the soul be the self-moving, and therefore of necessity unbegotten and immortal?" (Phaedrus, p. 286, also sees the "Phaedo", especially the introductory comments on the philosopher's proper concerns with death.) Is the 'origin of language' problem a theory of life?

[14] If Descartes' *cogito ergo sum* is considered carefully, it claims that each individual exists via thinking and language. But the problem of possibly understanding others remains a dilemma in this construction of the 'problem'. In the tradition of Plato-Descartes, the problem of 'communication' does not even arise, and language has a purely autonomous existence (Chomsky, 1968). For others (e.g., Cassirer), language enables communication; but, how it does remains unclear and will continue to do so, in my view. Scholars engaged in the 'origin of language' problem represent both of these views and talk 'past one another', because their underlying assumptions about the nature of language, and consequently of man, are different with respects to the nature and locus of 'mind'.

[15] While the notion of (human) consciousness seems intuitively correct, and self-evident, claims that (other) animals do not possess it, or are not 'conscious' or 'self-conscious', might direct one to rethink its nature. Just as language, the nature of consciousness is arguable, even though modern Psychology claims to be studying it (Miller, 1962). Instead, I have suggested that it may be a useful exercise to consider consciousness as: "the ability and willingness of an individual to cue in on a shared, multi-person picture of the world when it is situationally appropriate."

[16] My objections include a number of ideas which are developed in this essay. However, some of them have been argued only in others and will be left as simple statements here.

[17] For a journalist's review of the 1972 Animal Behavior Symposium, a debate with R. Allen Gardner, opposing P. Marler and N. Geschwind, see Linden, *Apes, Men and Language* (1975: pp. 240ff).

[18] There will, I suppose, always remain a question of whether nonhuman animals have any socially meaningful idea of what 'significant' might mean but, as we will see, most people who engage in the boundary disputes about human nature constantly are working for ways to preserve human uniqueness and will use any available method. Anyone who is so confused about human uniqueness as to have to defend its boundaries is hardly in a position to be objective about the language origin problem: often merely a metaphor about exactly those human-animal boundaries. Most of those who wish to 'protect' the uniqueness of man via the concept of language are responding to an 'inner urge' which has to do with politics, theology, and usually both (Adler, 1967).

[19] The Psychology of Development continues to be concerned with mind-body dualism in a way which parallels and virtually caricatures the 'origin of language' issue. The question which is generated by Piaget *et al.,* is how a 'biological-reflex creature' comes to be rational. I suggest that there is a potential Anthropology of Development in which it is obvious that children turn out to be mostly like their parents and families and communities.

'Rationality' is, in my view, some sort of statement about adultocentric views of themselves and the world. It is what the 'normal' community agrees is rational. The confusion is between the nature of growing up to be 'rational' vs. becoming 'adult'. Since rationality as a social process is not *a priori* delimited, the proposed Anthropology of Development is potentially a comparative discipline, while the Psychology of Development is not and cannot be comparative except within the confines of a particular definition of rationality. In a deep sense, the 'problem' is exactly about such a definition, and 'language' is merely a cover term for it.

[20] The use of the term 'speech' to designate what (other) animals utter verbally is opposed to 'language'; i.e., what humans supposedly do. The term 'speech', used this way, is merely an icon for the 'origin of language' problem. It has no basis in fact and is used, in my experience, to stifle discussion.

[21] Those who claim to study animal 'calls' have fallen into the thinking mode of animals-as-deficient-humans, without any clear acknowledgment of it. Marler's elegant exposition of the nature of (other) animals' 'calls' is a thought construction of humans about other animals, and it is irrefutable in its own terms:

"In animals the tendency is ... to pack as much information as possible into single, indivisible signals. Thus a bird alarm call is at once a symbol for a predator and a directive to escape. The 'rough grunting' of chimpanzees announces the discovery of food and also invites others to come and share. This incorporation of noun and verb function in the same indivisible signal greatly limits the possibilities of syntactical rearrangement of signals to create new messages" (Marler in Stokoe, 1975).

The 'callists' seem to have already decided that (other) animals do not have 'language'. Marler's definition of calls is merely an irrefutable way to defend this earlier decision. Once he has decided 'calls' are 'indivisible' (on what possible grounds?), he is free to go ahead and do what he wants with them.

My diagnosis of callists' thinking is that they have already assumed a simpler-than-human basis for (other) animals. They have made a jump in thinking to suggest that these calls are unitary and about behavior which tends to be **innate** [part of the notion of (other) animals as 'simple']. Calls are thus semantic but in the sense of the very limited 'intelligence' which humans are willing to impute to (other) animals.

In fact, on inspection of an oscilloscopic display of human and nonhuman 'utterances', human sentences and animal 'calls' do not appear very different. How have Marler *et al.*, **decided** they are indivisible? How did he conclude that animals' 'incorporation of noun and verb function in the same indivisible signal greatly limits the possibilities ... to create new messages'? I believe it had to have been decided in advance (see: Plato's *Protagoras* for an earlier version of the same story). It may or may not characterize (other) animals' verbal output — who knows?

My ultimate objection to the callists' thinking is that, by tending to over-simplify (other) animals, it has a parallel tendency to affect how we imagine humans to be. That is, the 'human nature enterprise' is never separable from the characterization of (other) animals. Statements such as Marler's (above) must be examined very carefully — not only for their basis in fact, but for their implications and entailments.

[22] One of the most fascinating aspects of studying (other) animals in their natural settings is that it is usually clear that we watch moving bodies. The fact that most behavioral scientists in the laboratory miss or dismiss the fact of bodies' moving is astounding to me. Of course, the idea that human language provides a direct route into the human mind assists us in this most current annotation to Plato's banishment of time, the body, and, I suspect, the possibility of new knowledge about the human condition (Chomsky, 1968).

[23] The 'origin of language' problem tends to urge a sense of human language which is autonomous; language *per se*. Thence, it is an easy jump to study 'language' (by whatever definition is 'selling') as if it represents totally that which is uniquely and distinctly human.

[24] A great deal of the discussions around this issue have to do with the issues of change and continuity; Thus the earlier discussion of time and language. I suggest as an overarching strategy that we ought to assume change and attempt at all moments to account for (apparent) stability.

This thinking strategy has a number of advantages: (1) it will force us to examine what we mean by 'ideal' or 'normal' essentialist modes of behavior; it provides an existential antidote to the Platonic propensity to 'fix' time; (2) it will force us to take certain aspects of the human condition (e.g., aging), and examine whether they are attributes of being or consequences of being social; (3) etc.

[25] If one looks beneath the surface of the theories of many ethologists, one may begin to note how heavily animal communication work is influenced by a 'mentalist' orientation, particularly when it comes to interpreting (other) animals' behavior. The intellectual shift which they (particularly Lorenz *et al.*) are attempting, is to take intellective functions and show that some/most are nonplastic, not susceptible to learning or other forms of change, thus innate-genetic in some deep sense. It must be admitted that Darwin's *Expression of the Emotions* ... sets up this possibility by assuming that the 'emotions' are inborn. It is no exaggeration to suggest that the 'calls' of the modern animal behaviorist are akin to Darwin's 'emotions' (Ekman, 1975).

It is not, however, sufficient to assume that the 'emotions' are inbuilt, or even that we have direct access to knowledge about them. In the history of ideas, they have been left in a kind of 'no man's land' between body (animal) and mind (human) to be used as a convenient residuum whenever dualist mind-body theories are seen to be at impasse.

In fact, many ethologists 'describe' (other) animal movement with very little sense for how they move, from a kinesiological perspective. Most could not, for example, distinguish a 'balance-maintaining' movement from a 'gesture'. Even 'careful' descriptivists, operating from a mentalist-dualist conceptual frame-work can 'disembody the body' while claiming to describe it.

[26] The field of human facial expression is part and parcel of the 'origin of language' problem. If one assumes, as does Ekman, following Darwin's *Expression* ... that the face merely expresses a set (2, 5, 8, ... 1,000,000?) of inborn emotions, the problem of understanding facial expression is to separate the observed expressions into their 'components'.

It seems, to me, however, that this view is a consequence of the 'origin of language' issue: by oversimplifying (other) animals, we tend to see man as intrinsically simple.

In my view, man and (other) animals must be assumed to be complex — else we will not even see what there is to see. That is, the observer who is — in his mind's eye — prepared to see or to sort, say, eight categories of behavior, will not continue to grow in his observational capacities. Most behavioral scientists claim, in defense of simple-mindedness, that one cannot handle the enormous complexity I believe to be there, then they want to simplify at all moments; for the sake of 'management' and 'control'. In order for observers to get better at their trade, they must be prepared to 'see more' at all moments. This is, in my experience, true of any complicated skill, where mere practice is not sufficient to achieve increasing skill. (Here, I speak as a violinist.)

The human face remains poorly described — both in terms of its surface and of its underlying tissues (Oyen, 1974).

[27] The visual aspects of human behavior — and for that matter tactile, olfactory, taste, kinesthetic — have also not appeared very prominently in human language theories. Vision is around — as a sort of enabler, in the knowing of space, the external objective world. But it tends to have been excluded when we think of language. Interestingly, the other 'senses' seem not even to be around when it comes to ideas about language: who has studied sentences as smell; touch, and the adjectives?

[28] Personal communication: Burton Shapiro, D.M.D., Ph.D. Chairman, Department of Oral Biology, University of Minnesota.

[29] It may be stretching the point to suggest that mentation does not occur (as far as I can tell) with an untensioned tongue. At this very moment, the reader or hearer may note that the incredulity he may feel about this argument is as surely in his tongue, as in his mind. It is also worth pointing out that people with peculiar tongues and/or peculiarly shaped internal mouths are likely to appear 'retarded' to most of us!

[30] The claims that man's mind is 'creative and infinite' is part and parcel of the 'origin of language' problem. It is, in one sense, merely another way of proclaiming man's uniqueness. Its theological relationships are clear: one has only to glance at the development of St. Thomas Aquinas' thought to watch the mind become the soul, using the argument of the presumed 'infinitude' of language.

If man is infinite because he was constructed in the image of God, it follows directly that (other) animals must be 'finite', at least for the dualist.

The 'creativity' argument is similar and claims that man (alone) is not tied down by his instincts. But this follows also from the notion of unboundedness which infinity presumes. (Other) animals are bounded, unfree in their 'thought'. It should be noted, in these particular forms of the 'problem', that theology and politics tend to merge with great ease and little notice; subtle and slippery.

[31] In my view, so-called 'retarded' persons are not necessarily intellectually 'inferior' to us 'normals'. In fact, it is the thinking which pervades the origin of language, which leads us to think of them as deficient, more animaloid, thus stupider. We tend to apply this thinking to all the 'less-civilized' peoples of the world, the 'primitives' who have appeared to be intermediate between man and beast.

Having observed mothers' interacting with several infant mongoloids (Down's Syndrome), I have several puzzles concerning the nature of 'retardation'. It is a case where the perception of 'different faces' leads us to believe that their minds are different and defective as well. But, if one is treated as if he is stupid or crazy by other persons, it would be difficult to determine whether the differences were due to inherent stupidity (e.g., brain 'damage'), or to how we tend to interact with persons whose appearance is 'strange'. How do people get to look like they do?

[32] Many modern linguists have been moving to the study of 'semantics', away from 'syntax'. Their error remains that they consider language to have some sort of autonomous existence. In the swinging intellectual pendulum — language and thought — we are moving rapidly toward the primacy of thought, language being how thoughts are expressed.

A detailed analysis of language, as it is presently conceptualized, cannot possibly yield more than a set of directions on where and when to observe social interaction. Language is a process, not an entity. But our techniques of linguistic analysis have been attempts to 'fix' time; not to account for how we might understand one another in the ongoingness of life. The 'body' of language has been as effectively banished from the study of verbal communication as the body of man and woman has been from the study of human nature.

Since thought construction obviously determines what we see, to an amazing extent (if the origin of language problem is any example) more observation is not the answer. In my view, the conceptualization of language (human or other) has been afflicted by the need to probe those aspects of speech which we believed to be uniquely human. This has always led to minimal theories about human language and tends toward an oversimplification of the human condition, especially in politically pessimistic eras such as the present.

The dignity and uniqueness of man do not require defense, they demand understanding. The 'origin of language' problem cannot lead us to an increase of understanding, but will always tend to push us into the political-theological framework which underlies the formulations of 'the problem'.

[33] People, speakers of language X, actually embody such distinctions. The idea of a language existing independently of speakers of it is a seductive, but very limited, concept. Language, to me, is a kind of collective statement about the fact that a lot of people share almost identical muscular habits, conceptual frameworks, understandings. The distinctions made 'in a language' are really in the habits and/or minds of a set of people who all speak in about the same way.

[34] This phenomenon was earlier accommodated under the rubric of 'juncture'. I think that a more dynamic view of language behavior would suggest that we pay more attention to these momentary changes. They seem to be patterned and studiable, conveying a great deal of potential information about what's to come, the structure in which the words are embedded, etc.

[35] This paper is only one among several which have been concerned with the relationship between language and evolution. Among the most outstanding previous writers concerned with this area are C. F. Hockett and Eric Lenneberg. Hockett (1964) assumes a unique man and hunts for differences in human and animal languages. This approach generally follows and extends prevailing beliefs. Lenneberg (1960) suggests that language is an important part of the evolutionary process — that genetics, in effect, does not stop at birth and is not purely biological in the usual senses. This paper agrees fairly closely with Lenneberg, but attempts to extend the restricted concept of language to a more general interactional-communicational framework.

[36] In this connection it would be very informative to have a systematic comparative study between groups of hunters and gatherers and similar groups of primates.

[37] It seems quite predictable that animal communication specialists who make the 'sudden leap' assumption will now begin to look for physiological and/or anatomical differences between man and other animals. Differences will be 'attributed to' symbolic or language abilities or 'account for such'.

[38] Research in this area is being conducted at Western Psychiatric Institute and Clinic, Pittsburgh, Pennsylvania. A slow-motion research film of a sleeping four-day-old was made by Dr. Donald J. Coleman. Parts of this film were carefully analyzed by Marilyn R. Cummings and Davyd Greenwood under my direc-

tion. Dr. Coleman plans to continue intensive work in this area. Those methods should, of course, be extended to infants of other species.

[39] Western Psychiatric Institute and Clinic, University of Pittsburgh, Pittsburgh, Pennsylvania (1962-66).

[40] Reviewed in V. C. Wynne-Edwards (1962).

[41] Personal observations in research on dynamics of spatial relationships in interaction.

[42] This line of argumentation was first presented to me by Ray L. Birdwhistell in a course of Kinesics at the University of Buffalo, 1959.

[43] In Buffalo, the upper lip appears essentially incapable of vertical movement and the upper teeth are rarely seen. In San Bartolome, the upper lip is raised when beginning speech, and then held fixed, with continuous upper teeth display. In both places, the upper lip tends to become very thin and essentially disappears in middle age.

[44] Mischa Penn, Personal Communication, 1967-68.

[45] The **assumption** – a counter-productive one from my point of view – is that the equation of Man:Language – Animal:Signaling System is part of an undercurrent in linguistics. The Scholars who are most involved in the origin of language are also interested in very basic questions concerning man's nature, including his **moral** nature.

[46] Act Psychology – an assumptive position concerning the nature of human behavior; i.e., that behavior is only broken up into discrete or particulate events. Behavior is then 'put together' from these units or atoms in some manner. The most cogent voices of the thirties and forties argued for the necessity of dealing with a serial or lineal ordering of events (Lashley, 1951) – whereas Chomsky's possibly most important contribution to theory is to argue that an underlying set of 'rules' can operate fairly independently of any order (Chomsky, 1959: 56). The major difficulty in working at any act psychology involves the 'selection' or 'discovery' of event boundaries. Most methodologies have defined event or domain boundaries essentially by consensus or foolproof verifiability criteria, while doing actual observing. If much of human behavior is 'eventized' (and there is every reason to think that it is – **partially**) then the form and organization should be part of a procedure which attempts to build models with observational experience, not prior to that experience. The inherent 'on-off' nature of speech or absence of speech lends itself too easily to an act model which (unfortunately) regards each speech **act** as an independent unit. Communication is then taken to be the exchange of speech acts between two speakers. The usefulness of this procedure for naturally occurring systems is highly questionable. Clearly any behavioral stream can be described in an infinitude of ways, but if there are rules of organization, by which we behave, only a very few descriptions will be generalizable to our behavior. I believe, after several years of close observation of verbal and nonverbal behavior, that we are merely beginning in this endeavor.

[47] This is a good example of how particular assumptions lent themselves to procedural priorities. Helmholtz **first** wanted to study the nature of his units and **then** 'whole sounds'. If his assumption is either wrong or only partially descriptive, it might well detract from more general insights and procedures, even as its methods and instrumentation have become more exact and professional. This is, according to Mol (1963), very likely the actual case in the history of the study of speech acoustics.

[48] Summer 1959 in Taos, New Mexico with George L. Trager; 1960-62 in Southern Mexico with Norman A. McQuown. One of the most unfortunate effects of the antidescriptivist Chomsky school of the past decade has been the loss of an extensive field work, interviewing-observation tradition. In dealing with a live unsophisticated informant who speaks an unknown language, the field linguist is forced to deal with a much wider range of problems — verbal, grammatical, and many others — than a formal analyst. Granted that many problems were never solved or even adequately handled by the field linguist, he was at least aware of them as problems and not as liable to opt for reductionist theories, methods, or solutions as is the 'pure' linguist.

[49] Herbert L. Pick, Personal Communication (Institute of Child Development, University of Minnesota, 1968).

[50] Whereas most dynamic signals are symmetrical (with respect to 'zero' or some reference point) and vary principally in amplitude and frequency, or component waves, vocal language varies in most complex manners. The bulk of the signal is related directly, in most cases, to the distance between speaker and listener; but the number and kinds of variables in any actual speech situation have not been specified, except as they were assumed to be peripheral to the speech signal (Trager, 1958).

[51] We are presently carrying out a study which takes tapes of a person talking to several others in the attempt to see (1) if listeners can detect the type of person the listener is, or is not; (2) the relationship between speaker and listener; and (3) the size of the room, and try to characterize and generalize these differences around a more general study of sound in context (Benjamin, 1969).

[52] While I studied with them at the University of Buffalo, 1957-58.

[53] At Western Psychiatric Institute and Clinic, Department of Psychiatry, University of Pittsburgh (1962-66), we spent a great deal of time working on the verbal (and nonverbal) portion of filmed interaction.

[54] A number of recent psycho-acoustic studies strongly suggest that there is an underlying structure to ongoing speech which aids in the 'perception' of contextual information (e.g., I. Pollock and S. M. Pickett, "Intelligibility of Excerpts from Fluent Speech: Auditory vs. Structural Context", *J. Verbal Learning and Verbal Behavior*, 3: 79-84, 1964). A more recent comprehensive review of this area of study can be found in J. L. Flanagan, *Speech Analysis, Synthesis, and Perception* (Springer-Verlag, 1963), esp. #7.5: 236-238.

[55] See, for example, Pittenger, Hockett, Danehy, *The First Five Minutes* (Ithaca, Paul Martineau, 1960).

[56] The use of the word-phoneme a/ey/ is fortuitous. Any monosyllable could serve as well, but a is a common symbolic term in the English-speaking world and is less complicated than, say, x/eks/.

[57] A 35mm camera, attached to the oscilloscope, took each a separately. Then the five photos from each sentence were reproduced as a set. Figure I is a set of drawings made from contact prints of these. Thus the distance between each a is not meaningful. In a few cases (e.g., 1.4), parts of two words were accidentally photographed together and appear as a complex. This is easily checked by comparing a 'double-display' with the preceding and following words to see which one is the same. In the case of 1.4, the ultimate word is repeated. The speed of the display is about 30 ms/division or about 30 cs per photo; this can be made precise, but is altered for ease and usefulness of observation.

[58] These pictures are copied from actual size, polaroid prints of stored displays. They were made at a speed of 5 ms (½ cs) per vertical division (5 cs across the entire photo). The advantage of the stored display is in seeing the part of the word which is to be photographed. The only way to see an entire word spread out to see the individual 'spikes' is through the use of a movie film which moves at a rate sufficiently fast to separate out the wave form. This would result in photographs several inches long per word and is useful once an understanding of the problems and instrumentation are well in mind. Otherwise the problem in proceeding is that the sheer amount of data would very likely be crippling to its analysis.

[59] The basic frequency is "the most important frequency component, usually the one with the largest amplitude" (P. Ladefoged, 1962: 111).

[60] Personal Communication, Frank Lassman, Audiology, University of Minnesota, 1969.

[61] For more insight into the 'world-view' of a fairly successful mongoloid person, see *The World of Nigel Hunt* (Hunt, 1966).

[62] Personal Communication, Martin Q. Peterson, Physical Anthropology, University of Nebraska, 1970.

[63] Although linguistics has been mainly concerned with the study of grammar, i.e., sentences (Chomsky, 1957: 11), there seems to be no reason to neglect the possibility that language might be composed (also) of other, larger units. If we examine larger pieces such as in the question-response system, it is clear that some very basic claims about, for example, development, thought, creativity in understanding 'new' sentences, must be recast or discarded.

As will be pointed out later, the Q-R system examination suggests a syntax in which word and/or phrasal elements are most productively seen as members of sets or subsets; these, in turn, relate usually to a **small** number of other words or sets. If this is a useful way of thinking, then the usefulness of the 'creativity' argument is in doubt (Chomsky, 1964: 17).

[64] 'Wrong' questions also occur; i.e., questions are also embedded in larger contexts. What we usually mean by wit includes the clever use of 'slightly wrong' questions. Obviously this implies that larger verbal (or nonverbal) units form part of an interactional behavior. It may well be, for example, that the main 'function' of questions is to help maintain an interaction and has very little to do with information exchange in most situations.

[65] The idea that sentences 'contain' implicit information may prove very productive in gaining insight into language-cultural phenomena within the same study area. Although linguists usually act as if sentences have full entity status if they are agreed to be 'grammatical', it nonetheless appears true that actual sentences take place in actual contexts, where much of the context is so clear, obvious, and shared, that it need not be — and is usually not — discussed **out loud**. It appears to be no less a part of that sentence, however, than if it had been said.

To treat these parts of the context as if they do not occur leads to an examination of **sentence**. But it appears that all such notions of sentence are dependent on consensual measures, and the borderline between an examination of **behavior** and a **system of interpretation** becomes quite indistinguishable.

In context, then, sentences may well occur, but may also include for their understanding or interpretation the information which is present in the situation. The exclusion of these possibilities from modern linguistic studies has been unfortunate.

[66] A restriction on the study is that strategy dictates dealing with questions first which contained a **question word**, not of the form which would get a **yes** or **no** response. These latter seem, situationally, to derive from a special case of the more formal question; i.e., *Are you going*? They suggest that the questioner is relying on much nonverbal information in formulating his question.

[67] *teno ... e*. The person marker *e* always occurs in phrases introduced by *te-*.

[68] W. L. Pew, M.D., Personal Communication, 1968.

[69] Even the most empirically oriented linguists seem to have been narrowly empirical in their observations as they have been practitioners of this tradition. 'Language is language' appears to be a typical statement of linguists regardless of their positions on other issues.

[70] The problem of what rationality means is a very complicated one which impinges on broader questions of epistemology. From a social-behavioral point of view, it might merely mean that this picture is that one which adult humans use as a model for raising their young. Perhaps they see the world in such terms; perhaps not. Recent linguistic work has, on the contrary, apparently accepted a notion of rationality which seems overly accepting of its own truth.

[71] The reader might watch himself saying this statement in a mirror, concentrating on the changes in his mouth as it might be seen by an infant or toddler; and attempt to say it much as he would, say, to a one-year old. It is also useful to 'mouth' the words without any sound, to enhance this sense of what is seen in the *vis-à-vis*.

[72] Blind and deaf children are of great interest in this context. How do they speak? How do the deaf handle their communication problems via such 'languages' as American Sign Language. In a recent conference on sign language (Center for Applied Linguistics, December, 1969; Wm. Stokoe, chairman), it was the consensus that a viable research enterprise examining communication among people (and chimps; Gardner and Gardner, 1970) must take an initial strategy of considering Language and Sign Language as equivalent modes of communication, rather than considering one as the 'surrogate' or substitute of the other.

[73] To better understand this point a musical analogy may be helpful. In a very real sense, singing or playing a musical instrument are physical, bodily processes. But the body 'serves musical ends'. The goal of playing is a musical one, and the body must adjust itself or even be forced in ways which contribute to good music — almost regardless of the contortion the body must execute. A simple example — it is musically necessary to draw the violin bow in a relatively straight line. Since the right (bow) hand moves quite a distance, this can only be accomplished by a set of wrist movements which can involve both side to side and circular movements — all to help insure that a bow at some distance away is moving smoothly, continuously and straight relative to the bridge (the string support), and at a particular distance from the bridge — i.e., at the point where it contacts the string. Obviously even this is compounded in moving the bow at different angles on the various strings, so the musician must 'know' a number of variables — muscular, spatial, and musical — all at the same time. Thus the musical production, like the skin of the face we see, is a by-product of muscular movements.

[74] There has been a fair amount of comparative study on facial expression; much of it a belated outgrowth of Darwin's behavioral studies (Darwin, 1872) — this volume is accounted by many as the forerunner of modern ethological

studies. As its title states, expression was, and to a great extent still is, considered to reflect the 'emotions' in some manner, direct or indirect. While this idea seems fairly innocuous on the surface, the history of the emotions (perhaps it should be called a 'folk history') gives it some special thrust. It appears that 'the emotions' are often given 'entity' status much like 'the body' and 'the mind' — they, like the body, are assumed to be more 'basic', more animal-like attributes, and ones which we humans might well share with other animals. It is in this context that a comparative study of emotions, their physiology and anatomy, has been a lively enterprise — but those attributes of the mind which have been reserved for humans, language, and mind (and soul), have been assumed not to be open areas for useful comparative study (Chomsky, 1966).

[75] It is fairly simple to construct a personal **visual phonology** using a small hand mirror, and contrasting words in minimal contrast settings; e.g., *bit, bet, bat* for relative openness of all the English vowels — the mouth is literally open wider for *bat* than for *bet*. The sounds /m, š, ǰ, č, ž/ are all 'pursed'; the sounds /t-, d-, n-, s-, y-/ have lips widened in word initial positions, but less so in word medial or final position. Contrast *latter* and *ladder* — the mouth is open more widely in forming *latter*

It is still unclear as to what this might contribute to forming speech sounds, but these visual-facial factors seem to be about as ordered, patterned, and constant as do other phonological features — distinctive features or others.

It is interesting to note that essentially all professional singers have their lips under a great deal of tension, as if this tension contributes to the proper formation of their sounds.

[76] Working with slow-motion movies and an analyzing projector we were able to note a finite and fairly 'long' (in micro time) interval; surely one which is longer than, say, a blink — from start to finish — and one which is almost undoubtedly perceptible in real life/real time situations. The fact that most of us seem to be unaware of such events is probably of no more consequence for its 'reality' than, say, our unawareness of the aspiration following initial voiceless stops in English.

[77] It is not unreasonable to suggest, in this context, that speech is 'expression' at a distance. One might assume that it functions in about the same ways as visual or other sensory information in communication or message transfer. In this case speech could be seen mainly as a 'garnish' in the *vis-à-vis*, with most information handled in other ways. Clearly this characterizes most interaction in households or other settings in which the interactors are well known to one another. The information is relegated to context — a subject which has been rarely studied and is still considered to be unstudiable at least as a proper concern of linguists. For a counter-view, see Benjamin (1969).

[78] This brief paper will concentrate on the face, if only as more appealing to linguistic interests. The remainder of the body should be considered in similar ways

[79] Cosmetics seem to enhance such contrasts, perhaps to change their nature somewhat. Eyebrows and eye liner seem to provide a contrastive 'setting' in which eye movement seems to be more obvious to the observer. A complicating issue here, of course, is the relationship between information of the sorts: "I am available!" vs. "I am your friend!" vs. "I am feeling fine!" In addition we must realize that attractiveness or beauty is part of the same package.

[80] The question of how faces come to look like they look is an interesting

one, if it is not immediately attributed to innate-genetic factors. Here, again, no systematic research has been done on facial development across human (or other) populations, in families, the same persons over some number of years, etc. Anecdotally, the changes which can occur when people move into different socio-cultural groups, seem to be quite large. My own relatives who left eastern Europe to settle in China early in this century, appeared, to the American eye, to be quite oriental-looking a generation later. Similarly, orientals in Mexico are said to 'disappear' within a generation or two at most. The question of which children come to look like which parent, or which parent's family also remains unstudied — although many people seem to spend a fair amount of energy making such judgments as part of their familial folklore. It is difficult to say, at present, whether children really look like one parent, or they come to look like him as they are treated as if they had originally — i.e., we might be dealing with a self fulfilling feedback system of observation and prophecy and reinforcement.

[81] In 1970 we conducted anatomical studies of skin and its relationship to bone, muscle, fat, etc. Ordean Oyen (Texas A & M), an expert dissectionist-anatomist, did baboon facial studies in two directions — from the outside-in, and from the inside-out. Anatomical studies do the former, but the latter are necessary in order to preserve the relationship of skin as a total tissue to the underlying structures.

[82] Much of facial (and other) muscular mobility seems to relate to 'practice' and/or to exposure in one's immediate social surround. The ability to wink or raise one or the other eyebrow are cases in point. If no one in one's reference community moves particular muscles it appears that mobility is severely limited early in life and difficult to regain. Anecdotally, I learned to 'curl my tongue' at age 33 — urged by my children who are 'native' tongue-curlers. This occurred first during a cocktail hour and may help give substance to what the notion 'to loosen up' might mean. It is worth mentioning that I have had many years' experience in bodily training and retraining as a violinist and know that practice helps to overcome what appeared to be completely impossible at some earlier date. My personal bias has thus always been toward the idea of plasticity — given the right circumstances. It is clear, on the other hand, that most people are not exposed to such circumstances except quite early in life and become apparently fixed in their muscular habits when quite young.

[83] This may help to account for the anecdotal reports which have spouses growing to look more alike, masters like their dogs, etc.

[84] Set may be considered as a relatively constant thing against which to measure and contrast movement. Yet we also have a sense of 'voice set' which is a similar notion, but it has not been used in this manner (Trager, 1958). It is, perhaps, more useful to qualify the idea of set in an interactional context as 'the picture of the speaking-moving actor which the listener has in his mind, and against which he is measuring contrastive differences'.

[85] There are exceptions to this. Chomsky (1968) and Hjelmslev (1961) seem to opt for a completely independent notion of language, surely independent of its function for communication. Many other linguists have taken its communication aspects for granted, but have urged that the study of language **structure** is to be granted priority in moving toward understanding interaction behavior. Saussure (1959), Bloomfield (1933), and the others unselfconsciously assume an S-R (speaker-listener) model.

The notion of structure ordinarily seems to imply an analysis which looks for units and attempts to show how they are put together to make up the whole (structure). The ways of forming larger pieces out of units are often thought of as functions in relation to the structure. If, however, as appears true for notions like Language and Communication, the structure is merely **defined** into being, declared to be an entity by consensus and/or tradition, then it is unclear as to what notion 'units' or 'functions' might mean beyond the fact that anything can be analyzed and recombined in an infinite number of ways. It is in this sense that all such definitions seem circular, or at least incapable of being disproved.

[86] Modern biologists have abandoned the Mendelian-progressivist view of evolution which has characterized Social Darwinist thought for the past century. As I understand the 'modern synthesis' in genetics, the 'problem' of the origin of language would be considered to be a pseudo-problem. Their formulation is that all species are equally evolved through adaptation into different species, but none is considered 'higher' or 'more evolved' than any other.

[87] A social biological model suggested by primate ethology studies (Altmann, 1967) suggests that 'speech' allows social interaction to occur and continue at distances. Normal biological variation ensures that some normal infants (families) will be born without an imperative for speech. A useful distinction for the reader between modern biological and nonbiological approaches may be characterized by the search for differences and variation for the first, and the methodological need to arrange and analyze data for the nonbiologists.

[88] Studying with Smith and Trager (Buffalo) and McQuown (Chicago) in degree studies, and with R. Birdwhistell for more extended periods.

[89] Creationism — in some sense of instant creation of man as opposed to a gradual evolution/change, with adaptation.

[90] In the history of Western thought, the dominance of the mind in the context of a mind-body oppositional dualism has effectively eliminated the body from consideration as being the essential **locus** of behavior control. Rather, the body has been considered principally as a repository for mind.

Most theories of behavior, even of interaction, regard the body as a 'vehicle' for carrying the messages and intent of the mind, not as 'being' in its own sense. This is parallel to theories of language in which sound (= body) is presumed to **carry** messages (language, word, thoughts, mind), but not to be meaningful in and of itself (Spicker, 1970; Vesey, 1965).

[91] The observations on music are derived principally from my own self-analytic experience as a violinist, amplified by talking with a few professional musicians; jogging, likewise. Observations on mongoloid infants were made at the University of Minnesota hospitals, and several home visits.

[92] To check common pulse rates, one person monitors (holds) the wrist pulses of the two interactants, simultaneously. I have asked several psychologists about the wisdom or validity of this procedure, but remain unenlightened.

[93] It has been suggested that at least some body or circadian rhythms are also social in some senses. To speculate, it might be suggested that rhythmic changes after air travel are heavily affected by trying to interact with a majority of people who are in a quite different phase of daily rhythms than oneself. Anecdotally, I have heard mention that isolated troops of sufficient numbers tend not to suffer body rhythm difficulties on long flights.

[94] If we assume and believe that our ears mainly perceive tonal relationships, then we are primarily sound/phoneme analyzers (Helmholtz, 1954). The grounds for this assumption are certainly open to question; its reception of continuing

loyalty tending toward dogma. It is a clear case of a popular move in human behavior study tradition: noting an interesting characteristic of humans, elevating it to central, thus primary status, using it to characterize very incomplete observations as if they were exhaustive, and even attributing it to all other animals. It has certainly obscured as much as it may have illuminated.

[95] To extend this even further, it does seem remotely possible that 'face-shaping' of any individual may have to do not just with the interactional feedback of others responding to one's expressions but also to the attempt to 'hold' one's face in ways which mold at least some aspects of sound in 'interesting' and 'comfortable' ways.

[96] I wish to suggest that the stream of sound is as full of variables as the violin. We can hear and distinguish — all simultaneously and often continuously — the personal identifying characteristics of one's voice, his age, sex, relationships to his interactants in terms of a whopping number of social-contextual variables; we hear continuity, room size, the 'profession' of the speaker as priest, professor, mother, student. 'Baby talk' is one personal dialect among many. And the reasons they have escaped our attention have to do with under- (or over-) estimating their subtlety, and assuming they were idiosyncratic (*parole*), thus uninvestigable.

[97] Although 'consciousness' has been attributed to the individual (mind), this is a useful way of thinking about it in interactional terms.

Consciousness: 'the ability and willingness of an individual to cue-in on a shared, multi-person picture of the world when it is situationally appropriate'.

This concept would imply, among other things, a broadening of current views of psycho-pathology; the rational possibility of handling popular notions such as 'levels' of consciousness, para-psychology and ESP.

[98] The notion of 'talent' is interesting here, because many violinists reach a series of plateaus where increased practice does not make for much improvement. Talent, I suggest, is in large measure a good analytic sense of one's body, trusting one's own self analysis, and in remembering his body scheme.

[99] In a study now being conducted by the University of Minnesota, Department of Special Education, a number of volunteer parents of such children are in a program of sustained, intensive face-to-face interaction with their Down's children — the hope being that their children's faces will come to 'resemble' the family more than it appears to be 'typically Down's', increase the supportive 'feelings' in the familial interaction, and better socialize the children.

[100] Most, possibly all of the research work on monocular vision seems to have been done with binocular people who hold one eye closed. Truly monocular people have few of the problems one might predict for them in operating in the real world; e.g., driving, playing sports such as squash, ski jumping, are not difficult for one-eyed people.

[101] The nature of **conservatism** remains completely problematic.

[102] With practice, one can get to hear (on purpose) the subtle differences between *marcato* and *staccato* in terms of how they 'fill' their temporal slots: both end well before the next sound is about to begin; *marcato* has an amplitude change (rise and fall) which is relatively large from beginning to end; staccato is much steadier in amplitude, just stopping quickly. Counting, saying the alphabet, or listing items are very much like *marcato,* and this seems to be a favorite thing for children, especially, to do; both linguistically and musically. (Marches are very exciting for most of us and are very difficult to 'get out of one's head'; but this may be a culture-bound observation!)

BIBLIOGRAPHICAL REFERENCES

Adler, M. J.
  1967   *The Difference in Man and the Difference it Makes* (New York: Holt, Rinehart, & Winston).
Altmann, Stuart
  1967   "The Structure of Primate Social Communication", *Social Communication among Primates*, ed. by S. A. Altmann (Chicago: University of Chicago Press), 325-62.
Anderson, Hans Christian
  1956   "The Ugly Duckling", *The Family Treasury of Children's Stories*, ed. by P. R. Evans (New York: Doubleday & Co.) 229-31.
Andrew, R. J.
  1966   "Evolution of Facial Expression", *Science* 142, 1034-41.
Aristotle
  1941   *The Basic Works of Aristotle*, ed. by R. McKeon (New York: Random House).
Ashby, W. Ross
  1956   *An Introduction to Cybernetics* (London: Chapman and Hall).
Bales, Robert F.
  1950   "A Set of Categories for the Analysis of Small Group Interaction", *American Sociological Review* 15, 257-63.
Baratz, S., and J. Baratz
  1972   "Black Culture on Black Terms: A Rejection of the Social Pathology Model", *Rappin' and Stylin' Out: Communication in Urban Black America*, ed. by T. Kochman (Urbana: University of Illinois Press).
Barrenechea, Ana Maria, and Mabel V. Manacorda de Rosetti
  1968   *Guias para el estudio de la gramatica estructural* (Buenos Aires: Instituto Torcuato di Tella).
Beer, G. R. de
  1940   *Embryos and Ancestors* (London: Oxford University Press).
Bergson, Henri
  1950   *Le rire, essai sur la signification du comique* (Paris: P.U.F.).
Benjamin, Gail R.
  1969   *The Non-Linguistic Content of Speech* (unpublished M.A. thesis, Department of Anthropology, University of Minnesota).
  1974   *The Non-Linguistic Content of Speech in Japanese* (unpublished Ph.D. dissertation, Department of Anthropology, University of Minnesota).

Benjamin, Gail R., and Chet A. Creider
    1973   "Social Distinctions in Non-Verbal Behaviour", *Semiotica* 14, 1, 52-60.
Birdwhistell, Ray L.
    1968a "Communication", *International Encyclopedia of the Social Sciences* (New York: Crowell, Collier, and MacMillan) 3, 24-9.
    1968b "Kinesics", *International Encyclopedia of the Social Sciences* (New York: Crowell, Collier, and MacMillan) 3, 379-85.
Blanshard, B.
    1938   *The Nature of Thought* (London: Allen and Unwin).
Blauvelt, Helen
    1954   "Dynamics of the Mother-Newborn Relationship in Goats", *Conference on Group Processes*, ed. by R. Schaffner (New York: Josiah Macy, Jr. Foundation).
Bloomfield, L.
    1933   *Language* (New York: Holt).
Boas, F.
    1940   "Changes in Bodily Form of Descendants of Immigrants (1910-1913)", *Race, Language, and Culture* (New York: Free Press).
Bronowski, J.
    1965   *The Identity of Man* (London: Penguin Books).
Bull, N.
    1945   "Towards a Clarification of the Concept of Emotion", *Psychosomatic Medicine* 7, 210-14.
    1946a "A Sequence Concept of Attitude", *J. Psychology* 22, 165-73.
    1946b "Attitudes, Conscious and Unconscious", *J. Nervous and Mental Disease* 103, 337-45.
Busnel, René F.
    1963   "On Certain Aspects of Animal Acoustic Signals", *Acoustic Behavior of Animals* ed. by R. F. Busnel (Amsterdam: Elsevier).
Cabanac, Michael
    1971   "Physiological Role of Pleasure", *Science* 173, 1103-07.
Carter, G. S.
    1957   *A Hundred Years of Evolution* (Amsterdam: Elsevier).
Cassirer, Ernst
    1946   *Language and Myth* (Tr. Susanne K. Langer) (New York: Dover).
    1955   "The Philosophy of Symbolic Forms", *Language* (New Haven: Yale University Press) 1.
Chomsky, N.
    1957   *Syntactic Structures* (The Hague: Mouton).
    1959   Review of *Verbal Behavior* by Skinner, *Language* 16, 1, 26-58.
    1964   *Current Issues in Linguistic Theory* (The Hague: Mouton).
    1965   *Aspects of the Theory of Syntax* (Cambridge: MIT Press).
    1966   *Cartesian Linguistics* (New York: Harper & Row).
    1968   *Language and Mind* (New York: Harcourt, Brace & World).
    1968a "Language and the Mind: II", *Columbia Forum* Fall, 23-5.
Chomsky, N., and Morris Halle
    1968   *The Sound Patterns of English* (New York: Harper and Row).

Condon, William S.
   1964   *Process in Communication* (Pittsburgh: Western Psychiatric Institute).
Crook, John H. (ed.)
   1970   *Social Behaviour in Birds and Mammals* (London: Academic Press).
Darling, F. F.
   1952   "Social Behavior and Survival", *Auk* 69, 183-191.
Darwin, Charles
   1872   *The Expression of the Emotions in Man and Animals* (London:
          J. Murray).
Darwin, C.
   1965   *The Expression of the Emotions in Man and Animals* (Chicago:
          University of Chicago Press).
Descartes, René
   1951   *Meditations on First Philosophy* (New York: Liberal Arts Press).
Eibl-Eibesfeldt, I.
   1968   "Zur Ethologie des menschlichen Grussverhaltens", *Z. Tierpsychol.*
          25, 727-44.
   1970   *Ethology: The Biology of Behavior* (Tr. E. Klinghammer) (New
          York: Holt, Rinehart and Winston).
Ekman, P.
   1972   *Emotion in the Human Face* (New York: Pergamon Press).
   1975   "The Universal Smile", *Psychology Today* (Sept.) 35-9.
Ekman, P., E. R. Sorenson, and W. V. Friesen
   1969   "Pan-Cultural Elements in Facial Displays of Emotion", *Science*
          64, 86-8.
Enlow, Donald H.
   1968   *The Human Face* (New York: Harper and Row).
Ervin, Susan M.
   1964   "Language and Thought", *Horizons of Anthropology*, ed. by
          Sol Tax, (Chicago: Aldine) 300-17.
Feibleman, James
   1946   *The Theory of Human Culture* (New York: Duell, Sloan and Pearce).
Fenichel, O.
   1969   *The Psychoanalytic Theory of Neurosis* (London: Routledge).
Flanagan, J. L.
   1965   *Speech Analysis, Synthesis, and Perception* (New York: Academic
          Press).
Fodor, J. A., J. J. Jenkins, and S. Saporta
   1967   "Psycholinguistics and Communication Theory", *Human Com-
          munication Theory*, ed. by Frank F. X. Dance (New York: Holt,
          Rinehart, and Winston) 160-201.
Frake, Charles O.
   1962   "Cultural Ecology and Ethnography", *American Anthropologist*
          64, 53-9.
Frank, Lawrence
   1957   "Tactile Communication", *Genetic Psychology Monographs* 56
          (Nov.) 209-56.
Fries, Charles C.
   1957   *The Structure of English: An Introduction to the Construction of
          English Sentences* (New York: Harcourt, Brace & World).

Frings, Hubert and Mable
1964   *Animal Communication* (New York: Blaisdell).
Gardner, R. A., and B. T. Gardner
1969   "Teaching Sign Language to a Chimpanzee", *Science* 165, 664-72.
1971   "Two-Way Communication with an Infant Chimpanzee", *Behavior of Non-Human Primates*, ed. by Schrier and Stollnitz (New York: Academic Press).
Gibson, J. J.
1966   *The Senses Considered as Perceptual Systems* (Boston: Houghton Mifflin Company).
Gilbert, E. N.
1966   "Information Theory after 18 Years", *Science* 152, 320-6.
Goss, C. M. (ed.)
1954   *Anatomy of the Human Body* by Henry Gray (Philadelphia: Lea and Febiger).
Gregory, William K.
1965   *Our Face From Fish to Man* (New York: Capricorn Books).
Grimm, Jakob and Wilhelm
1956   "Snow White and the Seven Dwarves", *The Family Treasury of Children's Stories*, ed. by Pauline Ruth Evans (New York: Doubleday and Co.) 1, 140-1.
Hall, Edward T.
1959   *The Silent Language* (Greenwich: Fawcett).
Hamburg, David A.
1963   "Emotions in the Perspective of Human Evolution", *Expression of the Emotions in Man*, ed. by Peter H. Knapp (New York: International Universities Press) 300-17.
Hartmann, R.
1886   *Les singes anthropoides et leur organization comparée à celle de l'homme* (Faris: Felix Alcan).
Haudricourt, André
1948   "Relations entre gestes habituels, forme des vêtements et manières de porter les charges", *La revue de géographie humaine et d'ethnologie* 3, 58-67.
Helmholtz, H.
1954   *On the Sensations of Tone* (New York: Dover).
Hjelmslev, Louis
1961   *Prolegomena to a Theory of Language* (Tr. F. J. Whitfield) (Madison: University of Wisconsin Press).
Hockett, Charles F.
1958   *A Course in Modern Linguistics* (New York: Macmillan).
1967   Review of *Biological Foundations of Language* by Eric H. Lenneberg with appendices by N. Chomsky and O. Marx (John Wiley and Sons), *Scientific American* 141-3.
Hockett, Charles F., and Robert Ascher
1964   "The Human Revolution", *Current Anthropology* 5, 135-68.
Hoijer, Harry (ed.)
1954   *Language in Culture* (Chicago: University of Chicago Press).

Huber, Ernst
    1931   *Evolution of Facial Musculature and Facial Expression* (Baltimore: Johns Hopkins Press).
Hunt, Nigel
    1966   *The World of Nigel Hunt: The Diary of a Mongoloid Youth* (Beaconsfield, England: Darwen Finlayson).
Jackson, J. H.
    1958   *Selected Writings* (London: Staples Press).
Jakobson, Roman
    1968   *Child Language, Aphasia, and Phonological Universals* (The Hague: Mouton).
Kawamura, Syunzo
    1963   "The Process of Sub-culture Propagation among Japanese Macaques", *Primate Social Behavior*, ed. by Charles H. Southwick (Princeton: D. Van Nostrand) 82-90.
Kortland, A., and M. Kooij
    1963   "Protohominid Behaviour in Primates (Preliminary Communication", *Symposium, Zoological Society of London* 10, 61-8.
Kuhn, Thomas
    1962   *The Structure of Scientific Revolutions* (Chicago: University of Chicago Press).
Ladefoged, P.
    1962   *Elements of Acoustic Phonetics* (Chicago: University of Chicago Press).
Lancaster, Jane B.
    1965   "Language and Communication", *The Origin of Man*, ed. by Paul L. DeVore (New York: Wenner-Gren Foundation for Anthropological Research) 71-8.
Lashley, K. S.
    1951   "The Problem of Serial Order in Behavior", *Cerebral Mechanisms in Behavior*, ed. by L. A. Jeffress (New York: John Wiley and Sons) 112-31.
Lenneberg, Eric H.
    1960   "Language, Evolution, and Behavior", *Culture in History: Essays in Honor of Paul Radin*, ed. by Stanley Diamond (New York: Columbia University Press) 869-93.
Linden, Eugene
    1976   *Apes, Men, and Language* (Baltimore: Penguin).
Litter, Victor A.
    1957   *Aproximacion experimental a la antropologia* (Buenos Aires: I.D.E.A.).
Lorenz, K.
    1965   "Preface", *The Expression of the Emotions in Man and Animals* by C. Darwin (Chicago: University of Chicago Press).
    1966   *On Aggression* (New York: Harcourt, Brace and World).
Luria, A. R.
    1968   *The Mind of a Mnemonist* (New York: Basic Books).
Malinowski, Bronislaw
    1944   *A Scientific Theory of Culture and Other Essays* (Chapel Hill: University of North Carolina Press).

Mandelbaum, David G. (ed.)
    1949   *Selected Writings of Edward Sapir* (Berkeley: University of California Press).
Mauss, Marcel
    1936   "Les techniques du corps", *Journal de Psychologie*, 34, 3-4. (Reprinted in *Sociologie et anthropologie* [Paris: P.U.F.] 1950, 365-86.)
Mayo, B.
    1954   "The Existence of Theoretical Entities", *Science News* (Harmondsworth: Penguin Books) 32.
    1956   "More about Theoretical Entities", *Science News* (Harmondsworth: Penguin Books) 39.
Mayr, Ernst
    1963   *Animal Species and Evolution* (Cambridge: Harvard University Press).
McLuhan, Marshall
    1964   *Understandia Media: The Extensions of Man* (New York, London, Sydney, Toronto: McGraw-Hill).
Mead, G. H.
    1934   *Mind, Self, and Society,* ed. by C. W. Morris (Chicago: University of Chicago Press).
Meillet, A.
    1925   *La methode comparative en linguistique historique* (Oslo: Aschehoug).
Mering, Otto von
    1965   "Provisional Parenthood, the Foster Child, and Neighborliness", *Pennsylvania Psychiatric Quarterly* Winter, 4.
Merti, Carlos A.
    1957   "Introduction al estudio del languaje de los monos mirikina (Actus Azarae)", *Anules de la Sociedad Cientifica Argentina* 163, 89-105.
Miller, G. A.
    1962   *Psychology: The Science of Mental Life* (London: Penguin).
Miller, G. A., E. H. Galanter, and K. H. Pribram
    1960   *Plans and the Structure of Behavior* (New York: Holt, Rinehart, and Winston).
Mol, H.
    1963   *Fundamentals of Phonetics: I: The Organ of Hearing* (The Hague: Mouton).
Morris, Desmond
    1967   *The Naked Ape* (New York: McGraw-Hill).
Moss, Melvin L., and Letty Salentijn
    1969   "The Primary Role of Functional Matrices in Facial Growth", *A. J. of Orthodontics* (June) 566-77.
Negus, V. W.
    1929   *The Mechanism of the Larynx* (London: Heinemann).
Nietzsche, F.
    1967   *The Will to Power* (New York: Random House).
Oyen, O. J.
    1974   *The Baboon Face: A Different Study of Growth and Development* (University of Minnesota: unpublished doctoral dissertation).

Pegis, Anton C. (ed.)
  1948   *Introduction to St. Thomas Aquinas* (New York: Random House).
Peiper, Albrecht
  1963   *Cerebral Function in Infancy and Childhood* (Paris: Consultants Bureau).
Perrault, Charles
  1956   "Cinderella", *The Family Treasury of Children's Stories,* ed. by P. R. Evans (New York: Doubleday & Co.) 1, 337-44.
Piaget, J.
  1952   *The Origin of Intelligence in Children* (New York: W. W. Norton).
Pierce, J. R., and E. E. David, Jr.
  1948   *Man's World of Sound* (New York: Doubleday).
Pike, Kenneth L.
  1954   *Language in Relation to a Unified Theory of the Structure of Human Behavior* (Glendale, California: Summer Institute of Linguistics).
  1957   "Towards a Theory of the Structure of Human Behavior", *General Systems Yearbook of the Society for General Systems,* ed. by L. Bertalanffy and A. Rapoport, V. II.
Pittenger, R., C. Hockett, and J. Danehy
  1960   *The First Five Minutes* (Ithaca: Paul Martineau).
Plato
  1928   *The Works of Plato,* ed. by I. Edman (New York: Modern Library).
Pokorny, J.
  1959   *Indogermanisches etymologisches Wörterbuch* (Berne-Munich: Francke).
Pollock, I., and S. M. Pickett
  1964   "Intelligibility of Excerpts from Fluent Speech: Auditory vs. Structure Context", *J. Verbal Learning and Verbal Behavior* 3, 79-84.
Pribram, K. H. (ed.)
  1969   *Brain and Behaviour 1; Mood, States, and Mind: Selected Readings* (Baltimore: Penguin Books).
Rasch, Philip J., and Roger K. Burke
  1963   *Kinesiology and Applied Anatomy* (Philadelphia: Lea and Febiger).
Rosenblith, Walter A. (ed.)
  1961   *Sensory Communication* (Cambridge: MIT Press).
Ruesch, Jurgen, and Gregory Bateson
  1951   *Communication: The Social Matrix of Psychiatry* (New York: Norton).
Ryle, Gilbert
  1949   *The Concept of Mind* (New York: Barnes and Noble).
Salus, Peter H.
  1969   *On Language: Plato to von Humboldt* (New York: Holt, Rinehart, and Winston).
Salzinger, Kurt
  1970   "Pleasing Linguists: A Parable", *J. Verbal Learning and Verbal Behavior* 3, 79-84.
Sarles, H. B.
  1966   *A Descriptive Grammar of the Tzotzil Language* (University of Chicago, Department of Anthropology: unpublished Ph.D. dissertation).

Saussure, F. de
    1949   *Cours de linguistique générale* (Paris: Payot).
    1959   *A Course in General Linguistics* (Tr. Wade Baskin) (New York: Philosophical Library).
Schaffner, R. (ed.)
    1958   *Conferences on Group Processes* (New York: Josiah Macy Jr. Foundation).
Scheflen, Albert E.
    1964   "The Significance of Posture in Communication Systems", *Psychiatry* 27, 4, 316-31.
    1965   "Natural History Method in Psychotherapy: Communication Research", *Methods of Research in Psychotherapy*, ed. by L. A. Gottschalk and A. H. Auerbach (New York: Appleton-Century-Crofts), 263-89.
Schleicher, A.
    1861   "Sprachliche Curiosa", *Beiträge zur vergleichenden Sprachforschung* 2, 392-3.
Schwidetzky, G.
    1931   *Sprechen Sie Schimpansisch?* (Leipzig: Deutsche Gesellschaft fur Tier- und Ursprachenforschung).
Sebeok, Thomas A.
    1963   Review of *Communication among Social Bees* by Martin Lindauer (Cambridge: Harvard University Press, 1961); *Porpoises and Sonar* by Winthrop N. Kellogg (Chicago: University of Chicago Press, 1961); *Man and Dolphin* by John C. Lilly (Garden City: Doubleday, 1961), *Language* 39, 448-66.
Shapiro, Burton L.
    1970   "Prenatal Dental Anomalies in Mongolism: Comments on the Basis and Implications of Variability", *Annals of NYAS,* 562-77.
Simpson, G. G.
    1966   "The Biological Nature of Man", *Science* 152, 472-8.
    1970   "Reply to Sarles 1969", *Current Anthropology* 11, 1, (Feb.).
Slobin, Daniel
    1965   "Language and Communication", *The Origin of Man*, ed. by Paul L. DeVore (New York: Wenner-Gren Foundation for Anthropological Research) 71-8.
Smith, W. John
    1969   "Messages of Vertebrate Communication", *Science* (July 11), 145-50.
Spencer, H.
    1867   *First Principles* (Boston, New York: Caldwell).
Spicker, Stuart F.
    1970   *The Philosophy of the Body* (Chicago: Quadrangle Books).
Spinoza, B.
    1948   *Ethics* (London: Dent).
Spitz, Rene A.
    1965   *The First Year of Life: A Psychoanalytic Study of Normal and Deviant Development of Object Relations* (New York: International Universities Press).

Spitz, R. A., and K. M. Wolf
    1946   "The Smiling Response: A Contribution to the Ontogenesis of Social Relations", *General Psychology Monographs* 34, 57-125.
Stebbins, G. Ledyard
    1965   "Pitfalls and Guideposts in Comparing Organic and Social Evolution", *Pacific Sociological Review* 8, 3-10.
Stein, L.
    1942   *Speech and Voice* (London: Methuen).
    1949   *The Infancy of Speech and the Speech of Infancy* (London: Methuen).
    1951   "On Talking", *Brit. J. of Medical Psychology* 24, 10-11.
    1953   "Stammering as a Psychosomatic Disorder", *Folia Phonietrica* 5.
    1958   "Analytical Psychology, a 'Modern' Science", *J. of Analytical Psychology* 3, 43-9.
    1962   "An Entity Named Ego", *J. Analytical Psychology* 7, 47-51.
    1966   "In Pursuit of First Principles", *J. Analytical Psychology* 11, 1-10.
Stokes, W.
    1861   "Reduplication im Altirischen Verbum", *Beiträge zur vergleichenden Sprachforschung* 2, 396-7.
Stokoe, William C.
    1975   "Sign Language Autonomy", Paper presented at the *Conference on the Origin and Evolution of Language*, New York Academy of Sciences (Oct.).
Stoller, Robert
    1967   "Effects of Parents' Attitudes on Core Gender Identity", *International Journal of Psychiatry* 4, 1 (July), 57-60.
Sturtevant, William
    1964   "Studies in Ethnoscience", *American Anthropologist* 66, 99-131.
Tinbergen, N.
    1957   *Social Behaviour in Animals* (London: Methuen).
Trager, George L.
    1958   "Paralanguage: A First Approximation", *Studies in Linguistics* 13, 1-2; 1-12.
Trager, George L., and Henry Lee Smith, Jr.
    1951   "An Outline of English Structure", *Studies in Linguistics*, Occasional Paper 3 (Washington: American Council of Learned Societies).
Vaihinger, H.
    1924   *The Philosophy of "as if"* (New York: Harcourt).
Vesey, G. N. A.
    1965   *The Embodied Mind* (London: George Allen and Unwin).
Virchow, Rudolph
    1962   *Disease, Life, and Man* (New York: Collier Books).
Waddington, C. F.
    1975   Review of Wilson's *"Sociobiology"*, *New York Review of Books* (August).
Washburn, Sherwood L.
    1959   "Speculations on the interrelations of the History of Tools and Biological Evolution", *The Evolution of Man's Capacity for Cul-*

ture, ed. by J. N. Spuhler (Detroit: Wayne State University Press)
21-31.

Weekley, E.
    1930   *Adjectives and Other Words* (London: Murray).

Whitehead, A. N.
    1929   *Process and Reality* (New York: The Free Press).

Whorf, B. L.
    1952   *Collected Papers on Metalinguistics* (Washington, D.C.: Department
of State Foreign Service Institute).

    1956   *Language, Thought, and Reality*, John B. Carroll, ed. (New York:
John Wiley and Sons).

Wittgenstein, Ludwig
    1958   *Philosophical Investigations* (Tr. G. E. M. Anscombe) 3rd edition
(New York: Macmillan).

Wolff, Werner
    1943   *The Expression of Personality* (New York: Harper and Brothers).

Wynne-Edwards, V. C.
    1962   *Animal Dispersion in Relation to Social Behavior* (New York:
Hafner).

INDEX

HARVEY SARLES earned his doctorate in anthropology at the University of Chicago in 1966. Since then, he has taught at the University of Minnesota, where he is now professor of anthropology, adjunct professor of American studies, and director of the Center for Comparative Thought. Sarles has also served as a visiting professor at the University of Sussex, SUNY Buffalo, and Cornell University.